The Essentials of CoreSinging

The Essentials of CoreSinging

A Joyful Approach to Singing and Voice Pedagogy

Meribeth Dayme

Edited by Cynthia Vaughn
and Matthew Hoch

ROWMAN & LITTLEFIELD
Lanham • Boulder • New York • London

Published by Rowman & Littlefield
An imprint of The Rowman & Littlefield Publishing Group, Inc.
4501 Forbes Boulevard, Suite 200, Lanham, Maryland 20706
www.rowman.com

86-90 Paul Street, London EC2A 4 NE, United Kingdom

Copyright © 2022 by The Rowman & Littlefield Publishing Group, Inc.

All rights reserved. No part of this book may be reproduced in any form or by any electronic or mechanical means, including information storage and retrieval systems, without written permission from the publisher, except by a reviewer who may quote passages in a review.

British Library Cataloguing in Publication Information Available

Library of Congress Cataloging-in-Publication Data

Names: Dayme, Meribeth Bunch, 1938- author. | Vaughn, Cynthia, 1957- editor. | Hoch, Matthew, 1975- editor.
Title: The essentials of CoreSinging : a joyful approach to singing and voice pedagogy / Meribeth Dayme ; edited by Cynthia Vaughn and Matthew Hoch.
Description: Lanham : Rowman & Littlefield, 2022. | Includes bibliographical references and index. | Summary: "This book presents a unique and innovative outlook on singing and voice pedagogy by one of the most important voice pedagogues in modern times, focusing on the five essential areas of energy, awareness, imagination, practice, and performance. Also included are case studies by CoreSinging teachers as well as other select writings by Meribeth Dayme" —Provided by publisher.
Identifiers: LCCN 2022005536 (print) | LCCN 2022005537 (ebook) | ISBN 9781538163993 (cloth) | ISBN 9781538164006 (paperback) | ISBN 9781538164013 (epub)
Subjects: LCSH: Singing—Instruction and study.
Classification: LCC MT820 .D29 2022 (print) | LCC MT820 (ebook) | DDC 783/.043—dc23
LC record available at https://lccn.loc.gov/2022005536
LC ebook record available at https://lccn.loc.gov/2022005537

You may give this part of yourself many names—persona, soul, and so forth. I describe this part as your core—the spirit that lives in you that no one else has. It is the very thing that makes you human. Your voice is the sound of your spirit.

Meribeth Dayme

Contents

Foreword by Nicola Harrison	ix
Eureka Moment	xi
Editorial Remarks by Matthew Hoch	xiii
Introduction by Cynthia Vaughn	xv

PART I: THE ELEMENTS OF CORESINGING

1	Basic Principles of CoreSinging	3
2	Energy	19
3	Awareness	35
4	Imagination	43
5	Practice and Performance	51
6	A Summary of Key Concepts in CoreSinging	63

PART II: CASE STUDIES: PRACTICAL APPLICATION OF CORESINGING

7	Why CoreSinging? by Rachel Velarde	71
8	The Body Knows How to Sing by Michael Hill	89
9	A House with Four Rooms by Elizabeth Blades	101
10	Using CoreSinging with Children, Tweens, and Teens by Aimee Woods	113

| 11 | Organized Fun by Trish Rooney | 127 |

PART III: SELECTED WRITINGS

Meribeth Dayme: A Biographical Sketch by Susanne Bunch Hill	147
Spring Birthday Walk (unpublished 1986 poem)	155
The Little Book about Singing: A Guide for Those Who Want to Get Ahead Fast (2006)	157
Creating Confidence: How to Develop Your Personal Power and Presence (1999, rev. 2006)	181
The Incredible Shrinking Singer: Rebuilding Your Confidence (1999) An Interview with Meribeth Dayme by Cynthia Vaughn	263
Suggestions for Further Reading (compiled by Meribeth Dayme)	267
Index	269
About the Editors and Contributors	277

Foreword

Nicola Harrison

If I had to use one word to describe Meribeth, it would be "aurora"—a sky full of brilliant and ever-changing light. She embodied—in her teaching, her work, and her own being—many of the highest qualities that we, as human beings, can possess. A fearsome intelligence coupled with integrity and deep intuition made for an exceptional educator.

I first encountered Meribeth on the floor of the University of Sheffield's music library. Sitting on a threadbare carpet and reading through operatic scores, I suddenly came across a copy of *Dynamics of the Singing Voice*. Cross-legged on the floor, I read it from cover to cover right then and there, and the effect on my thinking was nothing short of epiphanic.

A meeting in London soon followed with a session on postural anatomy that led on to lunch and a walk around Regent's Park. Then came one of Meribeth's legendary anatomy classes in Barnes, London, where I first met Cynthia Vaughn, now a lifelong friend. Further training followed, and finally, in 2010, a small group of us traveled to Annecy, France, to attend the first-ever CoreSinging course taught by Meribeth.

Contact with Meribeth continued via Skype, as it did for many of us. She was a masterful presence, supporting and connecting a joyful international community of singers and teachers. I think we all believed she would live forever.

Happily, despite her passing, Meribeth continues to connect us all through her enduring work, which we, as teachers, are able to pass on. The immense body of material that is crafted together here by Cynthia Vaughn and Matthew Hoch furthers this mission. *The Essentials of CoreSinging: A Joyful Approach to Singing and Voice Pedagogy* is a testimony to Meribeth's life and work and a powerful legacy of her genius and her love.

Nicola Harrison
Pembroke College
University of Oxford
September 2021

Eureka Moment

Meribeth Dayme

Suddenly in my seventh decade of life, I have had that "eureka" moment when my experiences and expertise converged with the promise of a new and exciting concept, and CoreSinging has been born. To say I am excited is an understatement! My passion in life has been the study of the voice and the practice of good singing. From singer to professor of voice to professor of anatomy of the voice, I have traveled a long and winding path in my quest to find an approach that could be germane to anyone who had the desire to sing. In recent years, I have immersed myself in spiritual and healing techniques, knowing intuitively that they would add to my repertoire of tools. The idea came to me when I was writing about the future of the teaching of singing in the new fifth edition of *Dynamics of the Singing Voice*—working with ideas that speak to our approach to learning, the language of the mind, developing talent, learning to trust the voice, and the awareness and responsibility that goes with teaching and singing.

Ever since I started to sing, I have been fascinated by the need for singers to combine their artistic creativity with technical ability of the highest standards. This led me to my PhD in vocal anatomy, enabling me to identify obvious practical issues in voice production. But increasingly I have realized the need for performers not simply to overcome practical barriers, but also to make the mental leaps which enable performers to communicate creativity through their art form, imbuing performances with an intense energy that dispels nerves and draws in audiences. I have therefore also drawn on my own experiences in the mystic arts and healing energies to create an approach to singing that will raise any performer and performance, whether you are a newcomer to the stage or an experienced performer looking to retain and enhance your power of performance. CoreSinging, I believe, will make a very real contribution to the joy and fulfillment that singing brings to our lives.

Meribeth Dayme
Veyrier-du-Lac, France
Letter to a Sponsor, 2009

Editorial Remarks
Matthew Hoch

Some "academic" projects are a chore, while others are a labor of love. Perhaps more than any project I have ever undertaken, compiling and editing *The Essentials of CoreSinging: A Joyful Approach to Singing and Voice Pedagogy* by Meribeth Dayme unquestionably falls into the latter category. I have placed the word "academic" in quotation marks for a reason, because I don't think Meribeth would approve of that designation. CoreSinging, as you will read, defies labels. It is broader in scope and more all-encompassing than traditional methodologies, an approach to singing that could only have been conceived by a spirit as adventurous and a mind as capacious as Meribeth's.

Meribeth's legacy in the field of voice pedagogy cannot be overstated. She was one of the last students of the legendary William Vennard (1909–1971) at the University of Southern California, where she earned her PhD in 1974. She then went on to earn tenure and the rank of associate professor at the University of Delaware before leaving the security of academia to continue her research at the Royal College of Surgeons in London on an NIH postdoctoral fellowship. In 1982, she published *Dynamics of the Singing Voice*, which is perhaps the most erudite investigation into the biomechanics of the singing voice published in between Vennard's *Singing: The Mechanism and the Technic* (1967) and Richard Miller's *The Structure of Singing* (1986).

Meribeth remained in Europe until 2016, where she built a solid reputation as a pedagogue and clinician in England, France, and Switzerland. During this time, she was named the 2001 winner of the Van L. Lawrence Fellowship and founded her own approach to singing and voice pedagogy, CoreSinging, in 2009. In 2004, she coauthored and published a "basics of singing" book with Cynthia Vaughn titled—simply and appropriately—*The Singing Book*, which quickly became one of the most-used class voice texts in higher education and private studios across the country and beyond.

Perhaps most significant, Meribeth was one of the only scholars of her pedigree and stature who was not afraid to pursue lines of inquiry that were not necessarily in line with the values of the establishment. I know of no other pedagogue, for instance, who has dovetailed the discipline of voice pedagogy with the bioenergy fields of Valerie V. Hunt or Tor Nørretanders's theories of human consciousness, to name only two of her more recent explorations.

Meribeth was kind and generous with her time when I was doing some research on William Vennard in 2017 and 2018. I enjoyed hearing about her experiences under his tutelage, and I was fully aware that I was speaking with one of only a handful of living "primary sources" who could offer firsthand insight into Vennard and his teaching, along with many other interesting anecdotes.

On an ordinary Saturday—October 26, 2019, to be exact—the postman left an unexpected box on my front porch. When I opened it, it contained an original 1967 hardcover version of Vennard's *Singing: The Mechanism and the Technic* with the initials "M. A. B." engraved on the back cover. On the title page was following inscription: "To Meribeth Bunch, with confidence that she will achieve her worthy and unusual ambitions. Cordially, Bill Vennard." (She certainly did.) The package also contained a rather thick stack of some of Vennard's research papers, which I assume he passed on to Meribeth before his death during her doctoral studies in 1971. I will certainly "pass them forward" as well when my time comes.

Meribeth passed away two days later, on October 28, 2019, an event that was unexpected—at least to us. I never had a chance to thank her, but the "gift" she had bequeathed to me suddenly made a lot more sense. She was ready, readier than we were, and she knew that the time had come to pass along her lifetime of wisdom to those whom she knew would carry her torch forward. Meribeth Dayme's legacy is preserved in the volume you are holding in your hands. Cynthia Vaughn and I are humbled and deeply honored to transmit her joyful approach to singing and voice pedagogy to a new generation.

Matthew Hoch
Auburn, Alabama
December 2021

Introduction
Cynthia Vaughn

I don't recall exactly when I first met the esteemed voice pioneer Meribeth Bunch, but it was online in the 1990s, and it was in the early days of the VocaList LISTSERV, a dedicated electronic mailing list for classical singers that was a forerunner of today's popular online discussion forums. In VocaList I recognized the name of Meribeth Bunch from my graduate school pedagogy text, the 1982 first edition of *Dynamics of the Singing Voice*.[1] The first thing that had struck me as a student was how thin the textbook was and how accessible and well-written the information about voice science and anatomy was—especially compared to the other dense and scholarly pedagogy books that were available at the time. Even in the early edition of *Dynamics of the Singing Voice,* the author hinted at ideas beyond physical voice science that she would embrace later in her career.

While I was intellectually curious about voice science and physiology, I graduated with a performance degree and was primarily focused on auditioning and singing. When I began teaching voice lessons in my home studio and joined the National Association of Teachers of Singing (NATS), my innate curiosity and desire for learning and collegiality grew when I discovered the LISTSERV mentioned above in 1986. I was a bit of a lurker at first, but I was thrilled that my Apple Macintosh Performa could connect me with voice professionals from across the country and world, including the famous "Dr. Bunch" in London. She was an early adopter of technology and when America Online was established in 1989, she found her way to an AOL "chat room" that I had designated for singing teachers.

The original AOL chat rooms were a bit like Facebook groups and private forums, except there was no feed or notifications and you had to connect via slow and noisy dial-up phone connections. Initially, you just dropped into the chat room hoping someone would be there from anywhere to talk about singing. Sometimes it was crickets. Other times it was quite lively! Eventually I scheduled some monthly chats and invited prominent guests. In the early days there was no video—the guest and attendees had to type their questions and comments in real time. Sometimes only a few people joined the chat, but when there were more—up to a dozen or so—I moderated the best I could to stay on topic with everyone "talking" (i.e., typing) at the same time. When I invited Meribeth Bunch to be a special guest, she surprised me by immediately accepting and staying up all night to join us at 2:00 a.m. London time.

After that, Meribeth and I became casual online acquaintances. I was becoming increasingly fascinated by her work in voice science and anatomy and her uniquely holistic approach to performance and the teaching of singing. A pivotal moment in my life was reading her 1999 book *Creating Confidence: How to Develop Your Personal Power and Presence*.[2] I read and reread this slim paperback, and it was truly life changing. Using my newfound personal power, I asked the editor at *Classical Singer* magazine if I could interview Meribeth Dayme about her book. I had been writing for *Classical Singer* for a few years as both a feature writer and associate editor, but had stepped away from monthly deadlines to begin a doctoral program at the age of forty-two. I was terrified at being the "oldest graduate student ever," so Meribeth's book had arrived at exactly the right moment in my life.

My former editor gave me the go-ahead to interview Meribeth and to review her book. My preference then, as now, is to conduct interviews via email for a paper trail, but Meribeth insisted on speaking to me personally on the phone, even though long-distance international calls were quite expensive at the time. I was shocked when I first heard her voice. I expected a London accent, but I heard a gentle, southern American accent that reflected Meribeth's North Carolina roots. To make a long story short, one phone call turned into many, and I learned about her life, career, and the research and spiritual influences that had led her to meld the study of voice science and anatomy with research in the human biofield and consciousness. The article and interview was published in the April 1999 issue of *Classical Singer* under the title "The Incredible Shrinking Singer: Rebuilding Your Confidence."[3]

The article was well-received, and Meribeth was pleased that I had captured the essence of her book—and had not misquoted her! Accuracy and context were important to her. While going through her papers recently, I learned that she had been quoted out of context in the early 1980s by a London tabloid and the piece caused quite a stir for Meribeth (supposedly) criticizing a prominent politician's speaking voice as "weak."

After the *Classical Singer* article was published, our daily phone calls stopped. Months later, unexpectedly, I received a phone call from London one evening. It was Meribeth. The new music editor, Maribeth Payne, at W. W. Norton & Company had reached out to her regarding a college voice class song anthology and textbook for nonmusic majors. The editor offered to send a list of vetted authors. Meribeth said, "No, wait. Before you do that, there is a voice teacher and author in Colorado that I would like to ask. We work very well together, and I like the way she writes and thinks." Years later I learned that Meribeth had also consulted a spiritual advisor before asking me to collaborate. It helped that I had years of experience teaching class voice, but Meribeth didn't know this at the time. And that is how a relatively unknown writer ended up coauthoring three editions of a best-selling voice class textbook, *The Singing Book*, with a renowned voice expert and author.[4]

Much of the information from *Creating Confidence* found its way into Meribeth's later books, including *The Performer's Voice: Realizing Your Vocal Potential*.[5] During this time, Meribeth was also developing CoreSinging,[6] which she described in a marketing brochure as "a trailblazing approach to vocal performance pedagogy that synthesizes performance, technique, and therapy into a joyful new way of teaching and learning to sing, including Eastern concepts, Western traditions, quantum mechanics, and recent studies on consciousness."[7] I had previously visited Meribeth in London in 2004 for one of her final vocal anatomy workshops, and in 2010 I traveled to her new home in beautiful Annecy, France, for her first CoreSinging teachers' certification course. The immersive course was forty-five hours over seven days and limited to nine participants. I was the only American in the group; my colleagues were from the UK, Switzerland, the Netherlands, Canada, and Scotland. Since CoreSinging is an approach that can be applied to many voice methods, our teacher's certification class included university voice faculty, a famous opera singer, a jazz singer, a pop singer, a Feldenkrais practitioner, Estill method teachers, and a children's choir director. Except for the fact that we were all women, we were as diverse as could be. This experience in France was a highlight of my life, and inspired me to teach singers of all styles, ages, and abilities.

In 2010 I hosted Meribeth at Magnolia Music Studio in Fort Collins, Colorado, for her first CoreSinging teachers' certification course in the United States. Meribeth, then in her seventies, traveled from France to Colorado one more time in 2011 before deciding that transatlantic travel was becoming too strenuous for her. She began to create online content and focus on European and UK introductory courses that required less travel. I assisted with one of her short courses for Voice Care Network UK in London in 2013 while we were supervising the accompaniment recordings for the third edition of *The Singing Book* at Trinity Laban Conservatoire of Music and Dance at University of Greenwich. Though I was twenty years her junior—and am now the age that Meribeth was when we first met—I could never truly keep up with her!

In 2016, after more than forty years of living abroad, Meribeth returned to the United States to be near her sister and family in California. The move was difficult, but she continued to grow her online courses and found a network of new friends and local business associates. Meribeth had spent her entire life forging new paths and starting over, even legally changing her name in 2004 from Bunch to Dayme, choosing a name that resonated with her literally, figuratively, and spiritually. Her brilliant intellect and generous spirit never dimmed, but her health began to deteriorate in the final years of her life. Meribeth once told me that she had always planned to live to be ninety-six—exactly ninety-six years old! However, when her doctors finally diagnosed her with late-onset advanced ALS (amyotrophic lateral sclerosis), she texted me that she was "relieved" and that "eighty-one is good." She argued with her doctors, however, that she would need "at least two weeks because she had things to do." She passed away a few days later in hospice with her family and her beloved dogs, Chip and Muppet, nearby.

As news of Meribeth's passing spread, tributes poured in from around the world. She touched many lives through her teaching, research, books, workshops, and friendships. One of the most profound and touching tributes was by NATS member and editor of NATS So You Want to Sing series, Matthew Hoch. Two days before Meribeth died, Matthew had received a surprise package. Knowing Matthew's interest in the work of the late William Vennard, Meribeth had arranged to have her early papers and work with Vennard sent to Matthew. This is just one of many examples of Meribeth's graciousness and generosity in her final days.

I deeply miss my friend and mentor, but she is still with me in countless ways. As a singer, I have learned to set intentions and "tune in" to awareness around and within myself. I regularly use qigong, dynamic balance, and energy testing practices before I walk on stage for a presentation or performance, and I am always aware of where my toes are pointed! Clearing the energy in a space is essential, whether it is my own studio, a guest venue, or even a hotel room. My students benefit from traditional vocal technique and pedagogy in addition to creative, fun, and empowering CoreSinging ideas. Technical or vocal challenges can often be overcome by an approach that includes "uhming and chewing" and miming the story of the song. Mentally adding a color to a phrase can completely change the vocal color or timbre. My favorite activity to do with students of all levels is to use colored markers and a flip chart or white board to draw their songs. I don't always get out of my head, but at least I am now aware when I am overintellectualizing or leaning toward self-critique and perfectionism.

CoreSinging forever changed my teaching and performing. I was able to integrate new ideas and awareness to my years of teaching knowledge and strategies. I already had a solid knowledge of vocal science, function, and anatomy. CoreSinging was the "missing piece."

It was Meribeth's request before her death that I would continue her CoreSinging legacy. I invited CoreSinging teacher Matthew Hoch to collaborate on this important project, knowing his work with Meribeth and his extensive experience as an editor. In January 2020, I traveled to California for a private celebration of Meribeth's life at the home of her sister Susanne Hill. With the family's blessing, I returned with Meribeth's archives: papers, books, journals, photos, poetry, musings, newspaper clippings, and original CoreSinging materials. In April 2021, as Matthew and I were planning this book, I flew to California again to retrieve the files from Meribeth's computer.

It is our duty and great honor to be the keepers of Meribeth Dayme's work and to share her legacy. We are grateful for the vision of Rowman & Littlefield publishers for recognizing the importance of preserving Meribeth Dayme's pioneering work in the voice field. During her lifetime, Meribeth insisted that she didn't want to write a CoreSinging book. She preferred to present in-person workshops and courses, and later, to work with individuals online as her health allowed. She then created a virtual CoreSinging course with written modules and videos. This book is the culmination of Meribeth Dayme's former online course materials as well as course materials from her in-person presentations. In addition, we have also invited five CoreSinging practitioners from around the globe to offer their perspectives on how Meribeth and CoreSinging have impacted their teaching and performing. Finally, we are including some additional writings that until now have been previously unpublished or are no longer available in print. Through these resources, it is our goal to share Meribeth Dayme's CoreSinging—a *joyful* approach to singing and voice pedagogy—with future generations of singers and teachers.

Cynthia Vaughn
Richland, Washington
December 2021

NOTES

1. Meribeth Bunch, *Dynamics of the Singing Voice* (New York: Springer-Verlag, 1982).
2. Meribeth Bunch Dayme, *Creating Confidence: How to Develop Your Personal Power and Presence* (London: Kogan Page, 1999). The contents of this book, long out of print, are republished in part III of this volume.
3. Cynthia Vaughn, "The Incredible Shrinking Singer," *Classical Singer* 12, no. 4 (April 1999): 14–15. This article later appeared in *Inter Nos* 53, no. 1 (Spring 2020): 13–17; it is reprinted, with permission of *Classical Singer*, in part III of this book.
4. Meribeth Dayme and Cynthia Vaughn, *The Singing Book* (New York: W.W. Norton & Company, 2014).
5. Meribeth Dayme, *The Performer's Voice: Realizing Your Vocal Potential* (New York: W.W. Norton & Company, 2006).
6. CoreSinging was a trademarked (™) and later a registered ® entity. In the interest of a cleaner look and smoother reading experience, we have not included these symbols in the copy of this volume. For consistency, we have applied this stylistic preference to other trademarked and registered entities as well.
7. Personal files of Meribeth Dayme, now in possession of the editors.

Part I

THE ELEMENTS OF CORESINGING

Chapter One

Basic Principles of CoreSinging

The CoreSinging approach has been developed over the course of my life journey through voice and teaching—an exciting journey that evolved through a passion for singing and performance, voice pedagogy, anatomy and life sciences, sports, and self-development in many directions—including the study of Eastern philosophies, qigong and tai chi, mindfulness, and courses in a wide variety of healing modalities. This chapter will explain the various modalities used in CoreSinging, their origins, and the ways in which they are incorporated into teaching and singing.[1]

CoreSinging is an approach that encourages teachers to follow their intuition, curiosity, and natural abilities to further their own pedagogy and performance. The approach is applicable to any style or level of singing and performance. It is formed of five elements: energy, awareness, imagination, practice, and performance. Each of these elements is present in all stages and levels of the singing experience—from beginner to professional—and changes the way singers and teachers at every level learn, sing, and perform.

Vocal lessons are life lessons. While some teachers work with professional singers, most do not. There are thousands of dedicated teachers who devote themselves to enhancing the lives of all ages and stages of singers. They are not only teaching singing; they are also providing multiple avenues for the joy and appreciation of singing and music, models for learning and discipline, nurture for students and their spirits, and healing. Teachers of singing are enhancing the lives of people in and on many dimensions. CoreSinging is dedicated to enriching the lives of teachers and singers and adding value to voice pedagogy and performance.

CORE PRINCIPLES

CoreSinging is based on principles rather than rules or prescriptions. It encourages a free, creative, and positive path to teaching and singing. While there are outstanding methods of singing to be explored and learned, over time they tend to get watered down as the methodologies spread. Methods are good for those who need rather strict rules. However, depending on the curiosity and knowledge of the teacher, there is a danger that those locked into a specific method may lose the creative and imaginary elements that encourage new exploration. *If you want everyone to be the same, just tell them there is only one way to do it.*

The CoreSinging teacher is guided by the following principles:

1. Have gratitude for each student and the opportunity to work with what they bring to the art of singing.
2. Refrain from criticizing students, other teachers, their methods, or their students.
3. Focus on positive energies, work, and self-development.
4. Honor the right of every person to study with whomever they choose.
5. Maintain a positive energy in the studio for each person.
6. Be supportive of other teachers of singing.
7. Be supportive of other approaches to singing.

And CoreSinging students need to remember the following:

1. There is nothing we are doing that you need to get right.[2]
2. Have gratitude for every sound you make.
3. Have no judgment regarding "past" singing or teaching, including what you have just done.
4. The more imagination and fun you have, the more interesting and useful your exercises will be. Curiosity is a great trait to have.
5. A silent mind and intuition are also great traits to have.
6. Using your voice from a place of inner silence and internal/external awareness will allow you to sing in ways you have never dared to dream.

When concepts related to energy are introduced into the teaching of singing, the teacher is able to help the singer transform themselves, their sound, and their performance into an experience of healing for both singer and audience. We have only touched on the possibilities that are available to us when we perform. Our four-hundred-year-old ideas and some of our current beliefs of what it takes to sing and perform are overdue for some changes. Working with appropriate energetic concepts will begin to provide those.

The CoreSinging approach emphasizes fun, play, and the use of the imagination in a collaborative environment. From the beginning, the teacher supports and encourages students to accept and enjoy their own sounds. Musical elements are gradually introduced with play and imagination. What follows is more specific information about each of the elements that make up CoreSinging.

HISTORY AND BACKGROUND

The work of CoreSinging is grounded in my childhood, particularly my love of singing and performance. Over thirty years of experiences in performance—on stage and in dance and sport—led to much thought about the various elements that comprise performance. These elements range from the simple joy that one feels through the act of singing to the heart of intent, mindfulness, preparation, and the exhilaration of being on stage.

From an early age, I had enormous curiosity about how things worked and loved the sciences. While I never expected to pursue science after high school, when working with William Vennard (1909–1971) at the University of Southern California I was presented with the opportunity to study anatomy at the USC dental school. The privilege of working with (and dissecting) cadavers and understanding anatomy gave me a profound appreciation and admiration of the miracle of the human body. Because of these experiences, throughout my university career I had the opportunity to teach anatomy in addition to singing and voice pedagogy. I taught anatomy to singers, dancers, speech therapists, physical therapists, dentists, and doctors. In the case of medical professionals, I attended their clinics and even observed surgery to better understand how to relate anatomy to their professions. This

Meribeth in London with the first edition of Dynamics of the Singing Voice *(1982)*
Courtesy of the editors

culminated in a National Institute of Health (NIH) Postdoctoral Fellowship to do research at the Royal College of Surgeons in London.

What followed next were twenty-five years in London (and later France) studying the works and philosophies of Eastern masters; learning tai chi and qigong; taking courses in counseling, metaphysics, meditation, craniosacral therapy, and neurolinguistic programming (NLP); and exploring the esoteric aspects of sound and singing. I read works written by scientists, physicists, and medical doctors who were exploring alternative systems, such as Valerie V. Hunt (1916–2014), Bruce Lipton (b. 1944), Candace Pert (1946–2013), Deepak Chopra (b. 1946), Gregg Braden (b. 1954), and Joe Dispenza (b. 1961).[3] I also read books in the field of self-development, by writers like Lynne McTaggart (b. 1951) and Carolyn Myss (b. 1952); studies in neuroplasticity by Norman Doidge (b. 1950); and works related to learning and creativity by Ellen Langer (b. 1947) and Ken Robinson (b. 1950).[4] This was only the tip of the iceberg. The joy was in looking at how all or any of this could enhance singing and performance.

Many questions began to arise about the effectiveness of our models of teaching singing and how we could enhance voice pedagogy. There has always been some polarity between the science of singing and the more empirical aspects. The singing voice as a science is well suited to the academic world because it provides numerous avenues for research, whereas the more empirical aspects depend on experience and tradition and are considered less suitable for the specifics needed in most research. The teaching of singing has become a very serious, sometimes narrow, endeavor for many. CoreSinging is dedicated to teaching that honors the science. At the same time, it goes beyond current preoccupation with the physical and moves into the realm of metaphysics and the human energy field, where the exciting possibilities become endless. A new awareness of possibilities and working with energy can change how we teach, learn, practice, and perform.

ENERGY

The human energy field is formed of photons (light particles) with intelligence, sometimes called consciousness. That is our essence. These photons have been around since the beginning of time, and we are composed of a field of such particles that have existed since then. When we consider this, many old concepts are no longer useful in describing what is happening on the physical level. The question "Why?" offers so many potential answers that the mind boggles. Usually, people approach the physical aspect of the energy field first because it is the most visible. However, it is the biofield—Valerie V. Hunt's term for the energy field preferred by some scientists —that surrounds, controls, and nurtures the physical aspect that we see. The physical aspect is less than 10 percent of the human energy field. Other aspects include the metaphysical, mental, emotional, psychological, psychic, and spiritual. When we look only at the physical aspects, we are missing 90 percent of the possibilities of answers. This knowledge cannot help but change the way we approach singing.

Chakras in the human body
Courtesy of the editors

The empirical study of energy has been studied for thousands of years. Western scientists and physicists are now proving and seeing what has been known for eons. Various forms of energy create a dynamic world.

What Affects and Transforms the Energy Field?

Thoughts and language have enormous influence over the energy field. Currently there is a large amount of research concentrated on the mind and the effect of intention, positive thought, and visualization. For some years those in sports psychology have regarded this practice as giving star athletes an added advantage. Now mental techniques are taught to children by their coaches. The work of Bruce Lipton, Joe Dispenza, Norman Doidge, and many others is showing how the brain can change at any age and build new neural pathways by intention and positive visualization.[5] The enormous field of self-development is looking at the power of intention to change any element of our lives. The research, currently led by Lynne McTaggart and others, is proving to be astounding with huge ramifications for the way we approach the teaching of singing and performance.[6] We know that thoughts count, and this knowledge needs to be emphasized and included in singing lessons. It is the most basic aspect of learning and performance that we can teach. Establishing an intent for what you are doing is vital to success in every field. Energy follows thought and the most important thing we can relay to a student is a positive and healthy mindset around singing—and life.

Fun and Imagination in Learning

We have established that intent is paramount to any energetic approach. So is *fun*. We've known for years that people remember things that are fun. Yet the field of education is only now returning to that concept. We have used things that were fun for children but forgot to honor the child in all of us. The desire for information about the voice and teaching has clouded intuition, spontaneity, and creativity in the studio. The more information we dole out to our students, the more confused they can become. Finding a simplicity of teaching, learning, and being is a primary goal of CoreSinging.

It has been known for centuries that experience is the best teacher when it is experiential and fun.[7] Children learn, and retain knowledge, when taught with imagination and fun. Many clever teachers use the art of fun and diversion to get students to sing without pondering the skill. By asking a student to do something like move or draw while singing, it allows them to concentrate on the action you have asked them to do, and they sing easily. Everyone is so surprised when they discover this. Diversion allows the natural and innate wisdom of the body and energy field to do the singing. There are many techniques that help singers get out of their own way and excellent teachers seem to have a lot of these up their sleeves.

Watching the excitement of a young child learn something new is one of life's most joyful experiences. Their enthusiasm and curiosity are unparalleled. Rather than exploring the wide world of possibilities available to us, our education system began to treat learning as something with right and wrong answers for everything. Looking at possibilities encourages imagination, research, and curiosity, and discourages rote learning. So many arguments and beliefs are based on the right and wrong expectations we developed in our schools, families, and cultures.

How do you learn to look at possibilities? The best way to see possibilities is to stop any judgment or preconceived ideas of how something happens or works. When we have expectations, that sets up those expectations to happen. It is easier as a teacher to stay open—with a blank screen, so to speak—and just see what happens when. By doing this, it will allow the student space to change and grow.

CONCEPTS OF LEARNING USED IN CORESINGING

The most effective learning occurs when using a multifaceted approach that includes as many aspects of the energy field as possible. This will enable a far greater retention of the music and text than a rote or single aspect approach to singing—or any subject, for that matter.

A soprano's drawing of Schumann's "Die Lotosblume," op. 25, no. 7
Courtesy of the editors

Practical Suggestions for a Multifaceted Approach in the Studio

Four aspects of any voice lessons are warm-ups, working with text, working with music, and teaching students how to practice. Warm-ups are best varied and not repeated in the same way each time. The teacher can make them fun by using improvised musical conversations—words, sounds, rhythms, movements, and so on. The same thing repeated over and over is not only boring, but also detrimental to flexibility of mind, body, and voice. Athletes are taught not to do an exercise the same way three times. It can lead to problems—especially when the coach or teacher is not there to give feedback. It is ideal to begin with something that does not have to be correct. For example, avoid beginning with a scale because scales need to be "correct." When you do get around to scales—and they are important—make sure scales are varied, fun, and have multiple elements to them as well as being accurate.

Regardless of the style, learning the text before the music allows the singer to be familiar with the emotions, the meaning, the imagination behind it, and enhances the authenticity of the message. When singers try to learn text, music, rhythm, and other elements all at once, it cheats the message, the music, and the audience; it is simply not enough. This is true for all the texts of popular music and many other styles that have lyrics that are repeated over and over. Each repetition needs to convey a new meaning. Song texts can be used as a game of charades—mimed, rapped, drawn—using different chairs for different characters, as well as danced and much more. Once you let the imagination loose on the text, there is no end to what is possible. This approach encourages creativity, flexibility, and focused play with words. Students love it because it does away with mindless repetition of the word. Imagination is the key to vocal color and emotion.

There are also things to consider when working with the music. Before learning the notes and rhythms, get the feel of the music in the body. Spend time listening and gently moving to the music, drawing the shape and movement of the music with colored pens, following the patterns of the melodic line with the hands, and using the space of the room to move. As the text is already learned, it is easy to begin to add the text to the music—at first without trying to be too accurate.

Finally, teach students how to practice. It is often assumed that they know how to practice; however, experience has proved that this is often not true. It is not necessary to create rigid guidelines; rather, use time wisely and make it fun. One-page handouts with suggestions are useful to students. At the beginning of a practice session, either short or long, set an intent for that practice. For example: "Today I will pay attention to how I am breathing." Suggest options for warm-ups, movement, ways to approach text and music, and one or two things specific to that student. Perhaps most important, always practice performance as part of practice—even if they know only two lines. A mock performance in front of an imaginary audience of hundreds where there is no going back—and no criticism—works wonders for nerves and the eventual live performance.

So many studio approaches are still carrying eighteenth- and nineteenth-century concepts that need to change—even in pop, rock, musical theatre, and various other genres of singing. We live in a world that has little attention span, and *perceived* little time. The more fun and enjoyable the learning, the faster it is retained at a profound level. When students have an experience that is unforgettable, they remember it forever. The intelligence of the energy field is unlimited. The contributions of Ellen Langer to the field of learning are immense. When we engage in a multifaceted approach rather than one that is primarily informational, the innate intelligence of the singer and the teacher can take over and create magical experiences in singing and performing.

ENERGETIC CONCEPTS OF BALANCE AND BREATH

There is an abundance of information on posture, balance, and breathing in the literature and methods of teaching singing. These are based mainly on physical corrections. There is interest in looking at the Eastern approaches to balance and breath and there have been small inroads to using those that are appropriate for singing. After regarding both areas energetically, I realized that many of the old teachings actually blocked the energy flow—or chi—of the singer. Instead, CoreSinging focuses on the position of the feet and using concepts of balance rather than posture. Working with the energy field makes breathing so much easier because the emphasis is not on overattention to muscular action while singing.

Balance: Being in a State of Readiness

CoreSinging uses concepts taken from qigong as a means of establishing balance as well as being aware and ready to respond. These include the ideas of "soft" joints, seeing eyes (not staring or focusing on a fixed point), and an awareness of your surroundings. Establishing this balance at the beginning of every practice or lesson is a key to a responsive and obedient voice. When one achieves "dynamic balance," the body and mind are in a state of readiness to sing. By using the mind and imagination to create invisible vortices of energy—that balance the body from the tailbone (coccyx), upper back, lower sternum, and the elbows—the biofield becomes strong, the body is in balance, the center is deep in the body, and the act of singing is easy and natural.[8]

Many cultures emphasize the need to make something happen. When something seems too easy, we think there is something wrong. The phrase "extra points for more effort" seems to have seeped into the vocal world as well. Teachers and their singers often are under the impression that they must do something extra to sing, and they go about proving it with excess tension while standing, breathing, phonating, and emoting. All these excesses block the chi and get in the way of singing and the spontaneous expression of text and music. Conversely, when you use the mind and awareness to create a state of readiness, the effort falls away. Cultivating these ideas is paramount to good singing and compelling communication.

The Energy of Breathing

As previously stated, we are—energetically speaking—a dense field of particles. It is therefore logical to assume that the whole human energy field is porous and "breathes." Working with this concept involves both imagination and intention. Various Eastern practices use a concept of breath in which we sense that we are "being breathed" rather than physically managing air. Because the collective consciousness of breathing for singing is dominated by hundreds of years of attention to physical and biomechanical aspects, the shift to energetic breathing can be a challenging concept to absorb. However, using the imagination can be helpful in understanding the energy of breathing.

AWARENESS

When we become aware, we open to a huge field of information and a new way of being. This awareness enhances the voice in multiple ways. The resonance expands to fill the space; there is a feeling of unseen support from the audience, the space, and all that contributes to what is being sensed. The singer is no longer alone on stage.

Working with External Awareness

Being aware is a must for excellent performance. So often performers are taught to block everything out, when what they need to do instead is open themselves up to all that is going on around them. Blocking awareness also blocks both the sound and your message. Expanding awareness does not negate the intention and focus of the message—it includes it. Filling space and creating energetic power in the voice means being open, aware, and mindful without judgment or analysis; it is the key to being centered and present while singing freely and compellingly. Whether you are preparing to teach or perform, simply sitting in awareness for a few minutes or less will help you set up a sense of space and feel comfortable within it.

Working with Internal Awareness

Internal awareness means getting in touch with the inherent rhythms of the body. These are key to feeling the music in profound ways. The obvious rhythms are breath and pulse. Finding the pulse and using that as a metronome (even though it is uneven) can help connect the singer and the song to the body. Most singers are so busy singing that real connection with themselves becomes lost. Every organ of the body has its own rhythm. While many of these rhythms are so subtle that it is difficult to physically discern them, it is always possible to connect to them through the imagination. Using a combination of external and internal awareness can bring enormous presence to the sound.

Now consider all sensory input as contributing to the creation of your personal orchestra. With that abundance of support, your sound, confidence, and performance will reach new heights. This concept is especially important to singers who perform in noisy environments. Rather than trying to block out the sounds, absorb these noises and allow yourself to be supported by them. Allow everything to become part of the music. This way of thinking can eliminate much of the anxiety that can accompany performance situations.

PRACTICE

When practice is fun, imaginative, and has variety, it is likely to be even more exciting than the lesson. Each of these three elements is vital to learning and practice. The collective consciousness around the word practice is something like tedium and is not conducive to effective learning or practice. Mindless repetition is a waste of good time. Sports coaches have learned that what is practiced exactly the same way more than three times actually hurts flexibility and spontaneity. This does not mean that something can't be repeated— only that it needs to be repeated with some slight variation each time. Practice is more effective when it's more like a game.

The importance of an energy-field approach to practice allows learning to be easy, fun, and effective. Pounding notes is not the way to learn or ensure confidence. I used to think/assume that a student would go away from the lesson with a clear idea of what to do. Much to my surprise, they would come in several weeks later and ask how to practice. I learned that you can never assume anything about what they will take away—no matter how carefully you plan the lesson. So, I created the following threefold guideline for effective practice in which there are three elements: tune *in*, tune *up*, and tune *out*. There are no set times for each element, and no dogmatic rules. "Tuning in" is a time to set an intention for the practice. "Tuning up" uses playful approaches to the words and music, including movement and mime to create color and expression. "Tuning out" invites the singer to get outside of their head and to practice performing a song or part of a song with no stopping or criticism. Practicing performing a song or part of a song at the end of every lesson or practice can alleviate performance anxiety. Many singers have found this approach to be extremely helpful in their performances and auditions.

PERFORMANCE

Performance isn't only about singing in public. It is about being in front of people in any situation and sharing a beautiful energy. Very few singing students end up as full-time performers, but they can use performance skills in so many different areas of their lives. Teaching someone how to prepare for performance can be one of the most valuable tools teachers can give their students. Sharing the joy of presenting the music and the message is the most profound thing you can do as a singer or teacher. When the singer/teacher achieves this, the audience/student experiences the same thing.

Preparation for Performance

Ellen Langer states that "noticing new things puts you in the present."[9] At the risk of being too repetitive, intent is everything. Athletes use it, those studying mindfulness learn to use it, Eastern philosophies have espoused it for thousands of years. Isn't it about time for those in the arts to take it into the mainstream of teaching and preparation?

From the moment it is known that a performance is coming up (this can be months in advance), begin to visualize being comfortable, knowing the message, and enjoying sharing it. Every time the mind wanders to the performance, use this visualization. This practice educates your brain to create what you want to happen. Students can do this for performance, auditions, exams. An example of an intent that I use is: "I want to create an atmosphere/energy in which the audience goes out feeling better than when they arrived."

Note: You cannot create something for someone else—you can only create the space in which it can happen.

The next step is to prepare your text and music in the most fun way possible. Dance it, rap it, draw it, use a ridiculous subtext, create Harry Potter spells with it, and anything else your wildest inner child can give you. The more fun you have, the easier it will be to retain and share it—play, play, play!

Remember, it is important to never leave a practice session without delivering a full performance to your thousands of fans. Stand and deliver—even if it is only one verse of something. Thank yourself and your "audience," and leave without analysis or criticism. It is amazing what this does for confidence and alleviation of anxiety.

Preparing to Go on Stage

While waiting to go on stage, do gentle grounding exercises. These can be deep breathing techniques, gentle movement, or some kind of mindfulness exercise. While you are doing this, make sure that your feet are firmly on the floor with your toes pointed forward. This will strengthen the energy field.

Next, become aware of the space: the sounds from audience rustling to various backstage noises, the surrounding air, and any visual aspects, odors, or physical sensations. Imagine that the energy field is as big as the whole arena. All the sounds and sensory aspects provide the orchestra that will contribute to the music. The audience is in the energetic home of the performer.

By increasing awareness, the energy field grows, calm ensues, and it is easy to become centered and in the "zone." It enables the singer and the audience to be in direct contact with one another. On the contrary, blocking everything out—as some have been taught—will shrink personal space and possibly prevent the audience from joining you. By the way, closing the eyes in performance does this too. The "zone" is a place of expanded awareness, not some kind of zombie state. The world becomes timeless, where the performer and the music become one. It is a special feeling that everyone deserves to experience.

All the intentions and visualization—together with your expanded awareness—allow the performer to walk out on stage knowing that it is theirs, it is home, and that the singer, fellow performers, and the audience are creating the concert together. If something happens that was not planned, in this state it can be accepted as a part of the whole and not dwelled upon. Finally, share the joy of music and performance and show gratitude to everyone in attendance, and especially to yourself.

After a lifetime of teaching and studying the voice, I have a few musings about the future of teaching performance. Teaching technique does not need to be separate from performance. Incorporating elements of intent, mindfulness, imagination, and play throughout the process of learning to sing brings out the explorer and the creator in teachers and singers alike. Performing at the end of each practice session or lesson puts performance squarely in the center of learning and gives added purpose to practice as well.

FINAL THOUGHTS

As more teachers embrace energetic concepts, self-development, and courses outside the field of singing, and find new approaches that enhance their lives, it is only natural that they will begin to include these elements in their teaching. These will gradually make their way into the studio and into the teaching of singing. This is happening now, and it is very exciting. Teachers love to experiment with new ideas; they sometimes need to give themselves permission. We can restore the balance of art, science, and performance by including concepts of energy in learning and teaching. Balanced singers and teachers become healers by their connection to the world around them. This is what the CoreSinging approach is all about.

NOTES

1. Portions of chapters 1–6 were previously published in Meribeth Dayme's chapter titled "The CoreSinging Approach," in *So You Want to Sing with Awareness*, ed. Matthew Hoch (Lanham, MD: Rowman & Littlefield, 2020), 123–42.

2. When someone perceives the need to get something right, they tend to become anxious and their energy tests low when muscle tested.

3. Representative works from these authors are as follows: Valerie V. Hunt, *Infinite Mind: Science of the Human Vibrations of Consciousness*, second ed. (Malibu, CA: Malibu, 1996); Bruce H. Lipton, *The Biology of Belief: Unleashing the Power of Consciousness, Matter, and Miracles*, tenth anniversary ed. (Carlsbad, CA: Hay House, 2016); Candace Pert, *Molecules of Emotion: Why You Feel the Way You Feel* (New York: Scribner, 1997); Deepak Chopra, *Quantum Healing: Exploring the Frontiers of Mind/Body Medicine*, revised and expanded ed. (New York: Bantam Books, 2015); Gregg Braden, *Human by Design: From Evolution by Chance to Transformation by Choice* (Carlsbad, CA: Hay House, 2017); and Joe Dispenza, *You Are the Placebo: Making Your Mind Matter* (Carlsbad, CA: Hay House, 2014).

4. Representative works from these authors are as follows: Lynne McTaggart, *The Field: The Secret Force of the Universe* (New York: HarperCollins, 2002); Carolyn Myss, *Anatomy of the Spirit: The Seven Stages of Power and Healing* (New York: Three Rivers Press, 1996); Norman Doidge, *The Brain That Changes Itself: Stories of Personal Triumph from the Frontiers of Brain Science* (New York: James H.

Silberman Books, 2007); Ellen J. Langer, *The Power of Mindful Learning* (Boston: Lifelong Books, 1997); and Ken Robinson, "Do Schools Kill Creativity?," TED Talk: https://www.ted.com/speakers/sir_ken_robinson.

5. Joe Dispenza, *Evolve Your Brain: The Science of Changing Your Mind* (Deerfield Beach, FL: HCI Printing and Publishing, 2007); Norman Doidge, *The Brain That Changes Itself: Stories of Personal Triumph from the Frontiers of Brain Science* (New York: James H. Silberman Books, 2007); Bruce H. Lipton, *Spontaneous Evolution: Our Positive Future and a Way to Get There from Here* (Carlsbad, CA: Hay House, 2010).

6. McTaggart, *The Power of Eight: Harnessing the Miraculous Energies of a Small Group to Heal Others, Your Life, and the World* (New York: Atria Books, 2017).

7. Confucius: "By three methods we may learn wisdom: first, by reflection, which is noblest; second, by imitation, which is easiest; and third by experience, which is the bitterest."

8. All the imaginary energy vortices go straight down to the ground except the one from the upper back (between the shoulder blades), which goes up.

9. https://www.leadinglearning.com/episode-97-mindfulness-learning-ellen-langer/, accessed January 22, 2020.

Chapter Two

Energy

We live in a dynamic world, one that is composed of various forms of energy. These vary from the gross forms—such as solar, magnetic, and volcanic—to the less obvious of life force: meridians, chakras, and particles so tiny and with such a short life span that the physicists build huge accelerators just to find evidence of them, as well as the invisible energies of the mind and higher consciousness. The activity of our world never stops. It reinvents itself by constant transformation just as we do.

As noted in chapter 1, we are energetic beings formed of photons (light particles) with intelligence. The light can become clouded with various aspects of our long history, as well as the present and future, and with the constant evolution of our physical, metaphysical, mental, emotional, psychological, psychic, and spiritual energies. It is therefore important to be constantly aware that we must reinforce the positive energies and clear the energetic negative memories we carry with us from a variety of sources. It is equally important not to create new unhelpful memories that become imbedded in our energy field.

It is much more likely that issues develop in the biofield outside the physical aspects long before we see their physical manifestation. This is the reason that what seem to be physical problems often do not change when treated or corrected (because the cause is not located there). Until the cause is found, the issue will remain, or at best be improved only slightly before it inevitably returns. It is possible to determine in which area a problem resides and make corrections. You can do this by using a simple muscle test—as long as you have no vested interest or expectation in the answer.

Chapter Two

ENERGY TESTING

Energy testing or muscle testing is also known as applied kinesiology and is a system that evaluates structural, chemical, and mental aspects of health using manual muscle testing combined with other standard methods of diagnosis. Muscle testing is a noninvasive method of evaluating body function that is used in the healing arts. Practitioners may include chiropractors, osteopaths, sports physicians, dentists, nutritionists, and conventional physicians who are first trained in their primary fields before studying applied kinesiology as postgraduates.[1] Muscle testing can be used to diagnose and treat nervous system problems, nutritional deficiencies or excesses, and imbalances in the body's "energy pathways" or meridians.

If you have visited a kinesiologist, you may have been muscle tested for foods or vitamins or suitable treatments. The practitioner may have asked you to hold out your arm and stay strong as they pushed down on your arm. Perhaps you were asked to think of something you really love, and your arm stayed strong and didn't release. Then the kinesiologist may have asked you to think of something you don't like at all and the moment you thought of that, your arm felt weak. The reason behind this is that when the energy field is negative or weak you will have that split second of the muscle letting go and your arm will go down.

While muscle testing is a fascinating concept to explore, I don't recommend that you do this with your students as a kind of lie detector test. That's not the purpose. However, it will help you a lot to learn how to muscle test for yourself as a way to get instant answers for things. One of the easiest and most common ways of energy testing for yourself is to use what kinesiologists call an "O-ring."[2] It's simple. Form an "O" by touching your thumb and your forefinger together. Then, with the other hand, hook your thumb or forefinger through the O-ring and pull to try to break through the O. Variations, such as interlocking two thumb-finger O-rings, can be seen in online videos.[3] When I ask a "yes" question—such as, "Is my name Meribeth Dayme?"—it will hold strong. Alternatively—for example, if I ask, "Is my name Janet Smith?"—my thumb or finger goes through the O-ring very easily.

When you are new to self-energy testing, I first recommend training yourself so that you learn to recognize your "yes" versus your "no." To achieve this, practice a repeated "yes-yes-yes-yes" and "no-no-no-no." If you practice this, eventually you'll find a definite strong hold for "yes" and a definite weakness (a feeling of "letting go") for "no." If you test strongly, no matter how long you hold it your thumb or index finger won't break through. This is something you'll need to play with if you have not done anything like it before.

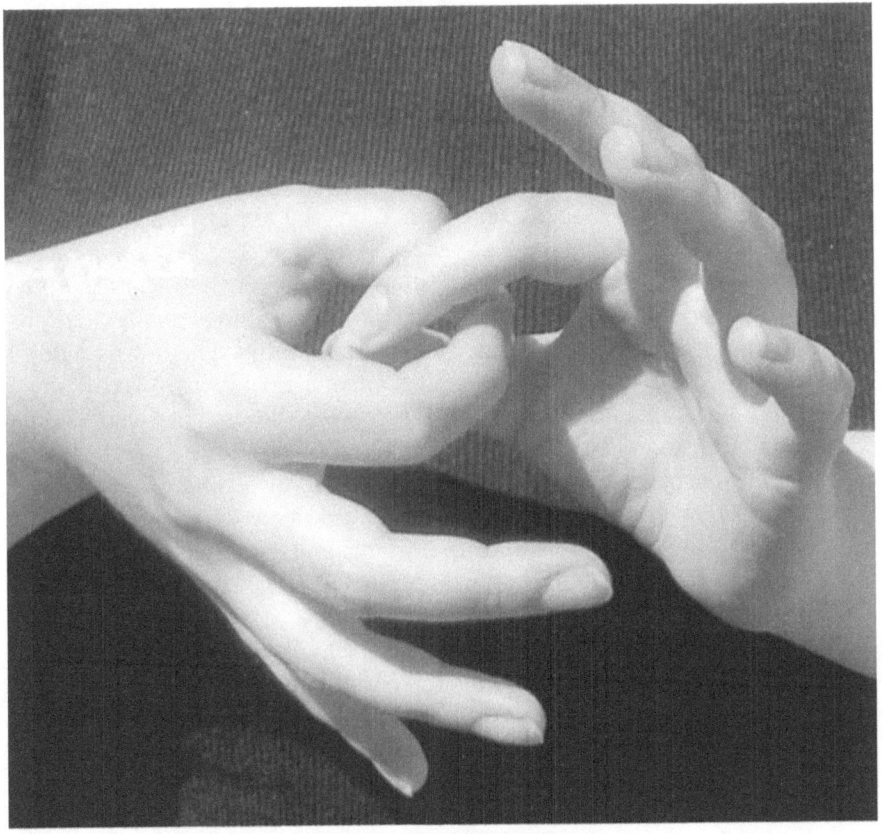

Bidigital "O-ring" energy test
Courtesy of the editors

There are other ways of self-checking energy, such as standing tall and using your body almost like a pendulum. If you feel a slight involuntary shift forward, that is strong. A slight involuntary leaning back is weak, and no involuntary shifting means that you are neutral for that question. But that is a little harder to trust at the beginning than something like O-ring energy testing, which you can both see and feel.

You may be wondering to whom (or what) you are asking your question. You are asking your higher consciousness. How you ask the question is important. The answer has to be "yes" or "no" (i.e, "strong" or "weak"). How you ask the question—and whether or not you are intimately involved with the answer to the question—also makes a difference. For instance, if you are asking something personal—like, "Does he love me or does he love me not?"—that's not going to work because you are too emotionally involved with the answer. Emotions act like superglue in the energy field and you will not get a trustworthy answer. If you ask the same question twenty times you may get a different answer at some point, but the answer you are getting is always for the present moment. If I asked about something pertinent—such as, "Is this music suitable for this student right now?"—and I get "no" as the answer, that doesn't mean that the music will not be suitable in a week or two weeks or a month or a year. You are always welcome to test again. If you check and it tests "yes," go with that. The best way to work with muscle testing is not to question it—accept the answer you are given even if you have no idea why. One of the wonderful things about energy is that there is no "why." There is only infinite possibility. That's why I don't even use that word "why" anymore. If someone asks "why," I will say I don't know because there are far too many possibilities. Or, I start listing some possibilities.

O-ring muscle testing is a simple approach to energy testing. Have fun with it, play with it, and don't worry if it doesn't work for you right away. If that happens, just let it go. If you are uncomfortable and thinking, "Oh, I can't do this," make an adjustment and instead (curiously) ask, "Hmm . . . What will happen when I do this?"

On a deeper level, energy testing can be used to clear energetic issues with singing or any other aspect of life that can originate from old and new emotions such as fear, grief, anger, guilt, and manic joy; the collective thought patterns of families, ancestors, and cultures; past relationships; past illnesses; and belief systems handed down over generations and more. Exploring these without emotional attachment to the outcome will lead to marvelous breakthroughs.

ENERGETIC ANATOMY

We are an energy field. It is part of the greater whole (or super-consciousness) and it furnishes our life force (or chi). The physical body that we see is only a small part of the great field that surrounds and feeds life energy to it. Energy is brought into the body via the chakras and its distribution is accomplished by the meridians, neurotransmitters, and other electrochemical elements. What Eastern cultures have known for thousands of years is now finally becoming more acceptable to Western mentality because of advanced research techniques that allow the recordings of very fine energies. Eastern medicines such as acupuncture, shiatsu, qigong, and many others are designed to keep the life force flowing. When the person is not well (or not functioning well),

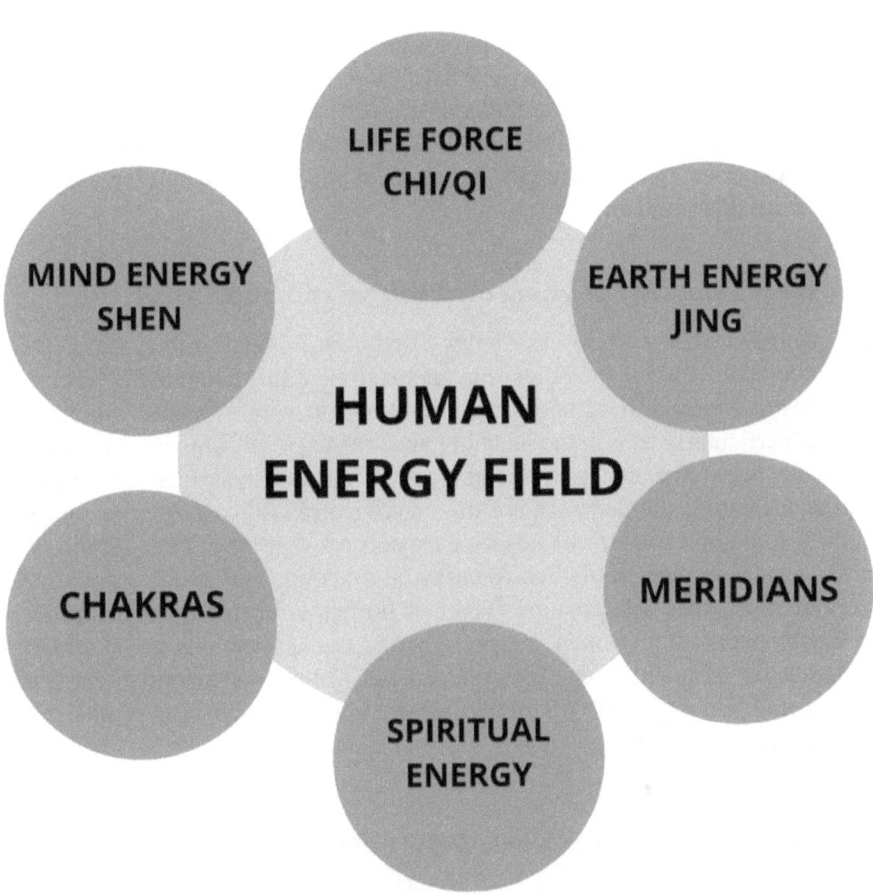

The human energy field
Courtesy of the editors

it is deemed to be a problem associated with blocked chi. The objective is to restore the flow of the life force. It is interesting to see how many of the old traditions in the teaching of singing—especially alignment and breath—actually block chi. When chi is flowing, singing is effortless.

Energy Work Begins with You

Gratitude is a great place to start. When we become grateful for what we are and for what we have (rather than critical or unhappy), we are able to start from where we are right now to build a new relationship with ourselves and others. It does not matter what happened in the past—good or bad. As long as we are tied to those thoughts and memories, we are being held in chains from the past. By starting with exactly what I have today, and being grateful for it, I will have a chance to change and progress at an unbelievable rate. This is the same as saying: "I will let go of all expectations and judgments based on past experiences or future possibilities and begin my life/singing/teaching anew from this moment."

The Ideal Language of Energy Is Positive and Supportive

Everything we think or say has energy and contributes to our reality. Once we understand this, it becomes our responsibility to maintain the integrity of a positive energy field and form a relationship with everyone around us. This is particularly true in the teaching and learning environment. In general, we have been educated and encouraged to use our analytical and critical abilities, often to the detriment of the creative and intuitive. As a result, our habit is to default toward the negative aspects of what we are examining. We often create negative thoughts, remarks, and actions and need to backtrack to remember what was positive. There is no place for this type of response in energy work. Being open, supportive, and transparent sets up an entirely different set of positive energies that do not need to be negative. Support, clarity, and nonjudgment will go a long way toward establishing mutual trust for teaching and learning.

WORKING WITH ENERGY

CoreSinging encourages working with mind energy. It is fast, effective, and noninvasive. When you work with the mind there is no such thing as time—it is instant. This means that you do not need to send your own energy anywhere or to anyone. Instead, you connect with universal energy and allow that to do the work. The success of working with the mind is determined by your ability to have no expectations or emotional involvement in the answer you get to your questions. Above all, do not question the responses you get. The intellect loves to get involved by questioning. After all, we have spent most of our lives learning to question every decision we make. Not here. Detachment and a state of being neutral are primary. Being detached is not the same as lacking sympathy or empathy. Being detached means that I have not prejudged an answer or person. I have no idea as to the answer before I test for it, and I do not react to it once I get it. I accept or clear the energy and move on.[4]

General Principles of Energy Clearing

The most important thing about working with energy is to remember not to become emotionally involved in the answer. You are merely seeking information; you must not care about the outcome. Checking energy begins with your complete detachment from the issue or situation with no vested interest in the outcome. Don't question the answer—just clear any issues if necessary. You *can* ask if your energy field is strong or weak to a situation. You can ask questions that can be answered "yes" or "no." You *can* command a change. When you work with energy in this way, you are asking your energy field (or higher consciousness) for the answer—not your own mind or previous experience. Always check to see if you have any energetic history of negative energy with any person you teach or meet. If so, ask how many, and clear each one. This will clear any subconscious or other history that may impede your relationship with this person.

Your Space

A welcoming, beautifully energized space is the nicest thing you can provide for your students. It is a tremendous gift to enter an atmosphere that feels like it is full of love and is a place where trust lives. Keeping your teaching studio energized and "clear" is of primary importance not only to you and your teaching, but also for each pupil who arrives at your door. Believe it or not, you can clear your studio space by mentally commanding it with the word "clear." It is important to do this at the beginning of the day and between each student. You do not want any old thoughts hanging around that might influence the next person who walks in the door. Doing this is silent and only takes a second to think; yes, your thoughts are that powerful. Many CoreSinging teachers use this frequent energy clearing and find that they are far less tired at the end of the day. Think of it as dusting your room after each person leaves.

There are many methods and rituals for clearing space. You may have one you use already. Try giving your teaching space a thorough energetic cleanse each week. Some people give a light sprinkling of salt, light candles, clap to clear negative energies, or envision the space filled with light (or a color). Once you have cleared your space, dedicate it to creativity, trust, or whatever value seems important at the time. You can energy test for this before you make the choice. What is appropriate for one day may be different the next. What is important is to make sure you clear your own thoughts—and any negative energy from the last person who has had a lesson—and begin anew with each student.

Every person who comes to your studio or office carries their own set of energies, some of which may be negative. You can clear these quickly before or as the person enters. This can be done in a matter of seconds by simply using your mind. Once this habit is established, the energetic health of your studio or home will become so important to you that "keeping it clean" will quickly become routine. Before beginning any activity, always test to see if your space is clear.

TYPES OF ENERGY

According to Eastern teachings, there are three types of energies: earth (*jing* for the Chinese), life force (chi or qi), and mind (*shen*). Earth energy or *jing* consists of all natural forces such as air, wind, fire, and water. This can include volcanoes, hurricanes, lightning, plants and trees, and much more. As you can see, these are very powerful forces. The life force or chi permeates all things and is considered to be far more powerful than earth energies. It is this energy that many healers call on in their work. The third energy is the mind or *shen*. This is the most powerful energy. Ideally, each person has a balance of these three energies. Qigong and tai chi are excellent ways to balance them.

I love practicing qigong and tai chi because they are all about flow and movement—as is singing. People who are in their head all the time demonstrate a lack of balance. Most of the time these people are not grounded at all. You will hear this in a voice that has too many high frequencies (and not enough lows). The best way to correct this is to make sure their feet are completely touching the ground. Chi or life force can also be blocked by the way we are physically aligned and balanced. An overly arched back or high breathing can block the movement of chi along the meridians and cause a lack of flow in the body. Energetic balance makes a huge difference in the ease of singing, quality of sound, and resonance.

Most of us have no idea how powerful our minds are. An ancient proverb says that "energy follows thought." In other words, nothing happens or is invented without first having the thought. This maxim has led to concepts of intention, visualization, the law of attraction, and many more philosophical ideas. Mind control is one of the most prominent topics of psychology coaching in both sport and business, and we are learning to use it for practice and performance in music. Establishing intent in whatever you are doing is vital to your success in any field.

One of the current areas of research and study is neuroplasticity. We used to think that the brain was not able to change. However, recent studies have shown that this could not be further from the truth. I recommend watching the 2008 documentary *The Brain That Changes Itself* by Norman Doidge. Our self-talk and the language we or our students use is vital to our own success. The sooner we learn this in the teaching of singing the better. Negative talk weakens the energy field. Using words like never, should, ought, right, wrong, try, and many more are sure ways of limiting learning and performance. Because your mind can issue commands to your higher consciousness, it is easy and important to begin channeling this energy toward healing and changing for the better. Stating what you want to happen is more powerful than you may realize. For example, if you fall, you shake up the energy of your body, which then becomes a feeling (i.e., you begin hurting). Just saying "clear trauma"—and thus reclaiming positive energy—can help to minimize physical pain.

CONSCIOUS, SUBCONSCIOUS, AND HIGHER CONSCIOUSNESS/INFINITY

There is an incredible amount of information fed to us every nanosecond of the day and night. The conscious mind filters nearly all of it, or we would not be able to function. The conscious mind is the part we use to speak, command, and consolidate information so we can make sense of it all. The conscious mind can deal with about 7–40 pieces of information per second; it is more typical to work with 7–15 bits of information. When we are using this kind of conscious attention, it is very slow and takes a long time to get a response. The fastest possible response is .5 seconds.[5] Singing moves much faster than this. When we are busy analyzing or thinking about each thing we do, we are slow, cumbersome, and essentially block the ability to be spontaneous and fluid. Trying to make everything happen is a nonstarter for learning and performing. The subconscious mind deals with millions, even billions, of pieces of information per second. This information comes from all our senses, the vast network of nerve endings in the body, and stored information from every thought or experience we have ever had. This quantity is mind-boggling. Imagine filtering all of that into seven pieces of information. The conscious mind is the ultimate filter!

The abstract noun "consciousness" is originally derived from the Latin *con* (with) and *scire* (to know). Awareness is often used to describe that infinite, knowing consciousness that is always with us. Others call it "higher consciousness." Mystic and some spiritual traditions teach us that everything we would ever need to know resides in our consciousness.[6] To access this aspect of ourselves, we must transcend the conscious mind and the subconscious.

This can be done via meditation, focus, breath work, and much more. We all have a higher knowing that gives us some valuable creative and practical solutions to questions we pose. (My answers often come in the shower.) Awareness is about listening—not talking. The more we become aware of this aspect of ourselves, the faster we acquire response and synchronicity. When this is achieved, seemingly magical things begin to happen.

The Collective Consciousness and How It Affects Us

Once you begin to understand that everything is energy and there is a continuation of what we think we see that is solid and the field of energy, you realize that everything is connected, and that includes our consciousness. Every thought, every word, every piece of information (in addition to prior knowledge) is surrounding us all the time. The collective consciousness refers to this and more specifically to our families, areas of study (such as singing), local culture, and national collective consciousnesses as well. That is unlimited information available. We tap into our collective conscious all the time without even realizing it. That is the way we often develop beliefs that are the same as our family, teachers, or spiritual leaders. We do not realize how often we are under the control of collective thought as opposed to that of our own.

The Art of Diversion

Have you ever noticed that when you are not thinking about something you can often achieve much more? How is that? One explanation is that the conscious mind is ponderous and slow. When we trust that what we want to achieve is possible, it can happen much faster. The best examples of this are athletes who practice with intention and perform in the "zone." Once you are in the zone, things just happen. Have you ever been in the zone while performing? I have, and it is truly like you have all the energy and all the skill you need. The song just sings itself. Wouldn't it be wonderful for that to happen regularly?

Many teachers use what I call the art of diversion to get students to sing without pondering the skill. Asking a performer to do something like move or draw while singing allows them to concentrate on what you have asked them to do, and—when they do so—they sing easily. Everyone is surprised when they first experience this. Diversion allows the natural and innate wisdom of the body and energy field to do the singing. This is one way to help us get out of our own way.

Learning to Trust the Inherent Wisdom of the Energy Field

When dealing with something seemingly invisible to us, our conditioning to what we perceive to be "reality" (or something solid) kicks in and begins to sabotage our ability to trust. For years we have been taught that "seeing is believing."[7] Once we can let go of our "reality" focus, it is astounding how many possibilities begin to emerge. We have lived in a "one right answer" world for a long time. The technology we have today is opening the way to many possibilities as opposed to only one answer. Every field—from physics to electronics to mindfulness to self-development—is influenced by the incredible quantity of recent scientific information. We are living in an age where there is an explosion of knowledge—and it will not stop. This is true in the vocal world as well. The singing profession continues to look backward, but the answers are not there. There is no need to negate the past, only to accept it as part of an ongoing evolution and enjoy the new along with it.

So where do we look for verification? First, your higher consciousness knows the answers you seek. A clue to whether an answer is appropriate for you is, quite simply, how you feel about the answer. Sometimes a thought is followed by a sense of warmth in the body, a feeling of elation, or a sense of comfort. Too often we cut off these sensations because we are too busy analyzing what is happening. We come by it naturally—we've been taught to do it. However, now is the time to learn to trust our inner instincts and allow the proof to unfold. There are answers we can tap by being mindful, meditating, or practicing qigong and tai chi. It takes a different kind of patience, understanding, and the profound knowledge that there is an answer available to you. Trust that it is a natural and valuable part of communication with yourself and your audience.

Mindful Preparation: Being in a State of Readiness

Preparing to sing is alerting the mind, body, and spirit to focus on the act at hand. Holistic preparation is the key to efficiency and shortened learning time, as well as focus, balance, centering and mental acuity. Athletes learn to do this early on in their training. Singers benefit from this approach by learning music faster, improving the ability to retain text and music, and greatly diminishing performance anxiety. Always set your intent before any lesson, practice session, audition, or performance. Recent research in the mushrooming field of neuroplasticity is showing how important our intent, habitual thinking, and ability to let go of past negative thinking is to changing the neural pathways in the brain. In my years of working with CoreSinging teachers, they report that this has made a huge difference in the learning and lives of themselves and their students.

In numerous areas of self-development, there is huge emphasis on mindfulness, awareness, and how the "law of attraction" brings to us what we are thinking. So, when we are busy negating ourselves, that is what we are attracting. Countering that with positive thoughts seems like an appropriate response. However, it is not sufficient because when you have a mix of the positive and negative, they counteract each other, and bring us some lessons we had rather not learn. Learning to use positive language and positive thoughts about your teaching, performance goals, and approach to life, however, can reap substantial rewards. It is important to insist that your students bring this into their lives and—if nowhere else—their lessons. The easiest way to alleviate negativity and achieve balance is to have no expectations. Never drag the past into the present. This is easier said than done because our culture teaches us to analyze and discuss problems. The CoreSinging approach focuses exclusively on what we want to achieve without any "extra" analysis, justification, or discussion.

Centering and Grounding: Dynamic Balance

Numerous habits can interfere with being grounded or "earthed." These include overthinking, nerves, lack of trust in our own resources, faulty perceptions of technique, and poor postural habits, to name a few. These are all things that take us away from being present in the moment. The quickest way to become grounded is with dynamic balance. "Dynamic" here refers to something that is constantly changing and moving—the polar opposite of static and rigid posture. Even when we are trying to stay still, our bodies are constantly in motion through our breath, heartbeat, blood pressure, organs, cells, and molecules.

The quickest and most efficient way to find dynamic balance (or alignment) for singing is to begin by putting both feet solidly on the floor, toes facing forward, slightly apart, as if Velcroed to the ground. It is amazing how good it feels to be connected to the earth. Think of bringing energy up through your feet. Next imagine invisible lines or vortices of energy connecting your body to the earth and beyond. Imagine an invisible line from your tailbone (coccyx) down to the ground. Then imagine a line up from your upper back between your shoulder blades. In the front of your body, imagine a line down from your lower sternum, and—finally—imagine lines down from both elbows.

As you imagine these lines of energy you may feel small physical shifts and movements that you are not consciously creating. Allow these adjustments to happen without analyzing them. Numerous breathing techniques from Eastern sources are also useful for centering. Some of these are specific techniques for yoga or healing and not necessarily useful for singing. I prefer to use something more analogous to singing, such as qigong.

Qigong

Qigong is an ancient movement form that began as a technique for healing three to six thousand years ago (depending on whom you read). The movements are designed to create flow in various meridians. There are many forms of qigong and many "masters" (as you might imagine for a system so ancient). Therefore, you will see many variations of the same thing with different teachers. There is not one right way. You can see some beautiful illustrations of the flow of qigong movement in the videos of Jesse Tsao. I particularly like Tsao's version of "Qigong Essentials: Eight-Piece Brocades (*ba duan jin*)."[8] One reason I like to use qigong is that in grounding there is a flow of breath and movement that is similar to music. Qigong is also healing.

In qigong, all joints are soft. I like this because it is much better than the idea of "relaxing," which is a state of collapse to many. The eyes are always open and seeing in qigong—not closed. Awareness is an important aspect of energy and communication, so the eyes are a key to presence, creating a space for the audience and for your connection to all that is around you. Outdated instructions—like "find a spot on the wall," "choose one person to focus on," "use a bobbly head to look around the room," "block out everything in front of you"—create blocks in the flow of chi and have a discernible negative effect on the resonance and quality of the voice. You can experiment with this idea by first singing with staring eyes glued to a point somewhere, then with your eyes closed, and finally with open eyes, using your peripheral vision to become aware of everything in your space. You will readily notice that peripheral vision significantly opens the sound.

In qigong, breathing is gentle and not audible. There is no need to prove that you are breathing. In general, you inhale as you gather energy and exhale as you release it. As in dynamic balance, your energy field is stronger when your feet are pointing straight ahead (like the number eleven). It is also a position of strength to place the tip of the tongue directly behind the upper teeth. By placing the tongue there, it connects two meridians running up the front and back of your body. While you can't sing with your tongue remaining in this position, it is useful when you are doing other things, such as walking on stage and preparing to sing. Creating intent by using any of the qigong or breathing exercises can be done in as little as a few minutes. It is helpful to begin lessons this way because it allows the student to come into the presence of your studio and immediately focus their energy in a way that is beneficial for learning.

WORKING WITH ENERGY VERSUS MANIPULATING MUSCLES

Centuries of various vocal traditions have given us many ways to approach the teaching of singing. Different cultures have emphasized a variety of physical alignments deemed critical to good singing. Many phrases are familiar to you: "chest up," "tummy in," "feet at angles one in front of the other," "hang like a puppet on a string," "lines of balance," "have noble posture," "tilt your pelvis," and so on. Some of these instructions have been handed down from teacher to pupil for generations without ever being questioned. When examined from the standpoint of energy, many of these techniques and suggestions actually block the flow of chi in the body and weaken the energy field. Many of the postures and alignments cause the singer to use more muscle than necessary to maintain balance. When that happens, the body is so busy helping the singer maintain equilibrium that it steals energy from the act of singing. It never ceases to amaze me that teachers do not insist on good balance in every lesson. The number of performers who are overworking and compensating for lack of balance is astounding. It is analogous to having a crooked scaffolding of a house. The extra support you would need for that house to stay erect would be phenomenal. Note: With students I use the phrase "invisible channels or vortices of energy." I have found that if I use words like lines, grids, or other similar vocabulary, they perceive something rigid and often feedback that they feel more constrained. I have to emphasize the words "invisible" and "energy." When they get it, they feel so much freer, it is easier to breathe, and easier to sing. The vocal instrument is so well balanced that the former hard work of singing is alleviated. Allow it to happen. The body knows how to sing.

WHAT YOUR STUDENTS NEED TO KNOW ABOUT ENERGY

As a CoreSinging teacher, your role is to guide students toward a positive relationship with their voice and singing. They do not need to know all that you know or understand about energy. However, the following reminders may be helpful.

Gratitude

Being grateful for what we have is taught in every spiritual and religious pursuit, and yet we tend to forget that it applies to everything in which we are engaged. This is particularly true of the art of singing. Make gratitude part of the language of the studio. When singers feel their voice is never good enough, they become quite skilled at being negative about any sound that they make, which blocks learning and creativity.

Use of Language

The most important thing you can help your pupils achieve is a change in the way they describe themselves and their singing. You can help them learn to reframe any negative or self-deprecating language as well as implement a studio rule that there is no negative self-language allowed. I call those negative self-predictions "curses"—it minimizes the potential for success. It is far better to think about the desired positive outcome than to devote energy to the negative.

Focusing and Establishing Intent

Focusing gives you and the student a chance to regroup before beginning to sing. It will bring you both into the present and establish a good habit for the student. This is useful for private and group sessions and does not need to take more than one or two minutes. Develop a goal for each lesson by focusing on what is wanted or needed based on the current state of the music or voice, and then determine what the student wants to achieve in that session. Other focusing exercises may include a simple visualization, a moment of silence, or a short breathing exercise. There are many more possibilities as well. Feel free to be imaginative, creative, and inventive.

Staying Centered

Staying centered means that the body, mind, and spirit are grounded and balanced. Many of the exercises used in CoreSinging will help you do that. Dynamic balance, breathing exercises, focusing, and visualization are all useful for centering.

FINAL THOUGHTS

Energy, while multifaceted and complex, is profoundly important to our lives, the lives of others, and the world around us. The perspectives on energy discussed in this chapter are foundational to the CoreSinging approach, paving the way for an in-depth exploration of other key elements. The following chapters will explore additional concepts that are essential to CoreSinging through in-depth discussions on four other elements: awareness, imagination, practice, and performance.

NOTES

1. The International College of Applied Kinesiology is an institution devoted to training these practitioners. https://www.icakusa.com.
2. https://en.wikipedia.org/wiki/BDORT.
3. https://vimeo.com/9454676.
4. It is important to remember that energy work is not at the level of consciousness. You may need to remind yourself of this frequently when first working with energy.
5. Bruce H. Lipton, *The Biology of Belief: Unleashing the Power of Consciousness, Matter and Miracles* (New York: Hay House, 2005).
6. While many religions speak about this, it is not a religious concept and is not to be confused with religion.
7. It is more modern now to say the reverse: "believing is seeing."
8. Jesse Tsao, "Qigong Essentials: Eight-Piece Brocades," https://www.taichihealthways.com/Qigong-and-Other/qigong-essentials-8-piece-brocades.html.

Chapter Three

Awareness

Awareness is the key to how you use space, allow spontaneity, and at the same time remain centered. It is a huge topic that is often neglected in the teaching of singing. On the contrary, in many cases singers are taught to block out everything so they can "concentrate." Energetically this is not a good idea. Once a singer begins to block out things, they are also blocking their own energy and expansiveness as well. It then becomes a two-way barrier, which is not something that is beneficial to optimal performance. The more aware you are, the more possibilities there are for expansion of your sound and your message.

In this chapter, we will be looking at some of the many ways to expand and use awareness and mindfulness in singing. There will be exercises for you to do.[1] We are going to explore energy and transformation in the sound by experimenting with our bodies, breath, and eyes as well as tuning in with all our senses and energetically connecting to our place. These practices will open your sound, awareness, and imagination in ways that immensely improve teaching and singing. One interesting benefit of this work is also the alleviation of performance anxiety. This was not a goal when these exercises were originally conceived; however, many teachers who have applied these CoreSinging ideas report that their singers now experience far less anxiety.

INTRODUCTION TO AWARENESS

Concepts, methods, and "secret" techniques of breath have existed in singing schools since they were first introduced several hundred years ago. It was likely fear of running out of breath that started the evolution of breath "control" in voice pedagogy. Now we are faced with myriad systems, all of which claim varying degrees of success. Many of these systems are based on the physical observations of accomplished singers.[2] In general, the methods that derive from such observations are usually related to the visible ramifications of breath use. That means that pedagogues have looked at the muscles being used and then try to devise a method for using those muscles to create what is needed for singing. As each person has different alignment, balance, and postural habits, breath patterns are a result of those habits. Breathing, therefore, is much simpler than we often make it. To begin our examination of this topic, I am going to discuss the physical act of breathing because there are so many misconceptions and misperceptions about it.

Physical Aspects of Breathing

The simplest thing one can say about breath is that air comes in and out subconsciously (or passively). We never think about our normal day-to-day breathing. If this were not true, we would not have time for anything else in our life. Various physiological balances in the body—such as pH and blood gasses—are dependent on healthy breathing. Various positions of the back, rib cage, and pelvis impact the movement of the muscles involved in breathing. The mechanism of that breathing is a signal from the brain that indicates a need for air, allowing the diaphragm to contract, which creates space and a negative air pressure in the lungs, thus creating a need to inhale again. This cycle repeats itself ad infinitum.

The operative system here is a balance of pressures in three chambers. The first chamber is the abdomen. While it is a closed system and not normally filled with air, it nevertheless plays a huge role in breath management. We include in this chamber the bony pelvis, sacrum, lumbar vertebrae, lower part of the rib cage, diaphragm, and abdominal muscles. I have used balloons to illustrate this: If you push on the walls of a balloon, the other side will move. In the case of the abdomen, there is a bone in the back, so the mobile parts are the top (or diaphragm), front, and small area below the pelvis. With stability in the abdomen, the subglottic pressure is adequate for vocal fold closure, and there is back pressure on the top of the vocal folds caused by some air being reflected from the palate, teeth, and inner cheeks back toward the vocal folds. This allows for a balancing of supraglottic pressure. When there is a lot of tension in the abdominal area, the top of the balloon will not move. That means the diaphragm will not move downward, and something in the pressure system above it (chest area) will need to move instead.

The second chamber is the chest cavity, which is almost completely closed as well. This area opens or closes depending upon the position of the vocal folds, which form a valve at the top of the respiratory system. This chamber is bordered by the spine, rib cage, and diaphragm. The position of the body, spine, and rib cage determines the possibilities of movement for breathing in this area. Obviously, the largest mobile area is the diaphragm, located at the bottom of the rib cage. You can feel the pressure in the chest when you hold your breath (glottis closed), and lightly contract the abdominal muscles.

The third chamber is a complex one: the mouth. It's a closed system when the lips are firmly closed, but otherwise it's a leaky-pressure system with openings in two places: the nose and mouth. You can feel the different pressure systems relating to each other when you firmly close the lips and puff out your cheeks by blowing on the inside of them. You can feel the pressures of the abdomen, chest, and inside of the mouth and throat. Any tensions and imbalances in the head and neck will affect this system.

When the three pressure chambers are balanced in singing, there is adequate stability in the abdomen, the subglottic pressure is adequate for vocal fold closure, and there is back pressure on the top of the vocal folds caused by some air being reflected from the palate, teeth, and inner cheeks back toward the vocal folds. This allows for a balancing supraglottic pressure. When any of the pressure chambers are out of balance, breath control is difficult, if not impossible. Some of the causes of pressure loss are as follows: perception of a need to aim air and sound out the mouth which negates the needed back pressure; abdominal muscles that are too lax or too tense; inadequate subglottic pressure; and poor physical alignment.

When this is not properly understood, voice teachers begin to tinker with various muscles in an attempt to fix the problem. For example, when there is inadequate back pressure from the mouth and the vocal fold valve is leaking air, all the attention on the abdominal muscles will do nothing. When there is too much abdominal and chest pressure, it closes the vocal folds (as occurs when lifting something heavy) and creates tension in the sound that results in poor sound quality. I think this is why the SOVT (semioccluded vocal tract) "straw" exercises are so popular now. You can do the same with lip trills, blowing through nearly closed lips, and so forth. Ultimately, it is all about balance of pressure of the three chambers.[3]

Allowing the breath to flow is a common issue with beginners as well as more advanced singers. You can give all kinds of reasons for struggling with this: gasping for perceived lack of air, having been taught to take a breath and then pause before onset of the sound, trying to control air at the level of the larynx, and many more. But the solution is simple. What we need to think is "air in, sound out." Simply that.

One way of achieving this flow is through a simple head-turning exercise. Begin by slowly—*very* slowly—turning the head from side to side while remaining conscious of the air flowing in and out as you turn. Do not allow any hesitancy in the movement of the head. Once you have established easy and slow movement of the head, add a gentle hum on the exhalation, still without allowing the movement to be hesitant (or stopping). When people think, they tend to stop the breath and the movement even though they are singing. Continue the exercise using phrases—speaking first and then singing. You can learn an entire song this way, and you will find that the breath will flow, and you easily will have enough air to sing each phrase.

Energetic Approaches to Breathing

I have found that the way to navigate through all the misinformation that is out there about breathing is to treat breathing energetically. This approach solves a lot of issues without the intellectual concentration on the mechanics of breathing. The following suggestions represent a few ways to accomplish this.

Being Breathed

I love to use the Hoberman mini sphere (or "breathing ball") to illustrate being breathed.[4] Sit quietly, two feet on the floor, imagining that every pore in your body is breathing. Do this for a few minutes, concentrating on the movement of the breath and the expansion and release. Allow it to happen—do not try to make it happen. The whole body/energy field expands with the inhalation and returns with the exhalation. It's a lovely feeling that can be calming and relaxing before auditions, concerts, lessons, and much more.

Once you have a sense of being breathed, experiment with that approach while singing a song. At first you will need to go phrase by phrase and have the patience not to rush to the end. All breathing exercises eventually need to be integrated into your song. It is not enough to just do the breathing. So many people do not know how to connect the dots between an exercise and its application to singing.

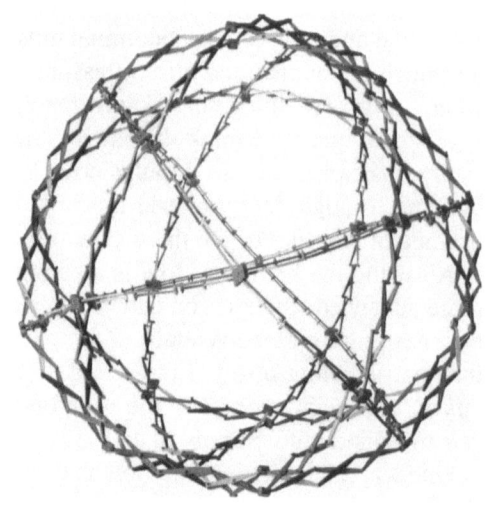

A Hoberman sphere
Creative Commons (CC BY-SA 4.0)

The Breath Loop

Next, explore the breath loop around the spinal cord.[5] This is a wonderful exercise that can be used for centering and calming; it's easy to imagine, and no one knows you are doing it. I suggest thinking of the breath loop while waiting for an event, performance, practice, or before an audition. Imagine that you are breathing in from the bottom of the spine/coccyx. The "in" breath travels all the way to the top of the head along the back of the spinal cord, and the "out" breath travels down the front of the spine—not the outer body—back to the coccyx. This is a very long, narrow loop. As with the other breaths, once comfortable with this, add sounds and phrases of the song on the exhale.

Using the Chakras for Breathing

When describing this to a student, it is not necessary to use the word "chakra." Alternatively, you can say lower back, solar plexus area, or heart. Energy enters the back of each chakra and exits the front. You can breathe the same way. Imagine breathing in from the back and breathing out the front of each chakra. Do this repeatedly, and—when you are comfortable doing so—begin to add sound. The lower chakras relate to the low frequencies in the sound, and the higher ones correspond to the higher frequencies. You can get a singer to add depth to the sound by imagining they are breathing in at the level of the second (pelvic area) chakra. It's a lot of fun to explore the different sounds you get with concentration of breath on each chakra.

Also imagining that you are breathing in from different combinations such as chakra 2 and 5, or 2 and 4. Later, be brave enough to use all of them at once. Breathing in through the back takes the emphasis off of all the need to concentrate on the abdomen and allows the whole system to work easily and naturally. I have had well-known teachers tell me that the spinal loop and chakra breathing worked better than all of the mechanical breathing exercises they had tried with their students. It is very important that you spend time *doing* all of the above for yourself—it's not good enough to just read this! There are so many ways to imagine breath that keep a singer centered. You can try many for yourself and your students. They can even grow roots and breathe from the middle of the earth.

Scalar Breathing

This approach to breathing is very advanced and not for everyone. Valerie V. Hunt was the first to discover that consciously thinking about breathing in the same frequencies or colors coming from opposite sides of the body creates a "bioscalar" energy inside the body. Hunt further discovered that the energy by all hands-on healers, craniosacral therapists, and psychic healers is bioscalar energy.[6]

The Orchestra Outside You: Working with External Awareness

Being aware is a must for excellent performance. So often performers are taught to block everything out, when what they need to do instead is open up to all that is going on around them. Blocking awareness also blocks your message and your sound. This does not negate the intention and focus of the message; it includes it. Filling your space and creating energetic power in your voice means being open, aware, and mindful without judgment or analysis. It is the key to being centered and present wherever you are and contributing to a compelling voice and performance. Whether you are teaching or performing, simply sitting in awareness for a few minutes or less will help set up your space and keep you comfortable in it.

On the subconscious level we are being bombarded with millions, even billions, of pieces of sensory input. Take time to tune in to each of your senses. What are you seeing, hearing, feeling, tasting, and smelling in that space? Write down as much as you can.

The first sense is *seeing*. Some questions you can ask yourself: What colors are bright? How many different colors are around you? How do they make you feel? What shapes are present? Are there people in your line of sight? Are you seeing movement of any kind? Are you able to see the large picture with your peripheral vision? Next comes *hearing*: What sounds are present—both outside and inside? Are there regular sounds such as ticking clocks or electrical buzzes? Are there sounds of traffic, or planes overhead? Are there voices nearby or in the distance? What's happening outside? Are birds singing? Trees rustling? Can you hear wind or rain? *Touching* and *feeling*: What does the air feel like on your skin? How do your clothes feel on you? Are they heavy or light? Are you aware of your skin all over your body? What different textures are present? Regarding *smell*: Are there odors in the room or space? Can you smell any flowers present? Is someone wearing oils or perfumes? And finally, *taste*: Is there a taste in your mouth? Can you taste the room? (I swear that I can taste a library.)

Once you have made your list, perform an experiment. Choose something simple to sing. Sing it first while blocking out everything. Sing it again, this time tuning in to everything. Imagine that everything around you contributes to your personal orchestra. What I have found is that when you use all the senses and all the input from those senses to form a kind of energetic orchestra for your performance (or practice), the singing expands incredibly.

A playful exercise to use with groups is to have someone sing while the leader instructs the group (secretly) to either begin whispering or dropping things. At first, the selected singer looks completely startled. Then once they catch on that they are to use the energy of the disruptions, something entirely different begins to happen. With children and adults, it is fun to assign sounds to the audience. For example, if someone is singing "Sheep May Safely Graze," I ask people to be the sheep, birds in trees, wind, or rustling leaves. It's a lot of fun and aids the imagination and expression of the singer. The audience loves participating in this way too.

Another favorite awareness exercise is to ask the singer to place both hands solidly on the piano, as if attached by Velcro. Then have them place an ear on the piano. Now ask them to sing while feeling the vibrations of the piano and staying tuned to the vibrations while the teacher or pianist plays. It's a wonderful feeling and allows the singer to tune to the music in a substantively different way. CoreSinging teachers have also reported that this exercise has greatly helped some students learn to sing in tune.

The Orchestra Inside You: Working with Internal Awareness

Did you know that every cell and organ in your body has its own rhythm and sound? These sounds are too subtle to hear, but they are always present. Energy is going on inside of you all the time. In an anechoic (i.e., "without echo") chamber the background noise in the room is so low that it approaches the lowest threshold theorized by mathematicians. Your internal sounds become audible, and you become the sound.[7] You can hear your own heartbeat. A ringing in your ears becomes deafening. When you move, your bones make a grinding noise. Eventually you lose your balance, because the absolute lack of reverberation sabotages your spatial awareness.

Since we don't have an anechoic chamber, there are other ways to tune in to our internal sounds and rhythms. First, focus on your breath. This is the most obvious pattern and one that is used in meditation and mindfulness as a starting point for focus. Tuning into your breath means just that. Do not try to manipulate the breath or study it—just notice it.

Next, find your radial pulse (next to the distal radius bone in your wrist) using a gentle, three-finger touch. If you press too hard you will not feel it. Note that your pulse is not a metronome and can be somewhat irregular. You can also find the carotid pulse in your neck just between your sternocleidomastoid muscles and the larynx. That one is usually quite strong. You can use the pulse for the internal rhythm of your song. If you play with this, you will find it to be centering. Sing with your pulse, even though it is a bit irregular. This exercise helps singers understand that rhythm is internal. It is a refreshing alternative to "toe tapping" or other external attempts to find rhythm.

Although there is indeed an internal rhythm to your organs, it is one that will have to be imagined. However, it is possible to access these rhythms once we are tuned in to them. It is always possible to sing while imagining that your internal orchestra is supporting you and your sound.

FINAL THOUGHTS

It is important to remember that external and internal awareness exercises are ultimately combined. Imagine that all the sensations are now fusing to make one wonderful energy field of you, your voice, the music, and the message. And—most important—remember to have fun!

NOTES

1. As you explore these exercises, please be prepared to sing and record yourself for best results. Even better, do this with several people and note the differences. You will need to see and hear this—not just read about it!

2. Richard Miller's *National Schools of Singing: English, French, Italian, and German Techniques of Singing Revisited*, second ed. (Lanham, MD: Scarecrow Press, 1997) is perhaps the most famous and influential of these studies, at least within the academic world of voice pedagogy.

3. Readers will note I have not said much about muscle movement. That is because I believe when you understand the pressure system (and can look at a person's balance) you can then begin to be logical about how the muscles are working. Many times singing is taught by directing students to focus on particular muscle actions, which is in effect looking at symptoms and not causes. Attention to muscular movement often confuses singers, causing them to overwork.

4. Hoberman spheres, originally designed by inventor Chuck Hoberman (b. 1956), are popular educational toys that resemble geodesic domes capable of folding down to a fraction of their size. See https://hoberman.com.

5. Adapted from the "cosmic breath" concept as described by Mantak Chia in *Cosmic Orbit: Connect to the Universe from Within*, ed. Lee Holden (Chiang Mai, Thailand: Universal Tao Publications, 2005).

6. Valerie V. Hunt, *Bioscalar: The Primary Healing Energy*, Audio CD (Malibu, CA: Malibu, 2008).

7. https://www.cnn.com/style/article/anechoic-chamber-worlds-quietest-room/index.html.

Chapter Four

Imagination

Watching the excitement of a young child learn something new is one of the most joyful experiences I know. Their enthusiasm and curiosity are unparalleled. I think I have kept enthusiasm for learning my whole life, and it saddens me to see anyone bored when learning new things. Somehow, somewhere along the way our education system began to treat learning as something that is very serious—with right and wrong answers for everything—rather than an opportunity to explore the wide world of possibilities available to us.

So many arguments and beliefs are based on the right and wrong expectations we developed in our schools, cultures, and nations. Tests were such that there would only be one right answer—and anything else was wrong. This led to our need to "get it right," and everything went downhill from there. This has carried over to learning to sing and has created a generation of efficient, boring singers who are busy "getting it right" while compelling stage communication has been neglected. Educators of young people know that when information is fun, it enables faster learning; however, there is a reticence to make things fun after a certain age. I believe we need to appeal to the child in every person. CoreSinging is dedicated to creating and promoting learning processes that are fun, effective, and create joy.

THE JOY OF LEARNING

Even the words "right and "wrong" weaken the energy field. Interestingly, when you muscle test the words "right" and "wrong," they both weaken the energy field. Right away you can understand that anyone working toward that goal is going to be weak. When being right is the goal, they start from a difficult place. One of my challenges when I first began to write books was changing my phrasing and replacing both of those words. That was quite a process. The best way to get rid of the need for being right is to have a veritable cornucopia of fun ways to teach. It goes back to the idea of diverting the concentration away from a specific way of doing something so that the body and higher knowledge will take over and allow the singing to happen.

The best way to see possibilities is to stop any judgment or preconceived idea of how something happens or works. When we have expectations, that sets up those expectations to happen. This kind of self-sabotage is often seen when students are auditioning. They predict that someone else will be cast and it weakens the energy of their own performance. How often does a teacher set up negative expectations for a student? Teachers often say things like "Johnny is never prepared" or "Pat always sings the high note flat." Instead of expecting a negative outcome, it is far more helpful for a teacher to stay open—with a blank screen, so to speak—and just see what happens. By doing this, it will allow the student space to change and grow without having their energy weakened by negative energy from the teacher.

How did we get so serious in the first place? As I said earlier, along the way, it became a perception that adult learning must be serious. This gradually crept into the whole school experience, which moved into the business world, and so on. The collective consciousness took over, and we became captive to all those thoughts. How can we get rid of that and move on to teaching and learning with joy and imagination? The answer lies in play and remembering that in play, nothing is sacred. The moment we think something is precious, we begin to treat it like fragile china, and we walk on eggshells. This simply does not work for singing.

Using Imagination in Learning the Text to a Song

When learning is fun, then there is not a need to remember. Instead, remembering happens through play and by doing the exercises. When it comes to learning text and music, there is huge variety in the CoreSinging approach. The exercises are fun and—more important—involve the entire energy field in the process. Groups love the CoreSinging exercises and spend a lot of time laughing while doing them. In my workshops, I put people in twos or threes and have them do the exercises for each other.

When you are teaching one on one, it is vital that you participate and share the activity with your student. Never give them the exercise and just observe them. That is the surest way to increase their level of self-consciousness.

CoreSinging approaches learning music by first beginning with the text. Unless the character and the words are really understood and expressed, it is hard to deliver the message with complete freedom. By learning the text as a dramatic monologue first, it establishes the imagination, the character, and the onomatopoetic properties of the words and sounds so vital to compelling communication. Only after you have honored your text can you begin to explore the musical aspects. You will find that much of your work has already been done by the process of developing the text and message of the song. Now—let's have some fun!

Creating a Character

Any song, no matter what genre or style, has a character (or characters). The first thing to do when exploring a new song is read the text and create the character. You do not need to know the character in advance—you are creating one every time you encounter a new song. This is less true in opera or musical theatre where the characters are clearly defined. In this case, you must thoroughly explore the emotions and make them yours.

To help a student develop a specific character, I have devised the following template, which can be used with any song or aria. When you are able to answer all these questions about the character, then you are ready to begin learning the song.

1. Who is this person/creature? What is their gender (or pronouns)? Age? Social status?
2. Describe every possible physical detail you can: length and color of hair, clothes they are wearing (including colors, textures, and style), shoes (or barefoot), skin texture and color, eyes, hands, posture, gait, and more—anything that you can think of.
3. Set the scene. Is it inside or outside? If it is inside, describe everything you can about the ambiance, set, decor, or furniture. What materials are these things made of—wooden, fabric, colors. Are there any odors? What is the air like—fresh or stale? Are these things old-fashioned or modern? If it is outdoors, describe everything around you. Is the character standing on cement, grass, or in a forest? Are there flowers and trees? If so, what kinds? Is it spring, summer, autumn, or winter? What is the air like—is it dry, humid, or windy? Are there clouds in the sky? Are there birds and animals there? Is there water, and if so, it is a lake, ocean, brook?

These questions and descriptions trigger the imagination in a big way. People think they know a character. However, most of them have never delved this deeply into it. You can create study sheets with these questions and more for your students to fill in as homework.

Working with (and Memorizing) the Text

Next, you can delve into the song text. This exercise can serve as a blueprint for how to learn a song moving forward. As an example for the exercises I use, here is the poem "Down by the Salley Gardens" by William Butler Yeats (1865–1939):[1]

> Down by the salley gardens my love and I did meet;[2]
> She passed the salley gardens with little snow-white feet.
> She bid me take love easy, as the leaves grow on the tree;
> But I, being young and foolish, with her did not agree.
>
> In a field by the river my love and I did stand,
> And on my leaning shoulder she laid her snow-white hand.
> She bid me take life easy, as the grass grows on the weirs;
> But I was young and foolish, and now am full of tears.

I first teach students how to chew and add sound in an exercise that I call "uhming and chewing." I then have the student speak the text of the song or poem inside the mouth while uhming and chewing. You must watch them carefully to ensure they do not stop the chewing process when words are added. As they continue the uhming and chewing of the text, instruct them to begin to try to say a few words. The mouth is still barely open, albeit only a few millimeters perhaps. The sound and words are still all contained in the mouth and vocal tract.

This process—a variation on a semioccluded vocal tract (SOVT) exercise—works the whole vocal tract and provides a lovely back pressure to balance the vocal mechanism. As they work their way through the song in this way, the student will often stop chewing or try to open the mouth and say the word. It is important to remember that the words are not supposed to be understood yet. Groups love this because the "nonsense" early in the process often sounds humorous. When you are one on one with the student, do it with them. It's fun to do uhming and chewing together and having company eliminates the need for self-consciousness.

Next, try "roller-coasting" the vowels up and down throughout the singer's range. Teacher and choir directors often talk about singing "on the vowel," but these types of exercises are usually difficult to do well, and the student may find them discouraging. Singing a song with only vowels can be a wonderful exercise but is not always easy. To work toward that eventual goal, here is an exercise that gradually builds in the vowels for you. Remember, this is spoken—not sung. Let's stay on the same poem, "Down by the Salley Gardens." Try saying the first line this way:

Imagination

D ah-ah-ah-ah-ah oo-oo-oo-oo-oo N
B ah-ah-ah-ah-ah ee-ee-ee-ee-ee
Th uh-uh-uh-uh-uh
S ae-ae-ae-ae-ae L ee-ee-ee-ee-ee
G ah-ah-ah-ah-ahr D eh-eh-eh-eh-eh NS.

Speak each vowel with a "siren" that utilizes the entire vocal range. In my text example below, I have drawn this out so you have a visual idea of what this may sound like. There is a tendency for singers to use the same pattern of pitch and direction for each word, but this is not ideal—it really needs to be like a roller-coaster. Other singers like to move their heads instead of the pitch. Remember that this all goes on in the vocal tract and nowhere else. No other compensatory physical motion is necessary.

Once you have finished this exercise, you can "beatbox" (or make sound effects) with the consonants of your song. Remember, this is *fun*—it does not have to be "correct." Students may be reluctant to try this, but encourage them to take a stab at it. After rapping the text, proclaim the words loudly in a kind of singsong that is exaggerated—like ancient Greek theater. Speak the words broadly and clearly as if you were in an outdoor amphitheater.

Next, mime the text silently, pantomiming the text (Marcel Marceau–style) as if you are playing a game of charades. Use your hands to fully show the text. There is a tendency to use the hands by waving them around, but this is

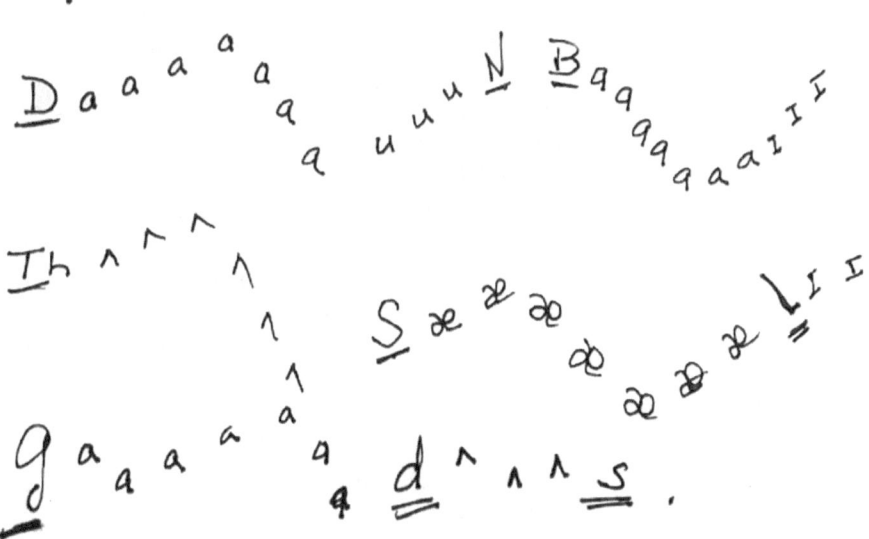

Vowel "roller-coaster" (hand-drawn by Meribeth Dayme)
Courtesy of the editors

not how it should be done. Rather, use the hands specifically, outlining things like trees, animals, and so on. This physical exercise will do more for expression than anything you can do with the text alone.

When you are ready, combine the previous two exercises by "singsonging" the text on one pitch while using mime gestures at same time. Remember to monitor the students' hands while they do this, making sure they are gesturing in the same expressive manner; we must *see* the words. Finally, stand and give a full dramatic performance of the text—to an imaginary audience of thousands. At this point it is very likely that the singer has learned and memorized the lyrics in a much faster and more lasting way than by mere rote repetition.

Students generally love to do these exercises, especially in a group setting. Other variations include having one person read or rap the text while another person interjects with scat or improvised sounds. When I use these exercises, I never give out instructions for all the exercises in advance (as a list). Instead, I give them sequentially—one at a time. Only after the person or group has finished one do I tell them about the next one. These exercises work for any song or aria. When singing in another language, the student must know the translation of every word—a general meaning will not do.

Learning the Melody through Movement

To begin this exercise, play a recording of the melody or a soundtrack, allowing your body to move gently as you feel the music in your body. This can be done while sitting in a chair. Gentle swaying or moving is all you need to start. Then move a bit more, as if you are dancing in the chair to the music. Ideally that dancing will propel you to get up and move around the room. Do this several times while listening to the whole song on each repetition. Next, dance around the room to the melody and draw the melody in the air with your hands.

Now add some sound by beginning to "uhm and chew" the melody. Don't worry if the melody isn't accurate at this point. Chew and mumble the words to the melody as if you are groggy and sleepy. Clap the basic pulse (*not* the exact rhythms) and mumble the words to the melody as you walk around the room. Finally, sing the song as best as you can at this moment. It may seem ridiculous at first, but learning a song this way puts it into your body. You can go back and clean up the notes and rhythms later, and remember—you already know the text (from the preceding exercise). These final steps will be relatively easy. Follow these steps in this order and you will be amazed how quickly (and well) you have learned your song.

Drawing Your Song

One of the most effective and demanding of any of the CoreSinging exercises is "drawing the song." I have seen this exercise work wonders with a singer; it occupies them so completely that they simply sing without any encumbrance whatsoever. Mannerisms drop away and the tone is lovely; they are so distracted that music simply happens. However, the singer must know the music extremely well to undertake this exercise. Trying to draw a song without thoroughly knowing the text and music first is usually too frustrating a task to be a positive experience.

Drawing the song is the equivalent of musical graffiti. The larger the area for drawing, the better. You can use a large white board or black boards in a classroom or a paper flip chart with a variety of colored markers. The rules are simple: The pen comes off the paper or board with every breath, while sustained notes mean continual movement of the marker on the paper or board. As long as the note is sounded, there is a movement of the pen for each syllable of the text and each note that moves. Ideally the contours of the phrases are maintained. When the song is fast or has a lot of runs or riffs, you then must make smaller movements with the pen or marker.

A group of CoreSinging instructors with their song drawings

Be careful to avoid extra movements that fall outside the parameters outlined above. For example, I have had singers add a lot of wiggles to the page, and—interestingly—they had the same wobbles in the sound. We stopped that by having them draw straight lines for each pitch or even dots. People who scoop tend to do the same on the paper—they don't scoop when drawing dots or short lines.

Some CoreSinging teachers who use this exercise have found that using the nondominant hand brings people up to pitch and using two hands can create a bigger sound. Notice how different colored markers affect the sound. You can also cap the markers and experiment with the singer "drawing" in the air. Your brain, energy, and voice respond as if the singer were still drawing on paper. Gradually, have the singer put down the markers and continue to sing. Notice how much more freedom and ease there is in the performance.

FINAL THOUGHTS

These are just a few suggestions of how to use imagination and play with your students. CoreSinging teachers often create variations of these exercises and invent their own interactive play-based learning games. When we play the game of "What will happen if we explore this?" it offers both teacher and student a variety of possibilities without setting up judgments of right and wrong. An atmosphere of imagination and playfulness greatly enhances the learning process as we are finding new ways to explain, visualize, and become more creative. As in childhood, imagination becomes an important part of learning—again.

NOTES

1. There are several well-known settings of this, which is Yeats's famous poem. The most familiar is the arrangement of the traditional tune "The Maids of Mourne Shorne" by Herbert Hughes (1882–1937). There are also original settings by Rebecca Clarke (1886–1979), John Ireland (1914–1992), Ivor Gurney (1890–1937), Benjamin Britten (1913–1976), and John Corigliano (b. 1938).

2. Salley (or sally) comes from the Gaelic word "saileach," which means willow.

Chapter Five

Practice and Performance

The importance of a whole-energy-field approach is as equally important to practice as it is to learning. When practice on your own is fun, imaginative, and has variety, it is likely to be even more exciting than the lesson with a teacher. The more practice feels like a game, the better. Sports coaches have learned that what is practiced exactly the same way more than three times actually hurts flexibility and spontaneity, but this approach has not yet become standard practice among musicians and within the voice pedagogy community.

The collective consciousness around the word "practice" is something like "tedium" and is not conducive to effective learning. This does not mean that something can't be repeated—only that it needs to be repeated with some slight variety each time. For example, a scale can be sung with different rhythms, on different vowels (or syllables or scat), or in modes beyond the two-mode (i.e., major and minor) system. Pounding notes on the keyboard or correcting wrong notes by singing a passage over and over by rote is not the way to instill confidence in yourself or others.

A NEW APPROACH TO PRACTICE

When I was a young teacher, I assumed that a student would leave a lesson with a clear idea of what to do before the next one. Much to my surprise (at the time), they would come the next week or several weeks later not having practiced—not because they were lazy, but because they didn't know how to go about doing it. I quickly learned that no matter how carefully you plan the lesson you can never assume anything about what students will take away. Because of these experiences, I created the following guidelines for effective practice. It takes in all the elements we have discussed in previous chapters.

Tune In, Tune Up, and Tune Out

There are three elements to effective, fun, and imaginative practice, which I have labeled "tune in," "tune up," and "tune out." There are no set times for each element, nor are there dogmatic rules. Different students may engage in different elements at different times. The following provides a brief overview of these concepts.

Tune In

"Tuning in" is for centering and setting the intention(s) for that specific practice session. For example, what would you like to have happen as you practice this song? It could be a technical challenge—such as classical melismata or pop riffs—working with language or style, memorizing a song or verse, or any number of specific intentions. After you have set your intentions, center your mind and body with exercises such as "dynamic balance" and use one of the CoreSinging breathing patterns, such as "being breathed" or the "breath loop." This is also a great time to do qigong exercises and clear the energy in the physical space before moving on to the next step. Avoid rote repetition by varying the order of your centering and intention choices.

Tune Up

"Tuning up" takes the centering and intention work we have just done and connects it to elements of the music. You might begin by "uhming and chewing" the spoken text and then adding the melody. Try using one of the breathing patterns; this can be done with a single phrase or for the entire song. This may mean taking the song out of context for a moment, and that is perfectly fine. Breathe in up the spine then sing and imagine the breath moving back down the front of the spine—air in, sound out. You may find that you have more breath available for the phrase when you aren't focusing on a rigid mechanical breathing exercise.

Singing scales can improve your musicianship and pitch accuracy. However, try to sing a variety of scales that are fun to sing. If you are practicing a new song, use some of the imaginative steps to learning text and/or music from chapter 4, including creating a character, "uhming and chewing" the text, roller-coastering the vowels, beatboxing the consonants, miming the text silently, dancing to the melody, and drawing the song. Rather than starting at the beginning every time, have fun with selected phrases from any part of the song. And as a reminder, focus on entire phrases and musical ideas—never single out one high note or a perceived problem note. That will only reinforce the negative, which is something you don't want to happen.

Tune Out

Now you are ready to play with the whole song. As you sing, draw your song with markers on a flip chart or white board. Have a variety of colored markers available to choose from. You can do this with a piece of paper and pencil if that is what you have with you at the moment. No paper? Use your finger to draw your song on an imaginary flip chart.

Now you are ready to *dance* to your song. It may seem silly, but when you are standing and performing your song, your subconscious will remember the freedom you experienced in your dance. Finally, perform your song as if you are in front of an audience of thousands.

Above all, remember this rule: *Never leave the practice room—or a voice lesson—without performing your song.* If you do not yet know the song, perform only two lines. It does not matter how long or short the performance is as long as you perform something. This is one of the keys to alleviating performance anxiety. When you are performing for your imaginary audience, there is no stopping, criticizing, or even comments of any kind—regardless of whether they are positive, negative, or constructive. When you are finished, simply accept the imaginary applause and then leave the practice session or voice lesson. Get in the habit of exiting the "stage" without automatically criticizing yourself or rating your performance against past or (imagined or ideal) future performances. A student singer should never leave a lesson without a short performance. Practicing performance sets up the brain to function that way. Conversely, practicing while always critiquing yourself sets up the brain to find fault in every performance.

While most performers are in the habit of practicing their performance, they tend to only do this shortly before the actual audition or performance date. Waiting until that late in the process can cause a lot of unnecessary performance anxiety. Teachers and former students who practice CoreSinging have repeatedly told me that this one element—always "performing" a song at the end of a practice session or lesson—has been a key component of their success and confidence in performance.

Vocal Warm-Ups

There are many ways to warm up the voice. I prefer to begin with activities that are not necessary to get "right." The very need to get something right blocks the chi. A scale needs to be correct; therefore, I never begin with a scale. Childlike vocal activities are great fun, a bit wild, and take the edge off the beginning of a lesson. It's so much easier to learn when we do not need to analyze what we are doing. "Uhming and chewing" is good for both warming up and cooling down.¹ It can be done anywhere—in the car or at home—without needing to be in a studio or near a piano.

It's also great fun to have a conversation using a variety of vocal sounds. You can choose two or three of your favorite sounds—or semioccluded vocal tract (SOVT) exercises such as lip buzzes or hums—and have an imaginary conversation. I usually suggest a topic like your favorite movie, what you did yesterday, or anything that is easy to talk about. However, you will not be using words—only the improvised sounds. Most people also gesture, adding hands for emotional emphasis. The more variety in pitch, range, and color there is in the sounds, the better. I encourage people to err on the side of exaggeration when doing these exercises. One fun variation is to have a conversion on scat syllables. Don't be afraid to be creative, and—above all—have fun!

Scales are an important part of learning the structure of music and understanding how it all fits together and "works." However, students overcompartmentalize and treat the scales, arpeggios, and vocalises they sing during their warm-up routine as separate entities than the repertoire they perform. If not used thoughtfully, warm-ups can become perfunctory and routine—things to "get through" before moving on to a song. Every aspect of singing should be done with intent—including warm-ups. Thankfully, a scale or arpeggio can be done in many ways. Try singing them on a variety of different rhythms, adding words to the pitches, moving using your whole body while singing them, or even drawing the scale or pattern while vocalizing. Many people refer to scales and vocalises as technical exercises or the "technique" portion of their lesson or practice session. For me, *all* of singing is part of the technique—I do not separate out any facet of it. In the end, it is all directed to performance.

If I were to recommend a single published set of exercises, I love the scales in Kim Chandler's *Funky 'n Fun* vocal training series.² They are accompanied and there is a great variety of fun vocalises to explore. She literally includes every type of scale and riff. If you can do all of them, you are quite an accomplished vocalist!

Student Action Plans

At the end of each lesson, I usually ask students to name three things they will be taking away with them. When you ask a question—like "Can you tell me three things you are taking away from what we explored today?"—it enables a quick mental review for them and gives you an opportunity to gauge how they have perceived the lesson. It is a great way to encourage the positive aspects as well. It is not helpful to ask something generic like, "What did you get out of the lesson?" Instead, be very specific. This kind of questioning is a great way to clear up any misconceptions or breakdowns in communication that may have inadvertently occurred. If they heard or interpreted something other than what you said or meant, you can clarify the matter. You may ask them to rephrase if necessary (i.e., if their response confuses you or is unclear).

After they answer this question, I then invite the student to create an "action plan" that outlines what they will do before the next lesson. This is important, and it is much better for the student to create their own action plan than for you to do it for them. It empowers them and they are more likely to feel a sense a responsibility to achieve their weekly goals. When there is something missing (i.e., something you feel is important that the student has not mentioned on their own), you can add it to their plan. However, limit your suggestion to one thing only. For example: "If you do not do anything else this week, I would love for you to remember to keep your feet straight while you are singing."[3]

I have a small "Prescription for Practice" notepad that I use to quickly write out the action plan, or anything else I want them to remember. For me, this is better than emailing a student notes. So much of our lives is digital

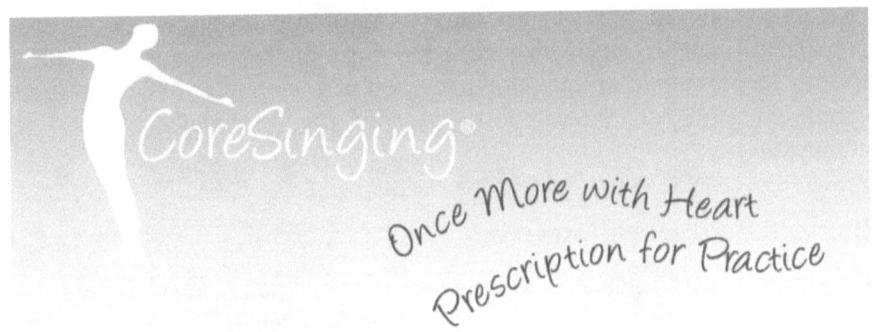

A "Prescription for Practice" note
Courtesy of the editors

these days (and perhaps I am in some ways old-fashioned), but I find that a short, handwritten list to give the student at the end of the lesson is beneficial.

Creating Student Guidelines for Practice

Some simple, clear guidelines for practice are very useful for your teaching. I recommend that you have a printed copy of these for everyone to use. Obviously, every student is different, so you will want to vary the exercises within the guidelines of "tune in," "tune up," and "tune out" in addition to practicing performing. Parents of younger students who have no clue how to help their children practice are grateful for some guidelines, and this may be a gentle reminder to allow their child to practice performing without parental critique.

GUIDELINES FOR OPTIMAL PERFORMANCE

Now that you have performed for your imaginary audience on a regular basis, you are ready to perform for a real (or virtual) audience. For many singers, performance is the ultimate reward. I don't know of anyone who does not like the applause of an audience; however, most teachers and singers do not prepare adequately for performance. They sing a lot and think of technique a lot, but they miss out on the mind and spirit of performing. There are some simple things that anyone can do to prepare for a performance, audition, or competition.

Before the Actual Performance

Preparing for performance occurs the moment you know you are going to do it. The process begins as soon as you know the date, details, location, and who will be in the audience. It doesn't matter if the engagement is in two weeks or two years—you are ready to start the journey toward that moment.

Start by setting an intention, just as you do for practicing. What would you like to experience? How would you like the audience to feel? How would you like to feel after the performance? Ask yourself how you would like to be perceived by the audience. Imagine seeing yourself on stage feeling comfortable, knowing the music, engaging with your coperformers, and thoroughly enjoying every moment. Do this every time you think of the performance. Instead of panicking, visualize the picture of yourself performing exactly the way you want to. This practice furnishes a strong message to the brain and energy field and paves the way for your desires to happen in reality.

From the moment you begin preparing the music, you should practice performing. Even if you know only one or two lines, begin performing it! Sing the text as if you are the finest actor on the planet. What story are you telling? What would you like the audience to feel or experience? Once you have that character or narrative established (and only then), begin to prepare the music. Whatever level you have just achieved in your lesson or practice session, perform it now for that imaginary audience of thousands before leaving the studio or rehearsal. Don't forget to imagine the applause as well. Remember: no self-criticism is allowed as you exit your imaginary stage.

There is, of course, a time and place for self-critique, appropriately noting what needs further work and preparation. The key CoreSinging concept, however, is to allow yourself one final feedback-free performance at the end of every practice routine. I also highly recommend that you regularly video record your practices. You need to know how you truly look and sound. It is too easy to fool yourself, and the mirror will not give you the same kind of feedback as watching a video. An added bonus is that the more comfortable you become practicing while videorecording, the less distracted and self-conscious you will be when an actual performance is being recorded or broadcast.

At the Actual Performance

While you are waiting to go on stage, do a simple qigong exercise. Find a place backstage or in the dressing room where you can have some privacy. Use any of the energetic breathing exercises you have learned, such as "being breathed," "breathing in a loop around the spinal cord," or "breathing into the chakras." Sit (if you are able to) with your feet firmly on the floor—hands on thighs and very still—and become aware of all that is happening around you. Enjoy the sounds and sensations you are experiencing and become a part of the whole. You can do this standing backstage as well. This is not the time to be frantically going over your lyrics and music. You are ready. You have practiced performing and you can trust what is about to happen because you have visualized it for weeks or months. Stay in the moment. To stay present, use any of the awareness exercises from chapter 3. What do you see, hear, feel, and smell?

As you walk on stage, completely immerse yourself in the experience. Be fully present in the moment and absorb the energy of the occasion. As you take in the energy, remember to acknowledge your audience—remember, the audience's energy forms a support for you and your music. Become part of the energy of any other performers who are on stage with you. You can ground yourself before singing while acknowledging the audience even before you take your first breath and begin singing. You can even use the dynamic balance exercise (from chapter 2) and no one will know except for you. You are there to share your music and your spirit, which are gifts you have the privilege of giving with great love and joy to your audience.

THE ROLE OF THE CORESINGING TEACHER

Before you can share this approach to singing with your students, CoreSinging must become a part of you. Take your time and try a few new things at a time. It should be more than an intellectual exercise. Gratitude is a great place to begin.

Energy begins with the way you, the teacher, thinks. Your energy is directly related to the words you use in lessons. You are the only one in charge of your energy. The basic elements of human energy are mind, body, and spirit.

Awareness begins with you, the teacher. Before you ask your student to do awareness exercises, can you feel your own pulse and sing at the same time? Can you tune in to your breath? How many sounds can you identify in the room?

Imagination and play begins with you, the teacher. Can you sing a blue song? How about a red song? Can you sing a duet with the vacuum cleaner or a bird? Can you pantomime or scat your lyrics?

Practicing that is filled with fun, imagination, and variety must first be modeled by you, the teacher. Can you "tune in" to set an intention for your own practice? Have you "tuned up" with one or two of the steps to learning text and music—or moved to a phrase or sung a variety of scales? Can you "tune out"—beyond the written music—by drawing or dancing your song or singing to an imaginary audience of thousands?

Focus begins with you, the teacher. Can you make a habit of focusing and clearing for thirty seconds (or fewer) several times a day, especially before and after each lesson you teach or meeting you attend?

Performance begins with you, the teacher. Can you ground yourself, be fully immersed in the moment, and feel the energy of the audience and other performers on stage? Have your students witnessed you sharing your own singing with great love and joy?

Introducing CoreSinging to Your Students

CoreSinging begins with you—the teacher. Whenever you are ready, you can begin to incorporate some CoreSinging approaches into your lessons. Energy test to see if you test strong. (Reminder: You don't need to talk about energy with your students.) You might begin with qigong exercises or some free movement with music. Set an intention by asking the student what they would like to gain today. As part of your warm-up, try improvising with conversation and sounds used in everyday speech, or play with sounds and rhythm. Don't worry about being "correct"—be spontaneous and have some fun.

As lessons progress, help your students get in touch with their pulse and breathing patterns. Can they sing to their heartbeat? Add awareness of outside sounds in the room or from the street (rather than blocking out such "distractions"). Teach dynamic balance as an alternative to "correct posture" and encourage your student to be aware of negative language and thoughts related to their singing—e.g., "I can't hit the high note," "I'm not a soloist," "I always forget the words," "I'm not good at ____." Those negative thoughts (which I call "curses") can become ingrained. Instead, ask your student to channel positive energy, focusing on what they want to happen and how they would like to sing.

From the very beginning, teach your student how to practice at home with variety, imagination, and fun and to end each practice with a performance, no matter how short or small. Invite the student to perform a song or part of a song for an imaginary audience of thousands at the end of each lesson, without you (as the teacher) stopping to correct anything. This will take some self-control, as teachers are conditioned to interrupt the student to fix things—for example, a wrong note, flat pitch, technical challenge, or mispronounced word. Resist the temptation to critique and allow your student to perform—even if it is just a few lines—without criticism or feedback.

After you establish these basic CoreSinging foundations, you can begin to share simple information about energy, awareness, imagination, practice, and performance. Introduce focus at the beginning of each lesson and teach one or two easy qigong or exercises. Get comfortable playing with conversation, sounds taken from speech, and other sounds such as babbling, lip trills, tongue trills, and sirens throughout the entire range of the voice. Improvise—both alone and to a rhythmic accompaniment—and add movement while singing or listening to music. Hum while focusing on different parts of the body (e.g., your foot, arm, head, etc.). Does the sound change as your focus shifts? Sing to the sounds you hear outside the room. You don't have to add everything at once. Follow the student's creativity and be aware of their own personal comfort zone.

You can also introduce simple concepts of dynamic balance—e.g., imagine balancing the right leg while thinking of the left (opposite) hand, imagine connecting your chin with your tailbone, and so forth. Talk about the powerful energy of language and thoughts as they relate to singing. Give your students written guidance regarding how they can practice and play at home and on their own. Encourage your student to practice performing at home and reserve time at the end of each lesson for the student to give a short "performance" of something—just for themselves and you (the teacher). After your student has practiced performing for a little while, encourage them to find opportunities to sing small public performances in the form of group sings—song shares, karaoke, or open mic nights—with friends or other students.

Continuing CoreSinging for Students

As students progress, I ask them to begin keeping a practice journal. Journaling is more helpful than a standard quantitative practice log that merely checks boxes for how many minutes and how many days a week a student practices. Journaling can include favorite vocal exercises and warm-ups, specific songs or techniques to practice and perform, singing activities outside of lessons, favorite singers and songs in different genres, favorite instrumental music, or anything the else the student wants to remember.

During lessons you can introduce qigong exercises and recommend YouTube videos to reinforce what you are exploring in the studio. Provide specific directions for dynamic balance and breathing with the room and energy field, feeling the whole body expand with each breath. Gradually add sounds like hums and short lines of melody, always allowing enough time to breathe the energy field. Invite students to feel energy (chi) by rubbing their hands together. Invite them to make rhythms based on outside sounds and then to their own pulse. Play with melodic motifs while singing them to a rhythmic accompaniment or drumming.

Help students to explore scale variations—including pentatonic, major, minor, and chromatic—using repeated notes in various places (e.g., 1–2–333–4–55555–4–333–2–1), as well as varied rhythms and sounds (e.g., "da dum doo-bi-doo doodle"). Add simple improvisation to chords and melodies; keep these very simple, using only a few pitches and rhythms—it is fine to begin with just one or two notes. Encourage them to add simple melodic improvisations to texts or create their own songs.

Advanced CoreSinging for Students

Encourage advanced singers to study qigong, tai chi, and yoga. They might explore playing another musical instrument and engage in other non-music-related personal self-development tools such as learning new languages, acting, writing, and painting. Work with dynamic balance and movement may be expanded alongside additional energy-field breathing techniques. Advanced students may challenge themselves daily by singing a variety of scales, arpeggios, chords, and rhythms.[4] They can also develop their own vocalises and improvisations, basing musical motifs on standard songs from a variety of styles. Once songs are thoroughly learned, they can be drawn on a chart or white board with colored markers as well as mimed. Advanced singers are ready to give public performances in front of large audiences.

Advanced CoreSinging for Teachers

By now you have probably guessed that this way of learning never stops. There is no end to what you can do and how much more you can learn. Being imaginative and playful is a birthright that you have full permission to use as much as you like. The discipline of following your thoughts—and probably reframing a lot of what you thought you knew—is one that never stops. Learning to find inner silence and listening for the innate wisdom that you have inside is a beautiful journey. This process will do wonders for your music, teaching, and performance.

As your CoreSinging journey continues, practice qigong, tai chi, or other similar mind–body connection methods on a daily basis. Explore breathing techniques from practices such as yoga, Feldenkrais, the Alexander Technique, and Body Mapping. These disciplines are intertwined with many of CoreSinging's essential principles.

It is important to understand how to practice . . . and play! Don't just read about it. Jump in and try everything you are asking your students to do. That includes playing with words and melody, enjoying improvisation without judgment, and singing without self-criticism. Strive to understand the use of space, simple concepts of energy work, and know how to "clear" and make corrections when necessary.

Above all, model becoming self-sufficient in learning and practice. Break out of your comfort zone and explore and enjoy a wide variety of styles of music, including the styles of music your students enjoy. Perform comfortably in front of others or with groups. And finally, take coresponsibility every time you have the opportunity to teach a student. Be sure to listen at least as much as you talk.

FINAL THOUGHTS

Musicians do not have to suffer to be good. If pupils are taught with joy and love, an entirely new type of performer will emerge. When we train students this way, they have the potential to create a healing energy for both themselves and the audiences they serve. This is the mission of CoreSinging. Welcome!

NOTES

1. The "uhming and chewing" exercise is explained in greater detail in chapter 4.
2. https://www.funkynfun.com.
3. Meribeth taught that pointing your feet/toes toward your audience strengthens the chi between you and the listener. She emphasized that energetically connecting to your listener is not the same as kinesic or nonverbal communication analysis. "Looking at body language from a cultural perspective is fascinating. Using it as a tool for judgement and analysis creates a number of communication difficulties. . . . Such interpretation invites unnecessary judgement and hinders the process of communication. When you are busy analyzing someone's body language, you are somewhere in your head and not fully present. You cannot listen to another person and analyze at the same time." Meribeth Bunch Dayme, *Creating Confidence: How to Develop Your Personal Power and Presence* (London: Kogan Page, 1999), 56.
4. See Trish Rooney's recommendations for practicing a variety of scales in chapter 11 of this book.

Chapter Six

A Summary of Key Concepts in CoreSinging

This chapter presents a concise review and summary of the five key concepts of CoreSinging—energy, awareness, imagination, practice, and performance—followed by a brief practical discussion of how to integrate the CoreSinging approach into your teaching and singing. It does not replace the previous chapters but is rather intended to be a "quick reference" to consult as you begin your CoreSinging journey.

FIVE KEY CONCEPTS

The following paragraphs present a brief summary of the information covered in chapters 2 through 5. Readers should feel free to consult these expanded commentaries for more information about each of these concepts.

Energy

Everything that exists is a form of energy/vibration. It includes both the seen and unseen. Western and Eastern cultures describe energy in different ways. Biologists see energy as qualities of human or animal life (such as breath and pulse), physicists as quantum particles, and Eastern traditions speak of prana, chi, and light. The importance of energy is recognized in medicine and various health professions using therapeutic and diagnostic tools such as ultrasound, electric pulse, shockwave therapy, and magnetic resonance imaging—to name only a few. In the field of complementary and alternative medicine energy, healing comes in many forms—such as hands-on work, natural energies (like crystals, magnets, and acupuncture), radionics, and life force or chi. What we see is merely a small part of what is. Scientists believe that more than 90 percent of the cosmos is invisible to our eyes and appears to us as empty space. This energy seems to be everywhere and always, having existed since the beginning of time. The human body, a dense quantum field, becomes a small part of the whole picture in relation to the vast amount of space that is perceived as empty.

The most obvious components of the energy field are what we see through the human body and our visible physical surroundings. To learn that the body and what we see is less than 10 percent of the whole is daunting. Our analytical/critical bias has insisted that we look at only those things that we can see or that offer sufficient statistical proof. We know now there is much more of value to us. We have spent a long time looking at only the 10 percent. This is true in the field of singing as well. Now is the time to broaden our horizons to include many more aspects of the energy field in singing and performance. When we do this, the results are exciting.

Awareness

The old sages taught their disciples to reach a neutral inner state so they could become more aware of what was happening around them. By being neutral, normal judgment—including emotions or disturbing thoughts—is not given importance. This results in being more internally and outwardly aware. Being neutral does not mean being unsympathetic; rather, you possess an inner stillness and are in a state of readiness. Such readiness allows us to respond with a newfound spontaneity that is difficult to achieve when we are working with preconceived ideas and expectations. Being neutral can be compared to being "in the zone" as discussed by top athletes today. Being in the zone demands complete detachment; it is something like a meditative state in which you feel as if a third person is viewing you and your actions from the outside. As an objective observer, the singer can then allow the music to tell its own story without interference. This is possible because simultaneous production and perception of the same emotional form cannot be carried out by the nervous system without some degree of interference. Ideal singing comes with the awareness of being at one with the self, one's surroundings, the music, and the spirit, coupled with a dynamic balance of the components of the vocal mechanism.

Imagination

Imagination is the key to a playful, free spirit that is needed in every aspect of singing. When the singer has the ability to play seriously, the resulting performance is compelling. Explore the creative aspects of your music and text as if you were a small child. Nothing is sacred in the world of play. Make gibberish sounds in place of the text. Make up new rhythms for the music and text. Dance and draw the music. Doing activities like this will result in new avenues of freedom opening for you and your singing.

Practice

Good results can be obtained in every practice session, whether it lasts for five minutes or more than an hour. The key lies in knowing what you want to achieve during each session. Take a moment to sit quietly and visualize the objectives before beginning the session or even each song. Practice first begins with a moment of focus followed by play and exploration. Producing sound that is not restricted by musical or vocal constraints (other than vocal health) promotes confidence. While notes, rhythms, and musical indications are important, it is much more freeing to begin with simple improvisation where correctness is not so critical. Later the need to be accurate can be addressed in ways that are positive and exciting. At first, however, you should sing for the love of it.

Practice and/or lessons are interesting and unforgettable when there is a combination and balance of information, imagination, and experience. Information goes into the analytical left-brain area and experiences are processed in the right, intuitive, creative brain. For example, the repetitive rote learning of the words to a song involves only the left brain, and the singer might have difficulty remembering them. However, by learning text using visualization, movement, color, and other techniques, the right brain and much more of the energy field is engaged, making it much easier to learn and memorize.

The element of play is also important to retaining what we learn. Perhaps Elousie Ristad said it best in her wonderful book, *A Soprano on Her Head*:

> It's strange what we assume about learning. How often we pretend someone must force it upon us, and that we in turn must force it upon others. We get all tangled up in concepts and instructions. Can you remember when you first learned to ride a bicycle? Did anyone really help by trying to explain it to you?[1]

Remember, learning is at its best when it is fun. Play, play, and play!

Performance

Performance must be practiced. Every practice needs to end with a full "performance" of something—even if it is one verse of a song. Sing for your imaginary audience as if your life depended on it every day. The resulting freedom on stage will amaze you. The moment a singer is free enough to allow their spirit to show in performance, that moment becomes something special—a moment when the balance of all energies is unified. Then the singer is "being sung." Every practice, preparation for lessons, or performance benefits from taking a short moment to clear all the "mind chatter," create a space for openness to learning, and foster an attitude of gratitude for those gifts and talents that are being encouraged and developed. When singers are too busy criticizing their voices, they lose the ability to be grateful and they destroy the magic of the moment.

APPLYING THE CORESINGING APPROACH

Ultimately, the beauty of the CoreSinging approach shines through when you integrate these concepts into your teaching, practice sessions, and performances. The following themes are among the most important.

Take Responsibility for Your Own Learning

Find ways to monitor your own learning. The most effective tool is video. Singers who do not want to see themselves are at risk of fooling themselves and not communicating with the audience. Do not be afraid to look at yourself—it is the only way you will know whether you are fulfilling your own objectives in singing and performance. Merely thinking you are doing what you intended is not enough; it can be a rude shock when someone ridicules your performance or does not like what you produced. Singers who perform in genres outside the classical arena seem to be comfortable in looking at themselves. However, classical singers are far behind in this aspect of their learning. Every singer needs a way to video practice sessions, lessons, and important rehearsals and view them objectively afterward.

Take Responsibility for Your Thoughts and Language

Your energy field (and that of those you are around) reacts strongly to the language used, whether in thought, written form, and in verbal expression. Both singer and teacher will profit immensely when they take responsibility for their thinking and use of language in the studio, and in their practice sessions and performances. The language you think and verbally express has a powerful effect on the energy field and whether goals are achieved. "Mind chatter" while singing is the equivalent of trying to perform in competition with a radio—it stifles awareness and spontaneity. Perceptions of music being difficult, notes being hard to reach, or fear of making a mistake will all perpetuate the problem. Using visualization with mental focus can eliminate self-fulfilling prophecies.

Be in a State of Readiness

Inner stillness and awareness combined with dynamic physical balance will give you the ability to respond with clarity, spontaneity, and intuition—all needed for optimum learning and performance. Readiness implies a mental, physical, and spiritual balance and awareness in what you do and becoming neutral—not letting the thoughts or emotions you have about something interfere with your centered state.

Pay Mindful Attention to Each Practice and Lesson

Every practice session and every lesson needs to have proper mental preparation. Preparation for singing includes creating an atmosphere or energy field that is supportive of a positive relationship between teacher and pupil or simply a good energy for accomplishing short-term goals. This can take the form of a short meditation, a moment to focus on each piece of music, or thirty seconds of stillness before beginning. Practice your performance at the end of each session.

Treat All Colleagues, Peers, and Teachers with Respect

Have positive thoughts and actions toward colleagues, peers, directors, and teachers. In the heat of a competitive environment, always stay centered within your own energy field. Do not waste emotions by getting involved even when they do not do the same for you. Negative emotional attachments can play havoc with your energy field and performance. Feeling sympathy is not the same as becoming emotionally attached—or better still, a state of neutrality.

Be Grateful for Your Voice at All Times

A relationship with music and your voice that is based on spirit, art, humanity, and gratitude rather than self-importance, ego, and vanity will pay huge dividends in your singing and teaching. I love the following quotation by the great Ella Fitzgerald (1917–1996): "I know I'm no glamour girl, and it's not easy for me to get up in front of a crowd of people. It used to bother me a lot, but now I've got it figured out that God gave me this talent to use, so I just stand there and sing."

FINAL THOUGHTS

We rarely take on anything unless we can see it for ourselves. While new ideas might be accepted intellectually, putting them into practice requires taking personal risks. Once we have taken that chance, we can then weigh the options and choose what is most useful at the moment. This book offers new perspectives, suggestions for taking small, nonthreatening risks, and many options for thought, experimentation, and change.

Enjoy the journey.

NOTE

1. Eloise Ristad, *A Soprano on Her Head: Right-Side-Up Reflections on Life and Other Performances* (Moab, UT: Real People Press, 1982), 193.

Part II

CASE STUDIES: PRACTICAL APPLICATION OF CORESINGING

Chapter Seven

Why CoreSinging?

Rachel Velarde

When I met Meribeth Dayme in person for the first time at the 2017 NATS Winter Workshop in San Diego (called "I Sing the Body Electric"), she had already been a huge inspiration to me. Both *The Singing Book*, coauthored with Cynthia Vaughn, and *Dynamics of the Singing Voice* had been influential. I specifically utilized *Dynamics* as a guide for my 2013 dissertation, which explores the connection between voice science and traditional voice pedagogy—validations especially that were later reaffirmed through research by the end of the twentieth century. When I met Meribeth and had a chance to speak with her, she encouraged me to work with her. I was hesitant; my financial life was not very stable at that time, but I took the plunge, and the investment was completely worth every moment. She forever changed my approach to teaching singing, in the very best of ways. Jumping into the deep end of something I did not fully understand exemplified the CoreSinging principle that everything is connected and every decision affects outcomes, sometimes years down the road. Today, the connectivity of energy, action, and humanity is foundational to my teaching.

BACKGROUND: MY PERSONAL JOURNEY

I started teaching in the way many young teachers do: by imitating what my first teacher did with me. In this vein, I had a sheet of ten vocal exercises that I handed each student. I had them follow me up and down the piano as I attempted to play every note for them, and I often sang along with them as well. It took me another twenty-four years of exploration through voice science and pedagogy to find a place where all that I am—a combination of intellect, emotion, and spirituality—became connected via the principles of CoreSinging. These principles are embodied in Meribeth's teachings.

For me, I had felt as if I knew how to connect well with students and that the "right" prescriptive measures, based on my own personal experiences, would best lead them to desired outcomes. With CoreSinging, my perspective on what concepts and modalities allowed the singer before me to find their own outcome was broadened exponentially. Meribeth was someone strongly rooted in the science of the singing voice who also demonstrated the necessity of going beyond the science and into the metaphysical to truly become the teacher who could fully serve the human standing in front of her, asking for assistance in improving their singing voice. Through CoreSinging, my understanding of what a teacher could and should be was transformed.

As a result, I have continued to explore both aspects of my understanding of the human voice: the scientific and the metaphysical. As before, I apply it to my own singing—to develop a working depth of understanding so I can encourage my students to find their own understanding and response to a given stimulus—but I no longer tell students that my experience must also be their experience. Rather, I give them space to explore by offering my thoughts and experiences, but then encouraging them to find comfort and ease for themselves. Most recently, I finish my lessons with, "Ask me a question," which leads to questions about technique, pedagogy, or even questions about my favorite color or what I'm going to have for dinner that night.

Recently, I have delved into the exploration of somatic practices and motor learning. This exploration was spurred by my personal journey with muscle tension dysphonia (MTD), exacerbated by a congenital defect in my left temporal mandibular joint. My MTD led me to a lesson with Meribeth one week prior to her passing, in which she counseled me— wisely, as usual—with scientific fact underpinning her deep knowledge of connectedness to the world. With this encouragement in mind, in the following months, I delved into various somatic practices, eventually deciding to become a certified teacher in one modality I find readily applicable in the voice studio.[1] I directly ascribe this willingness to explore areas which seem "outside" the prescribed realm of singing to my training in CoreSinging, which opened my mind and my soul to other modalities and concepts, and how they could, and should, be applied in the voice studio.[2]

Above all, application of CoreSinging principles in my teaching (and my life) guide me to increased respect for the human in front of me. How can I best guide them to their own awareness of their voice? How can I help them to find the vocalization habits that support their vocal goals, whether they be tonal, emotional, communicative, or habilitative? Therefore, I use every tool available: knowledge and understanding of the function of the human voice, yes, but also a substantial amount of metaphysics—creating a space where play, exploration, and curiosity are standard tools through which to find vocal outcomes. Creating a space where the possible is infinite and the path to infinity is lined with joy.

INTEGRATION OF CORESINGING INTO MY PEDAGOGY

How do I approach teaching and continued learning? I feel that CoreSinging, at its core (no pun intended, or maybe pun *intended*), honors a deep knowledge and love of science with an open mind to investigate everything that can help illuminate better connections for singing. This concept speaks to me especially, because as the daughter of a reference librarian a deep conviction of the intrinsic worth of knowledge has been integral to my development as a teacher. I must recall regularly that there are necessary limits to my desire to learn and learn and then "bestow" that knowledge upon my students. Rather, each time I learn a new concept, I need to play with integrating that idea into my teaching in an intriguing and exploratory way that excites the singer in front of me to explore the thought for themselves, so that their sensibility and precision of action expands, along with an increase in their understanding of the limits of what is considered natural and normal for them (to paraphrase the words of Moshé Feldenkrais).[3]

Some of the initial ideas I began to integrate into my teaching were the energy principles present in CoreSinging, those of chakra, qi energy flow—that energy which flows between and interconnects us all—and the concept of clearing of energy between students. I found these philosophies intimidating for students who are not yet at a place to recognize the interconnectedness of the energy of the universe. Therefore, bringing in elements of Newtonian mechanics, quantum physics, and chaos theory all served to assuage feelings of uneasiness around "woo-woo" mysticism that arose. The following are some examples.

Newton's Third Law

Rather than encouraging a student to feel the energy of the earth supporting their body (a concept I gleaned from Babette Lightner's "Wholeness in Motion" work), I speak about Newton's third law: for every action there is an equal and opposite reaction. If we are standing on the earth, then the earth equally is supporting us. I challenge the student to find a time when the earth fails to support them. Sometimes, a student will call me out and say, "What if a cliff crumbles from underneath me?" and I acknowledge their point, but also remind them that eventually the earth will again be there to catch their body—gentleness is not guaranteed. (Humor is always appropriate in the voice studio, as it leads to the creation of positive energy.)

Quantum Physics

Quantum physics (in extreme layman's terms) is about how particles and waves move and interact. What is sound except waves? What is the interconnectedness of the energy of the universe, but entanglement as described in quantum physics? Quantum physics states that entanglement is nonlocal: "The results of measurements made at a particular location can depend on the properties of distant objects in a way that can't be explained using signals moving at the speed of light."[4] In the voice studio, I can integrate this scientific understanding to help a student feel more connected to her audience, or to better understand the sense of energy that one receives from another, even though no words are spoken nor direct communication made. Quantum physics also helps to "normalize" and explain the sense of qi energy flow that can be noted within oneself, and which, when released from blockage, can dramatically increase free-flowing sound production.[5] According to preeminent voice scientist Ingo Titze, "The whole universe may be pulsing,"[6] leading to voice vibration. The extrapolation of the entire universe pulsing is that we can sense those pulsations and connect our internal vibrations to those of others, both near and far. With this sense of vibrational integration, singers then can connect to their audience in a foundational way, going beyond mere sensation and into metaphysics.

Chaos Theory

Chaos theory, introduced to me by Robert Sussuma, is even more fun for me to play with in the studio. It allows me to observe the student in front of me and sense their "initial conditions," which can be explained as their current mental and physical setup for singing.[7] Are they in a place where they will accept the language of energy with which I speak to them, or do I need to couch the terms in scientific explanations? Additionally, I use concepts of chaos theory, and the interconnectedness of our body as a fully functional and complete system, to direct attention to one aspect of the sound or sound production while desiring to change another part of the system, much like misdirecting attention in a shell game. Thus, if I want to release jaw tension in a singer, I might guide them through a brief somatic exploration around spinal flexibility. Because of the interconnectedness of the system, relief in one part of the body can readily bring about change in another part of the body.[8] Directing a student to "release the jaw" rarely works—first, because it does not tell the student *how* to accomplish that release; and second, because of the tendency of the human body to overfocus on and overwork to "correct" a perceived "fault."

What Was It?

So often, as a singer strives for improvement, sound production is defined by what the sound is not: not good enough, not easy enough, not repeatable, not . . . not . . . not. One of the first books recommended to me by Meribeth in my CoreSinging training was *The Magician's Way*, which explores this conundrum.[9] Through my increased understanding of the power of accepting rather than resisting failure, I began speaking to my students and asking, "What *was* it?" in relation to sounds just made, rather than focusing on all the ways that sound failed to "meet expectations." In the studio, we do not actually care what it was not. Our focus is on the outcome produced. When a singer can identify specific qualities of the sound, they can better understand the possibilities of that sound, as well as better identify options for modification. They no longer need to resist the idea of failure, because failure is not on the table for discussion. Every sound is a successful sound, because it is something that occurred, rather than a nebulous ideal to constantly strive for. This question of "What was it" helps remove judgment from the outcome and instead focuses on the process of obtaining that outcome. The singer can then follow their progress and find success, rather than a sense of continual failure in never succeeding to reach an ever-changing ideal.[10]

How Was That?

A related, yet different, question is, "How was that?" This relatively neutral question allows the singer to notice what they notice, rather than rely on me, the teacher, to direct their locus of attention—which outcome the singer may or may not have been able to sense.[11] With this type of guidance, the singer increases agency over their sound outcomes and thereby improves willingness to explore in the practice room and find joy in the journey. Prior to CoreSinging, these types of questions never occurred to me—*I* directed what the student should or should not notice, what they should sense, and what they should hear, all determined by my own specific vocal journey. After CoreSinging, I often have been astonished by what individualized sensations and intricacies of singing my students become aware of while singing. The vocal development gained by these students also has increased exponentially as a direct result. The singer is in charge of both noting and determining their own outcomes, rather than being dependent upon me, their teacher. I am now a guide, a facilitator of learning, rather than a maestro directing each predetermined outcome.

Procedural Learning

In addition to awareness of what the singer senses in general, an increased focus on improving the sense of noticing internal movements of the body, through questioning and guided awareness, and how they affect the sound has been foundational in my application of CoreSinging principles within the studio. By questioning, we become aware of habits that perhaps no longer serve us.[12] By experiencing through somatic opportunities, our procedural thought processes are stimulated, and knowledge is gained through heightened sensory experience. Procedural learning "refers to learning physical skills (procedures) by doing and is inclusive of both those innate movements with which we are born, like crawling, and advanced skills like learning to ride a bicycle or play a musical instrument."[13] Specific processes allow students to "hack their nervous systems" and find options and opportunities not previously available.[14] Rather than me, the teacher/maestro, telling the student what to do and what to feel (declarative learning[15]), a process such as "Velcro hand"[16] (my nomenclature) can guide the student to an inner awareness of how their body responds and find a spinal length and body alignment that works for them, in that moment. If I tell a student to "stand up straight," they may try to comply by manipulating their body in ways which are suboptimal for both efficiency[17] and economy,[18] conceivably leading to maladaptive habits which may then lead to excess stress or strain (and be a factor in the possible development of a voice disorder). The effects of nonoptimal behaviors sometimes cannot be noted for multiple years (as occurred when my body compensated for its congenital temporomandibular joint defect, first diagnosed at age ten, which led to my muscle tension dysphonia—but not until thirty years later). When a singer discovers ways by which to tap into their subconscious mind, ways to "hack the nervous system," they then have choices by which to move. Increased choices, counterintuitively, can lead to decreased anxiety and an expanded sense of self-identity.[19] What is initially a distraction,[20] an impediment to movement, can become an avenue of inquiry, of exploration, which allows the singer to find alternate ways to reach a desired goal.[21]

Ask Me a Question

Finally, as stated previously, a statement that I have added at the end of every lesson for my students is, "Ask me a question." This deliberate choice of closure to the lesson gives opportunity for the student to come with prepared questions, ask about something that occurred during the lesson, or even to ask what my favorite color or food is. In this way, the student increases their individual agency,[22] the expert–novice barrier is weakened, and power disparities within the voice studio are reduced. An integral aspect of CoreSinging is that we are all human together and we can and do learn from each other. As a teacher, I see my primary job in the studio and the classroom is to develop levels of exploration in the student, to inspire a passion for investigation guided by the singer's curiosity. I must, therefore, be open to return inquiry, and even challenges, from my students. When I, as the expert in the room, open the floor for open-ended questions, increased parity develops within the relationship, and I often see aspects of singing that had not previously occurred to me because my thought patterns vary from those of my learners. When my students ask a question, I may gain insight into their experience, but I also am challenged to explain concepts in various ways. In this manner, continual learning is both modeled and expected, emphasizing that areas of individual interest for the student themselves are of utmost importance. *Their concepts and understanding are at the forefront of their learning experience.* "The artist's role is fulfilled, at least in part, by simply operating within the realm of inquiry."[23] So . . . ask me a question.

CASE STUDIES[24]

Case Study #1: Energy, Intent, and Imagination in Text and Music

Bennett, a twenty-three-year-old tenor aspiring to be a musical theatre performer, came to me as a high school singer who never realized that singing lessons were an actual option. One of the early CoreSinging tools that led to a breakthrough—and that he continues to use at home—is drawing while singing. He terms it, "The coolest visualization for singing ever." Visualizing what the voice is doing, how it's working while singing, in what directions the phrasing moves, strongly connects him to what he's singing and why, giving a motivation for how the song is supposed to look. The visual aspect of the tool is vital to the outcome.

The use of imagination is key to meaningful communication and expressive voice use.

One of the biggest breakthroughs he had was the idea of, "Don't sing—*communicate.*" and that the singing will come as a result of the communicative intent. He finds that connecting the text and the music makes his singing much less effortful, and that was a new concept for him. He tells me that when he figured the concept of communication above all else was the moment he realized, "I can do this in the industry. I can make it in the industry. I have the skills and the knowledge to keep going and work towards bigger things." He has found that connection to the text gets him further when sounds come out naturally and effortlessly *all* the time.

To get to communication, we do a lot of research, seeking the actual reason why the character would be singing a certain phrase. Why is this character singing this song at this time? This involves figuring out why every word is being said, why every note is being sung, why certain accidentals are included, why the writer wrote the lyrics they did, and why the composer wrote the notes they did. It's all there for a reason. Once the full picture is understood, Bennett finds it becomes much easier to convey the message and get it told in a way that he's satisfied, which will then satisfy the audience. The first time he realized that he could really be a professional actor in music theater was after a show where character development was key to the directing, and people strongly responded to his performance.

Remove the intellectual mind from singing.

Bennett says that when he's able to think about the character in the moment, it all connects and meshes together and makes the most sense. If *he* believes what he's singing and saying, it comes out better and is more convincing to the audience receiving it, whether that's in the practice room or he's singing to four hundred people while on stage. Once he gets into the mindset of thinking about why he's singing what he's singing, using the least amount of everything needed to sing it, he's able to do so much more with it, keep it going, and do it again if needed. An example is if he doesn't sing efficiently he can get through maybe one full run of "Moving Too Fast."[25] If he's thinking about how Jamie is feeling, why Jamie's singing this, how much of a cocky #^&* he is, and just getting into that mindset and *then* singing the song, he can sing that song four or five times in a row, and it feels like the first time every time.[26] When he focuses on the notes written on the page and the rhythmic accuracy, he's rarely able to get through it even once. But when putting himself in that mindset of Jamie—*not* thinking about the music per se but rather thinking about why, in that moment, he's singing all these words and why he needs *all* these words to come out at this one time and why he's put each word after another—he sails through the roller-coaster of the song, feeling like it's 100 percent about the character (e.g., "The character took a step. The character touched his face. The character sang a song."). This approach makes everything easier.

The universe is breathing me. Tune in to internal awareness.
The cells, the breath, the heartbeat, the organs all have their own vibration.

Another benefit of CoreSinging Bennett has realized is staying grounded with the earth and his body, ensuring everything's in "a good place." He finds ways to sing in a variety of postures, because in a show it's not always possible to do it the same way every time. Whether sitting, standing, or moving around, he ensures the body remains centered and grounded so that optimal sound production is available. This body awareness has been demonstrated consistently in his early morning Saturday lessons (at 8:30 a.m., often after performing the night before). Bennett can sing a four-minute tenor ballad ten minutes after waking up because he finds the appropriate physicalization necessary to reset his body.

When he's not at his best—for example, when slouching—Bennett also finds ways to "reset" his body. These practices open his stance, increase his sense of confidence (even in a room of random strangers), and make him feel that "if something horrible were to happen in that moment, my body would be ready to react to it." An example of his physical awareness leading to positive outcomes is the time he fell down the stairs while running to backstage places in a production of *Dirty Rotten Scoundrels*. As he ran, he reported that he was aware that he felt pretty connected to the earth. Then, he missed a stair, fell down about nine stairs, and got up and kept running. He said he was asked, "You just fell down a flight of stairs. Are you good?" And he responded, "Yeah. I'm great. Let's do this dance number." We had just worked in our lesson that week on sensing the support of the earth, the sense of grounding and how the earth will never fail us, that connection to the universe. He has reached a point where he doesn't need to think about it anymore—his norm is being in that state of connection and "groundedness."

Case Study #2: Believe in Your Students So They Begin to Believe in Themselves

Anna is a twenty-three-year old full lyric soprano who studied with me as an undergraduate student from 2016 to 2018. She is now a voice teacher herself, but is still striving to fully develop her voice. She wants to readily hit high notes and sustain an open sound, enjoying the fullness of her voice for long periods of time. She aspires to sing a ninety-minute recital in multiple styles—mariachi, musical theatre, opera, art song, even some blues—without really taking a break. She feels that singing is about feeling free and being whole, letting go of whatever happens outside of the studio.

*The language of energy: mental thoughts by the teacher
affect student energy.*

When I first started teaching Anna, I was her third teacher in four semesters. She had been told she didn't know enough and that her voice was too loud, and she had interpreted those criticisms to mean that she was not a good singer and should think strongly about changing her major. From the beginning, I heard something in her, a potential of an amazing full lyric voice, and I believed in her possibility with everything I had. So, I gave her Puccini's "Un bel dì, vedremo"[27] to sing and we explored ways for her to find and trust her instrument so that she could credibly perform it.[28]

We explored moving while singing, especially the time-honored tradition of squatting for the high notes. She remembers singing the ending of the aria and squatting for the high note (B♭5). She no longer felt stiff and afraid. In that moment, she found openness, freedom, and the realization that she *could* sing it over and over again. When she wasn't trying to make it happen, and just let her body do what it had found to do, it "clicked" and she was suddenly able to consistently produce the operatic sound required to "sell" the aria.

"Un bel dì, vedremo" helped Anna solidify her mental tools. The focus on what was helpful—on the reality that she *was* able to sing the way she dreamed—helped her mental blocks slowly go away, which gave her musical freedom. In the studio, she was allowed to make mistakes. We focused on the fact that she is allowed to have freedom away from the notation on the page, to make music, and that the notes are not set in stone. One of the primary issues was that we needed to foster acceptance of imperfection and failure. She says, "Some of my lessons are going to suck. That's normal, and I'm a human being. I'm allowed to make mistakes." In this allowance, she found the ultimate freedom to explore her vocal potential and to be bold in her musical choices.

*Foster a <u>cooperative</u> effort toward a <u>central</u> goal
rather than remain in a teacher–pupil dynamic.*

As a teacher, Anna has brought the principles of CoreSinging into her studio practice. She asks her students questions such as: "Are you with me today?" "Are you having issues?" "Are you stressed?" "Did you not practice, or do you not know how to approach this?" She works on being communicative, open, and willing to try different things to give the student alternatives using positive language—rather than "I suck," "It's dumb," or "I did it wrong." She affirms that humans have emotions, that things come up in life that affect the singer physically, mentally, and emotionally. Anna creates positive energy in her teaching studio. For example, she gives herself permission to admit that this may not be the day to try a certain thing and instead encourages students to put something aside and come back to it later. She strives to give the student the option to choose what they want to do, and she follows the student's lead.

Anna credits her teaching principles to the fact that she was allowed to make mistakes—this new concept, first introduced in our voice lessons together, also helped her deal with life. She uses CoreSinging techniques daily, allowing herself moments to center and take time to breathe, and appreciate what happened to her that day and understand that whatever it is, it's OK. She has developed increased openness to possibilities, ideas, and concepts, always finding a variety of ways to reach the same goal.

Anna states that, for her, singing felt like trying to tame a wild horse. In our lessons, she has freed herself from a rigid structure and learned an availability and willingness to be curious and try new things. Even if she doesn't do them well or end up liking them, at least she's tried, and that's what's important. When she takes time to process and understand things, she sees that there are always options, which fosters a mindset that there's not just one set way of doing things.

Case Study #3: "Permission to Do Whatever"

Kristi, a fifty-year-old voice teacher and musical theatre professional, wants to sing until she dies: "Carry my dead, cold body out of the studio . . . I want to sing forever." Before coming to me, she had consistently been taught through a "traditional" voice lesson mindset, where it was about achieving the goal of a specific sound that the voice teacher—the "expert"—decided was correct. She thought she had acquired useful tools for singing. However, these tools were always specific and technical, such as "lift your palate here" or "drop the jaw a little bit more there." It was never about exploring the instrument and its possibilities. Kristi would sing a song a hundred times on a lip trill, then sing it only on the vowels, then practice one phrase over and over again ad nauseam. She felt the mindset was always "brace yourself and get ready to perform." She likens prior lessons and studio classes to "battle" for which she had to gird her loins and prepare in the hope that she would be "fabulous."

Expectations and assumptions <u>kill</u> response and spontaneity.

As singers, we listen, imitate, and have judgments about our sound that may or may not be true. The somatic focus Kristi finds through CoreSinging energy awareness throws judgments away and allows her to work in a completely physical way, disrupting an old idea that she had. She believes that CoreSinging is transforming her instrument in ways that were never possible through conventional voice lessons.

In teaching her own students, Kristi thought she had to explain to them everything that was going on with them physically. She now is doing that a lot less, encouraging her students to give themselves permission to make discoveries rather than meet objectives. She reports that students are now moving through repertoire quickly and effectively. If something isn't working, they put it down, move away from it, and go on to something different. In addition, when the voice begins doing something unexpected, she encourages students to continue exploring, whereas before she would have stopped immediately and redirected the student toward the expected outcome. Kristi and her students feel they now have permission to sound however they sound instead of having a goal in mind—in other words, a specific auditory destination.

> *Be willing to experiment.*
> *The life of an artist is that nothing is ever finished.*

Kristi's biggest takeaway is shifting her judgment from an auditory-focused goal to a physical sensation, and she finds it life changing. She thinks the way she sings now is more fun. She's finding new colors and different ways to tell her stories, and practice is about finding out what her instrument is going to do in a variety of places. She already knows what *doesn't* work in a specific song, but she's willing to find new things that don't work. She has likened her exploration to the idea of scuba diving—just swimming to see what happens. There's a whole ocean and her voice can go anywhere in the ocean. The goal is the experience, and this mindset is allowing new things to occur vocally. Asking the questions is a shift for her; her practice sessions are a sequence of playing with ideas, one after another. She no longer tries to drive and control her practice sessions; instead, she explores possibilities.

Kristi says that these concepts changed *everything* about her voice. She describes her singing as more honest and open, and she is more confident and comfortable with herself. She feels less "guarded" than before. She feels like whatever was wound tightly in her is uncoiling, and she just wants to do it more. In her words: "When we're in a safe space, the net is there, so we are willing to let go of the trapeze, fly through the air, and see what happens—and if we fall, it's OK. It's not scary or intense. . . . It's fun."

She feels a gentleness and an economy that hadn't existed before. It's softer and gentler, like a hammock or a rocking chair as opposed to a war or a battle. But staying in a hammock feels like she could explore singing all day and be safe. She has found she can go deeper when she feels safe. Until recently, Kristi never had a teacher that she hadn't been trying to impress with her goals and her memorization and her whatever she was coming in to do. She finds the kind of person who can give someone permission to just be whatever they are in the moment to be transformational. That's what she wants to be—a person who makes others feel safe. She recently said to me, "You know, I don't think they teach teachers how to be that." In CoreSinging, however, that is a foundational principle.

Case Study #4: Voice Lessons as Life Coaching

Jennifer is a twenty-eight-year-old attorney who sang in school choir and college a cappella groups. She came to lessons seeking to reincorporate music into her life. Jennifer self-describes as a "very type A" personality. She found vocal work in the past had always been a very prescriptive sort of thing, where she heard instructions like, "You're going to do it this way, and that's the right way. . . . That's what we expect." In our lessons, if she was having an "off" day, we would talk and figure out why it felt off. We would then do something fun and creative that she was not expecting, or just do something altogether different. We talk about ideas for real life, and she feels like she is an involved part of the curriculum.

Drawing sounds and songs can be a lot of fun.

At a recent lesson, we did a classic CoreSinging exercise when Jennifer had gotten stuck singing a piece the same way every time. As she tried to make adjustments based on things we had discussed, it was becoming really hard for her to find options, because she had practiced it so much in a certain way. So, we pulled out a piece of paper and some colored pencils and she started drawing as she was singing. I had her draw with long strokes, then big curves, then with pointy, angular shapes, and then with "fairy lights," also while changing colors each time from warm to cool and back. This exploration helped her get out of her head, get into the music, and helped her realize that she had a multitude more options, that there's a whole lot more available, than when her brain tried to intercept and modify every single note. Doing exercises like that, where she can, without even noticing it, just shut her brain off, gives her more freedom and makes her feel like she's doing a lot less work. Her brain is totally focused on something else, and it can't get in her way. Jennifer even reported that she took those drawings and put them up with magnets on her fridge, and having it there made her rethink and want to reengage with that process.

I will let go of all expectations and judgments based on past experiences, or future possibilities, and begin my life/singing anew from now.

Jennifer finds that the principles of CoreSinging play into her everyday life in myriad ways. She realizes that there are other ways to do things than just one correct, right, prescriptive sort of way. Being able to do that in voice lessons opened a door to more freedom, not only in her voice, but in her daily life—she's been able to get more comfortable with setting boundaries and setting limits in terms of what she wants (and doesn't want) to do and how far she allows work to intrude on life. We spent an entire lesson speaking about answering emails before getting out of bed and the electronic tether that a smart watch had become. By consciously removing those energetic distractions, she was able to find ways to experiment out of her "type A–ness." She finds this new mindset to be uncharted, like the Wild West, and so she finds it somewhat scary, because she doesn't know what is going to happen.

Although Jennifer doesn't know what sounds are going to come out when she sings, she finds it to be lots of fun once she gets started and realizes that so many different things can happen. She especially loves it when—once we have explored new ideas—she realizes that her voice is still working; it hasn't just evaporated or freaked out or been "bad" just because we've been experimenting. This results in a feeling of freedom—the feeling that everything's going to be OK, even if not done "right" the first time.

She finds the idea that these exercises—where we just get the brain to shut up and stop trying to be a dictator—demonstrate that that is possible to accomplish things in our life without working so hard and without the brain stressing so much about every single detail. That has been a revelation for her. Jennifer said that once she realized that stressing out is not required for success, she wanted to continue chasing that feeling—not just in voice lessons, but everywhere. She has found that maybe she doesn't *need* to be working so hard, maybe what's going to come out is going to be wonderful without unnecessary controlling, grabbing, and anxiety. As a perfectionist, she finds this realization extremely liberating. She feels that CoreSinging has dramatically increased her self-confidence.

FINAL THOUGHTS

The primary CoreSinging characteristic that consistently emerged throughout these interviews is that the principle of mindfulness and mutual respect leads to students who feel empowered to explore and discover new concepts and areas of voicing *for themselves*. An energetic relationship fostered in inquiry and discovery creates an open and transparent environment in which the singer finds *security* in the unknown and an environment of neutrality is created, where there are neither expectations of nor emotional involvement in the answer. The journey is the goal and artistic flourishing becomes the norm.

The ideal language of energy is positive and supportive.

CoreSinging has changed who I am as a person. My training with Meribeth, in the months shortly after my husband's stroke at age fifty-three, opened me up to new possibilities and gave me tools with which to meet life, not just do better in the voice studio. CoreSinging has become a daily approach to living and connecting with humanity in all its glory. I am thankful every day for the trajectory of growth that Meribeth helped set me on, and I know that her energy surrounds me as I continue to teach and learn.

NOTES

1. My exploration included Feldenkrais-guided voice lessons with Robert Sussuma. In the search to find ways to apply the relief and knowledge learned within my own lessons, I encountered the Feldenkrais-inspired practice of "Bones for Life," created by master Feldenkrais teacher/trainer Ruthy Alon, and became a certified Bones for Life teacher in October 2021. My research on the pedagogical application of this method was presented at the 2021 Virtually PAVA symposium.

2. "What you feel [sense] alters your sight and hearing. Interoception in the moment is more influential to perception, and how you act, than the outside world is." Lisa Feldman Barrett, *How Emotions Are Made* (London: Mariner Books, 2017), 79.

3. "Every time that we expand the limits of our knowledge, our sensibility and the precision of our actions increase and the limits of what is considered natural and normal also expand." Moshé Feldenkrais, *Awareness through Movement* (New York: Harper One, 1977), 87.

4. Chad Orzel, "Six Things Everyone Should Know about Quantum Physics," *Forbes* (July 2015), accessed August 27, 2021. https://www.forbes.com/sites/chadorzel/2015/07/08/six-things-everyone-should-know-about-quantum-physics/.

5. "When you overthink and overfocus, it interferes with the qi flow." Xie Ling Welch, Hug the Moon Qi Gong Studio. Personal correspondence with the author (Fall 2017).

6. Ingo Titze, *Principles of Voice Production* (Denver: National Center for Voice and Speech, 2000), 94.

7. "Beware of 'Initial Conditions.' Sensitivity to Initial Conditions Can Also Mean Life and Death for a Product." Ziauddin Sardar and Iwona Abrams, *Introducing Chaos: A Graphic Guide*, fourth ed. (London: Icon Books, 2013), 114.

8. "The brain is organized by chaos. . . . Although we know that certain regions of the brain perform certain functions, activity in one area can trigger more neuronal responses throughout a large region. . . . A healthy brain maintains a low level of chaos which often self-organizes into a simpler order when presented with a familiar stimulus." Sardar and Abrams, 142–43.

9. "'But the trick in learning to trust is learning to allow failure.' . . . Resistance to failure—when you say to yourself, 'I can't afford to fail'—will put you in your swing circle every time, because in your mind the only guarantee of success is control.'" William Whitecloud, *The Magician's Way* (Novato, CA: New World Library, 2009), 108.

10. "Pay close attention to the sensations, gestures, and postures associated with this behavior. Aim to use physical words, rather than words about emotions. . . . If this work of paying attention is challenging, that doesn't mean you're failing. In fact, it probably means you're on precisely the right track." Amanda Blake, *Your Body Is Your Brain: Leverage Your Somatic Intelligence to Find Purpose, Build Resilience, Deepen Relationships, and Lead More Powerfully* (Truckee, CA: Trokay Press, 2018), 260.

11. "The language of body and action may teach us a simpler way to do things and reveal knowledge we had within us but had not suspected. . . . Art is the act of balancing: knowing what to prepare, what to leave to the moment, and the wisdom to know the difference." Stephen Nachmanovitch, *The Art of Is: Improvising as a Way of Life* (Novato, CA: New World Library, 2019), 15.

12. "We need habits if we are to act appropriately and quickly. But habits used blindly or as if they are laws of nature, i.e., cannot be changed, are just perpetuated, agreed ignorance. The possible alternatives in our array of means, functions, and structures are staggering. Yet all unhappy sufferers 'are made like that,' i.e., like their habits. These make them blind to the enormous choice of alternatives available to them. Because habits are so useful and economic to use, we prefer not to change them." Moshé Felenkrais, *The Elusive Obvious* (Berkeley, CA: North Atlantic Books, 2019), 118.

13. Lynn Helding, *The Musician's Mind: Teaching, Learning, and Performance in the Age of Brain Science* (Lanham, MD: Rowman & Littlefield, 2020), 72.

14. "The important issue is that no alternative means anxiety. Free choice means having at least another way. Free choice is meaningless when we are compelled to adopt the one and only way we know. Free choice means having an alternative mode of action available, so you can then choose the way you want most. To elect not to act is really no choice at all—it is not life.

An intentional voluntary movement, say with your hand along a trajectory, can be stopped, recontinued, reversed, or moved to do something else. A voluntary movement means free choice. A defensive, reflexive movement is of the all-or-nothing type; it is primitive and without intention. Such a movement is valid only in the face of danger and self-preservation, and when there is no time for choice." Feldenkrais, *The Elusive Obvious*, 148.

15. "Declarative learning . . . is information that one can speak about, or 'declare.' . . . Memory for words and life episodes [fall] under the category of declarative learning." Helding, 72.

16. Rachel Velarde, "Velcro Hand," Accessed August 27, 2021. https://youtu.be/q5ImFY3S9Uw.

17. "Efficiency: the ratio of the useful energy delivered by a dynamic system to the energy supplied to it." https://www.merriam-webster.com/dictionary/efficiency, accessed August 29, 2021.

18. "Economy: efficient and concise use of nonmaterial resources (such as effort, language, or motion)." https://www.merriam-webster.com/dictionary/economy, accessed August 29, 2021.

19. "Anxiety handicaps your intelligence. When fear takes over, you feel as if you are in a blind alley, that you must break out at any cost, and so you tend to be swept into an irrelevant compulsive aggression. . . . Your nervous system . . . will continue to perpetuate that same limiting habit unless you address it, once more, in that same language designed for decision-making. You bring your nervous system . . . to the primal state of mind of open search, when you invite it to cope again with the raw material of the unknown and check it from different points of view. During this encounter with a new perspective, enriched with new options—especially if they offer more comfortable and more attractive solutions—a remarkable thing happens. Your blind alley no longer appears threatening as you begin to perceive that you have a choice of breakthroughs. Your hurried, self-defense impulse is replaced by a functional consideration. Your system updates its old decisions on its own. Habit loses its status of determined decision and regresses to a role, respected though not exclusive, alongside another, newer solution. It is not process which offers the more relevant solution, but your healthy response to a wider choice of possibilities sprouting forth in you spontaneously, autonomously and beyond the control of your consciousness. . . . When your self-righting mechanism sharpens, you are oriented to progress. . . . You are actually training your sense of daring in the art of how not to cease striving towards more satisfaction, how not to relinquish vitality. Acquaintance with the method of recovering choices encourages you to continue to refine your actions. . . . The motivation to refinement becomes a way of life." Ruthy Alon, *Mindful Spontaneity: Returning to Natural Movement* (Berkeley, CA: North Atlantic Books, 1996), 40–41.

20. "First, we learn to flow with distraction, like that blade of grass bending to the wind. Then we learn to use distraction, inspiring ourselves with what initially would have thrown us off our games. Finally, we learn to re-create the inspiring settings internally." Josh Waitzkin, *The Art of Learning: An Inner Journey to Optimal Performance* (New York: Free Press, 2007), 200.

21. An example I use regularly is learning to find a new route to the grocery store. We often have a set route to get somewhere. If, someday, that route is blocked, we must find an alternate route. Somatic inquiry is the discovery of that new route, which we may find we like much more than the prior, habitual route. Even more, oftentimes the new route has increased pleasure associated with it—perhaps the view is more pleasant, or you drive by a friend's house. This increased pleasure is something the brain will latch on to and want to repeat. This is the same way with practice. When

we find a new way to produce a desired task, and that way is more pleasurable, more sensual, more joyful, then we will want to repeat it. What happens if, in the practice room, we define goals by what feels good, feels right, feels pleasurable to the senses? In my experience, that is when practicing becomes a joy, and students (and I!) *want* to practice, spending time exploring our vocal abilities. And that is the magic where boundless improvement occurs.

22. "Agency is crucial to making sense of the world . . . from the cradle, we're learning cause and effect." Dennis Proffit and Drake Baer, *Perception: How Our Bodies Shape Our Minds* (New York: St. Martin's Press, 2020), 28–29.

23. Helding, 27.

24. Throughout this section, I reference information provided to me by Meribeth, from both a printed (unpublished) teacher certification workbook/manual and personal notes taken during my CoreSinging training process in February and March 2017.

25. "Moving Too Fast" is from *The Last Five Years* (2001) by Jason Robert Brown (b. 1970).

26. Which we did in a recent lesson, each time focusing on a different goal for communication, to continue to explore trusting the feeling of ease and connected discourse.

27. "Un bel dì, vedremo" is from *Madama Butterfly* (1904) by Giacomo Puccini (1858–1924).

28. And she did! Her senior recital included this aria, a set of mariachi pieces, for which she put together a small banda, and a set of contemporary musical theatre songs. All of these were styles she had previously been told she couldn't or shouldn't sing.

Chapter Eight

The Body Knows How to Sing
Michael Hill

A few years ago, a speech and language therapist shared her thesis with me on vibrational energy medicine. Until that point, I had only studied what I considered to be evidence-based approaches to voice training, so this felt rather "out there" to me. I did have a certain level of curiosity toward what I would have considered "ethereal" approaches—my native Scotland has a glorious yin-yang history of superstitious tales and level-headed pragmatism—but I couldn't quite get over my self-conscious, cynical inner voice, sirening the word "woo-woo" at me![1] However, this fascinating, well-researched thesis came from someone I considered a voice of reason, working within the health service and informed by the latest medical research on treating voice issues. Not only that, she told me that the great Meribeth Dayme, in my mind the last word on vocal anatomy and function, was now a key voice in this emerging field of singing as a vibrational, energetic, metaphysical practice. Had she moved from voice science to sorcery? Surely not.

MY PERSONAL JOURNEY: DISCOVERING A NEW APPROACH

Our knowledge of how the voice works has advanced dramatically in recent years. Trailblazing researchers, voice methods, and models have helped to reveal the invisible human instrument and develop practical frameworks to explore the myriad possibilities of the human vocal tract. Voice teachers now have access to an overflowing well of ways to troubleshoot almost any voice issue and facilitate mastery of vocal styles. Personally, I have found myself "geeking out" on voice science with colleagues around the world, hopping down endless research rabbit holes and discovering how much truth there is in the oft-paraphrased paradox, "the more we learn, the less we know." At best, these explorations are exciting, rewarding, and provide teachers and students with new possibilities; at worst, they create "die Qual der Wahl": the torture of choice. What technique will work best for my student? What if the technique I am using is deemed "wrong" by new research? What if I am missing some important new knowledge? Amid this existential angst, it is easy to forget a rather crucial aspect of singing and teaching singing: it's fun!

I have had a number of discussions about this with teaching colleagues. There is a duality to being a problem-solving pedagogue and a creative, curious artist. Sometimes, finding a path between these two facets of our identity can be a challenge. Singer-teachers in particular appear susceptible to the downsides of this duality, sometimes leading to crippling music performance anxiety (MPA):

> The MPA experienced in performances and in classes was often triggered as a result of self-induced pressure because of these singer-teachers' pursuit of tenure (specifically the need to acquire enough performing opportunities), their vocal insecurities in front of colleagues and students, and having to prove themselves worthy of their position on faculty.[2]

Teachers in higher education must prepare students for theory exams—technical tests decide which type of singing is of a high enough "standard" to merit a particular grade—and students spend their academic year gearing up for a high-stress exam or dissertation. At the same time, we are there to guide performers as they explore the great potential of their artistry, something very difficult to quantify with a number or grade. These numbers, perhaps reflecting another duality of artistry versus analysis, seem to follow singers doggedly, even into their professional careers. How many tickets have been sold? How many streams did the track receive? How much merchandise do we still have to sell? Is that chart position good enough?

COVID-19 exacerbated these issues, given the tremendous anxiety around lack of work and the almost overnight disappearance of live performance. It is understandable amid these pressures and conflicts that teachers and performers might lose the fun, joyful nature of connecting with the voice. Is the new paradox, "the more we learn, the less we enjoy"? A Taoist philosopher might well respond, "maybe."[3] Western notions of dualism see things as opposite, sometimes warring forces, whereas yin and yang are in harmony, inextricably linked, flowing back and forth in balance. I have always found religion and philosophy fascinating and, taking stock of my career to date, I found myself reflecting increasingly on these concepts. Even the nature of my career: the work and play of being a voice teacher and singer. Coincidentally (maybe), I found out much later from Cynthia Vaughn that Meribeth had a big interest in Taoist principles.

I started to wonder whether I had been spending too much time on the work part and not enough time on play. Was I getting stuck in "paralysis through analysis"? Perhaps it was time to explore some of Meribeth's sorcery. My initial plans to participate in CoreSinging courses in the UK were stayed by those "life getting in the way" moments: bereavement, a new job, and house renovations. I wrote to Meribeth to let her know that I was keen to begin studying, but just hadn't gotten round to it yet. She replied, "It will happen when the time is right." Her response struck me quite profoundly. Perhaps it resonated with my aforementioned yin-yang Scottish mindset; "Whit's fur ye'll no go by ye" is a very common philosophy (i.e., "whatever is meant for you, will come to you.").

Around that time, I discovered that there was a whole world of research around what I previously considered to be dubiously unscientific "woo-woo": energy fields, mind-body healing, even the power of prayer to reduce depression and anxiety.[4] In fact, the Scottish scientist David R. Hamilton, formerly an organic chemistry researcher in the pharmaceutical industry, wrote the book *Why Woo-Woo Works*.[5] If a scientist and fellow pragmatic Scot was exploring this work, maybe the time was now right for me to open my mind to new possibilities.

Meribeth's CoreSinging principles are now becoming an intuitive, habitual part of my teaching, a natural complement to the technical and performance coaching work I do with singers. In particular, I find the techniques useful for helping singers "get out of their own way," letting go of the self-criticism that can block creativity and finding play within the work of honing one's craft. I would like to share a couple of case studies of times when these principles have helped singers in this way.

CASE STUDIES

Case Study 1: A Musical Theatre Singer and Actor

I had been working with an actor and musical theatre singer for a few months, on and off, before starting Meribeth's CoreSinging course online. He had previously been told he had a relatively low voice, but wished to explore whether it was possible to increase his range in order to be considered for some of the modern, pop/rock-style musicals that he was auditioning for in London. He was a logically minded student who eagerly devoured any knowledge of anatomy and acoustics I gave him. He also liked to work on specific technical exercises and leave each session with a detailed practice guide. It was a joy to work with such a diligent, enthusiastic singer, and—over the course of a few sessions—we had some real "eureka" moments.

As it happened, the label of having a low voice had led him to cultivate a very strong, resonant sound, which didn't move comfortably above F4 on the piano. Given his enjoyment of anatomical explanations, I talked about the work of the vocal folds in higher pitches, the cricothyroid muscle and how his current vocal strategy might not be the most efficient one for the range he wished to explore. We worked on lighter sounds and he responded particularly well to twang-based exercises,[6] such as imitating a teasing playground voice or a "nyuk nyuk" Stooge sound on pitch glides.[7]

Within a few weeks—a testament to his focused work ethic—he had developed a thrilling, flexible higher range and felt ready to try out some of the more challenging modern musical numbers. We worked on "Waving through a Window" from *Dear Evan Hansen*, and, having demonstrated some warm-ups to well beyond the range of the highest part of the song, I thought it would be a walk in the park for him. However, every time we tried the song, he would freeze on the high B-flats, experience a tight abdominal area and a sensation of excessive pressure. We would then work on getting the lower belly to soften, gliding around in pitch on a vowel, and apply this to the difficult section. This would work, but then the same issue would arise in "performance mode." The session ended positively, with the singer determined to integrate this newfound abdominal freedom into his practice.

After a few weeks of working on building up repertoire, we returned to the song and the same thing happened. His reaction was, "I should be able to do this, but I'm doing something wrong with my breath support." Meribeth's research highlights why—from an energetic, vibrational perspective—this paralysis through analysis doesn't work: Getting stuck in our heads blocks "chi," which means we can't possibly be in the flow state we need for singing. In Western terms, we have entered the realms of fight, flight, or freeze. I decided to take a different approach:

Let's forget about wrong; your body knows how to breathe.

A key solution I took from the CoreSinging course is intent setting and I felt we needed to reset the intention of the session. It was clear that the singer was striving for perfection and was using negative self-talk. An important aspect of intent setting is that it should be driven by fun or by play. I was directed to the book *The Art of Possibility* in Meribeth's reading list and I was delighted to read about "Rule no. 6": "Don't take yourself so g--dam seriously!"[8] I needed to heed that advice as much as the client.

Firstly, I decided we should shake out the negativity, making whatever uncoordinated movements and noises felt useful. Then, I suggested we play a game of "getting it wrong": deliberately making the silliest sounds we could make at the climax of the song. I started by making some yodels, roosterlike crows, squawks, and hoots, encouraging the singer to do the same. Before long, we were enjoying contagious fits of giggles together! With the energy of the session now lifted, I encouraged him to "forget about technique for now." I knew this would be outside of his comfort zone, but we focused instead on a new intention: to keep things flowing.

I remembered Meribeth's video demonstration of the Hoberman sphere expanding and contracting. I asked the singer to orchestrate his hand movements with his breath like the sphere, making sure there was a continuous movement following the breath. This combination of a practical focus and a clear intention for singing the song seemed to provide the logic the singer enjoyed, while taking away the desire to get things right. It also offered visual feedback of whether he was flowing or freezing: if his hands stopped moving, or sped up, he knew to shake it off and return to the intention of the song. He managed to complete the song with much more ease and freedom and this gave him the confidence to perform the song at an audition a few weeks later, at which he was given great feedback.

I believe that the right techniques, tailored to the singer, can help facilitate their artistic wishes. In this case, however, technique had become associated with right and wrong, and we needed to find another way. The analyst in me wondered later whether I had used the approaches "correctly." As well as remembering Rule no. 6 of *The Art of Possibility*, I realized I also needed to remember number 6 of Meribeth's nine general CoreSinging principles:

The more imagination and fun you have, the more interesting and useful your exercises.

CoreSinging training, according to Meribeth, is like the scaffolding of a house; it's up to you what you put in it. This was one of the first times I applied CoreSinging concepts to my work and I found great joy in having permission to play, to work intuitively and in a nonstriving manner. I began to see how this approach could complement the work I did with clients in many ways, even outside of the practice of singing.

Case Study 2: An Actress and Voiceover Artist

For many years, I have applied vocal technique and musicality principles to accent, dialect, and character voice work. I was fortunate enough to present some of my ideas and pedagogical findings at the World Voice Consortium Congress in Denmark in 2017. I was fascinated by psychologist Diana Deutsch's work on the "Speech to Song Illusion," whereby listeners begin to perceive a repeated spoken phrase as music.⁹ It's striking how rapidly neural plasticity is possible in our perception of sounds and, working with actors and public speakers, I have found that a musical perspective to accents and languages can speed up learning—and make the experience more fun!

This work is often very playful and creative, with exercises on musicality coming to me from the many corners of my imagination: performers pretending to trot around the room on a horse to find a Received Pronunciation (RP) English accent; people channeling their inner rap artist to fine-tune the rhythm of a standard American accent; and a class of Scottish Gaelic language learners doing a strathspey to find the "Scotch snap" or Lombard rhythm of Celtic prosody.

There are still occasions when a performer will get stuck in an analytical mindset. With accents, there is a real pressure to get it right; nobody wants to be the actor whose ropy RP is forever preserved on film! An actor can spend months working on, and subsequently mastering, the vowel sounds and stresses of their target accent or language, but then comes the big challenge: putting it all together into one, flowing "song." If one is too focused on getting it right, it does not flow, and the listener hears that something is off.

I worked with an American actress, living in the UK, who was advised to work on her RP for auditions. Although she didn't consider herself a singer, she enjoyed working with melody and rhythm and made good progress, moving from shorter exercises to applying the accent in a monologue for future auditions. Whenever we reached the stage of running the monologue, the tongue and lip positions of her native accent would sneak in, the melody would change, and the pronunciation would quickly return to what she knew best. We worked on rediscovering the vocal tract shapes of RP and playing with the musicality, but some uncertainty remained about putting it all into practice. When I asked her what she felt was getting in her way, she said: "I think I like being a good student, so I don't like making mistakes."

Let's not be good students; let's be fun students!

Meribeth talked in her training course about having a "veritable cornucopia of fun ways to teach" as a way to get rid of the need for being right. It was clear in this session that we needed to get back to playing. So many of us associate the learning experience with serious outcomes; a good student can also be described as a serious one; good musicians are also called "serious." I don't think I've ever heard of a school parents' evening where a child was complimented on being "such a playful student"!

I thought it might be fun to incorporate some elements of the CoreSinging "Ten Steps to Learning Text" into our accent play. I asked the client to forget the words and "uhm and chew" the text with me on the pitches and rhythms of the words. This led to a few attempts to complete the paragraph without laughing! We then tried saying some of the words, always going back to "uhming" if any thinking about pronunciation crept in. I asked her to try the words, but in a "roller-coaster" fashion, exaggerating the pitch rises on stressed words and subsequent falls. I always ask people to listen to the London Underground's "mind the gap between the train and the platform" announcement and how dramatically the pitches leap around from stressed to unstressed sounds.

With that in mind, we then found our most exaggerated, dramatic, RP voice, reading the words like we needed to project them to the other side of the city. It became a fun game to "out-ham" each other! This took her very far from any notion of getting it right and, of course, from her native accent patterns. As a change of pace, I asked her to then mime the text, imagining it sounding just as she wanted, thinking of the expression the text required, the nuances of voice and intonation. We stayed here for a little while, giving time to the imagination.

Finally, I asked her to perform the text, focusing on her interpretation as an actor, with no mention of accent work. I was delighted to find that the accent was much more fluid and consistent. After the reading, the client said, "I think that went pretty well." Crucially, she began to trust herself and move away from being a "good student." In subsequent sessions, progress was much faster and it was much easier to fine-tune details and suggest specific exercises for home practice. She went on to use the accent in a prerecorded audition. This was an important step, as it showed she now saw the accent as a real possibility rather than something that was stuck in the "classroom."

There are other nonsinging applications to these tools we have been exploring. As a Gaelic speaker, I sometimes teach language classes to groups and individuals and I find it a helpful task to compare the song of one's own language with the song of the Gaelic language. Students often end up creating "melody maps" of how they interpret the sound, the rises and falls, stresses, and cadences. Then, if a student is particularly stuck with pronunciation, I might ask them to draw the melody, on a piece of paper or a board, using the color(s) of their choice. Meribeth suggested this as a more advanced exercise in CoreSinging, but it seems to be quite manageable with short sentences of speech, where breath is not really an issue.

Students are of course free to explore what works for them individually, but with Gaelic one of the main focal points is the length of vowel: If there's a long vowel, the melody line the student draws needs to keep going; shorter sounds get a shorter dash. This is particularly important in the language, because an incorrect vowel length might cause some confusion or even embarrassment: for example, "fèis" [feːʃ] in Gaelic is a festival, whereas "feis" [feʃ] means intercourse. Perhaps there are some festivals where the two go hand in hand, but knowing the difference is very important! Encouraging learners to draw the sounds with their hands seems to help them feel the nuances of the sounds. It's also fun to create a multicolored representation of sound.

Meribeth stressed that CoreSinging is designed to function as an adjunct to other ways of working, and as a teacher I feel that I am just beginning to explore the many ways these tools can be applied. At the very least, I am reminded of the importance of play in learning, to trust one's inner instincts (the teacher's and the student's) and, as Meribeth says, "allow the proof to unfold." Play is important; in fact, it is a human right, enshrined in law as Article 31 in the United Nations Convention on the Rights of the Child.[10] As adults, we seem to forfeit our right to play.

With that in mind, I now begin lessons by setting clear, positive intentions for my teaching and I invite the singer to establish positive intentions to implement into their singing practice. We then collaborate on playful, "not-getting-it-right" exercises, such as the "uhming and chewing" or improvised noise making, humming and moving, drawing sound: whatever instinctively is useful for the client. These fun exercises remind us not to get too serious about everything. They also get positive results, whether one explains them through physical or metaphysical concepts. As Meribeth wrote in her CoreSinging course:

> *Your role is to guide students toward a positive relationship with their voice and singing. They do not need to know all that you know or understand about energy.*

Is intention setting explained by sports psychology?[11] Is unblocking chi simply exercising your prefrontal cortex?[12] Is the flow of energy between people the quantifiable work of mirror neurons?[13] A Taoist would answer: "Maybe." Maybe it's both; perhaps this is another case for the harmony of duality. I'd like to think perhaps there was a little bit of sorcery going on, though!

REFLECTIONS

There was a fascinating interview with Barbra Streisand by Anthony Tommasini in the *New York Times* a few years back, trying to unpick the mysteries of her considerable vocal abilities.[14] When the interviewer tried to uncover what she did to get her voice to achieve such technical and artistic feats, she simply said:

> *I didn't do it intellectually. . . . I did it intuitively, unconsciously. I kind of like that.*

Streisand's will drove her voice. If she wanted to hold a long note, she would hold it. A voice geek like me would have once viewed these comments as frustrating. Surely, she must be doing *something*? In the field of human energy research, that something is quantifiable. Goldman talks about how "intent is the energy behind the sound. It is the consciousness we have when making and projecting a sound."[15] Valerie V. Hunt, who was professor emeritus of the Department of Physiological Sciences at UCLA, also states that "will directs all energy."[16] Could this mean that the energy required to sustain one of Streisand's superhuman twenty-second belt notes comes more from the will to sustain the note than any particular method of "breath support"?[17] Physicist-turned-baritone Thomas Hemsley further explains in his book, *Singing and Imagination* the following:

> My conclusion is that the ability to sing long phrases . . . is, to a very large extent, a matter of the singer's ability to imagine long phrases . . . and to maintain mental (and consequently, physical) concentration.[18]

Technique plays a very important role in singing, but there is also something about the energy of possibility, of meaning behind the sound, that can create vocal magic. Often, asking the singer to explore the text, create a character, and give meaningful intention to the song can work in ways where technical exercises might only scratch the surface. One might call this work acting through song; in CoreSinging, it could be working with energy and focusing intent.

Inspired by the CoreSinging course, I began to explore in more detail some of the techniques Meribeth endorsed as beneficial for energy and focus, particularly meditation and mental training techniques. Of the practices I tried, I found autogenic training (AT) resonated with me most and went on to postgraduate certification as an AT therapist. I have seen it help clients in overcoming performance anxiety, increasing creativity, and reducing negative self-talk. In many ways, it's another way of working with energy and intention. In fact, autogenic therapists often give "intentional formulae" to clients to repeat at the end of a training course.[19] For singers, this could be something like, "my voice is flow," "my voice brings joy," or whatever feels right for the person. In CoreSinging terms, everything is energy and our intent directs this energy, so a singer who meditates on a positive intention such as this will surely amplify it into their singing practice and connection with the audience.

Voice science has perhaps not yet embraced the diverse field of energy research. In years to come, it could become common knowledge, just as we now talk about formants and harmonics, or neural networks governing sensorimotor control of speech and singing.[20] Maybe we shouldn't worry about what might happen. Taoism and maybe again! From this perspective, the universe is always changing, therefore knowledge is always changing:

> True knowledge cannot be known—
> but perhaps it can be understood or lived.[21]

There is enough negative energy out there in the collective consciousness and singing teaching can only contribute to this if the balance tips too far toward analysis, right and wrong. The American neuroscientist and pharmacologist Candace Pert described the brain and its functions as a "receiver" and "amplifier" of collective reality.[22] What could we, then—as teachers and singers—be amplifying in our practice? What could we help students, or the audience, receive?

I feel that my role as a teacher is in creating a space where the student can create, explore, and recognize their innate intelligence. Singing provides so many social, mental, physical, and spiritual benefits and I now see my role as a teacher as something beyond technique and performance coaching: I have a responsibility—albeit a really fun one (!)—to help amplify positivity and remind singers that they have the answers within themselves.

The body knows how to sing.

I never actually got to meet Meribeth; she passed before I completed the course and I finished my final CoreSinging interview online with Cynthia Vaughn. Although I was switched on to energy research back in 2012, it took me a while before I felt ready to explore it. As it happens, the person who introduced me to Meribeth's work moved away from voice into other areas and I have never been able to find her again. Perhaps our paths were only meant to cross for a short while. Maybe it all happened when the time was right, just as Meribeth said.

NOTES

1. This term is used commonly in the British Isles to describe anything considered "out there." https://www.merriam-webster.com/dictionary/woo-woo.

2. Cupido, Conroy. "Music Performance Anxiety, Perfectionism and Its Manifestation in the Lived Experiences of Singer-Teachers." *Muziki* 15, no. 1 (2018): 14–36.

3. See "The Parable of the Chinese Farmer," a Taoist tale often attributed to the English philosopher, Alan Watts.

4. Boelens, Peter A., Roy R. Reeves, William H. Replogle, and Harold G. Koenig. "A Randomized Trial of the Effect of Prayer on Depression and Anxiety." *The International Journal of Psychiatry in Medicine* 39, no. 4 (2009), 377–92.

5. Hamilton, David R. *Why Woo Woo Works: The Science behind Crystals, Reiki and the Things That the Age of Reason Tried to Quash.* Hay House UK, 2021.

6. A number of approaches work with the idea of twang as a piercing, ringing character produced by epiglottic narrowing, and it is a discrete "voice quality" in Estill Voice Training. Emerging research, however, suggests there may be different ways to produce this sound. See Perta, Karen, Youkyung Bae, and Kerrie Obert. "A pilot investigation of twang quality using magnetic resonance imaging." *Logopedics Phoniatrics Vocology* 46, no. 2 (2020), 77–85.

7. On reflection, it's worth noting that the exercises that worked most effectively were the playful, fun ones!

8. Zander, Rosamund S., and Benjamin Zander. *The Art of Possibility: Transforming Professional and Personal Life*, London: Penguin, 2002.

9. "Speech-to-Song Illusion." Diana Deutsch, personal web page, accessed July 27, 2021. https://deutsch.ucsd.edu/psychology/pages.php?i=212.

10. Unicef UK, Children's Charity: For Every Child in Danger. Accessed July 27, 2021. https://downloads.unicef.org.uk/wp-content/uploads/2019/10/UNCRC_summary-1_1.pdf.

11. Healy, Laura, Alison Tincknell-Smith, and Nikos Ntoumanis, "Goal Setting in Sport and Performance," *Oxford Research Encyclopedia of Psychology*, 2018. https://doi.org/10.1093/acrefore/9780190236557.013.152.

12. Kotler, Steven. "Flow States and Creativity: Can You Train People to Be More Creative?" psychologytoday.com (blog), February 25, 2014. https://www.psychologytoday.com/us/blog/the-playing-field/201402/flow-states-and-creativity.

13. See, for example: Schober, Patricia, and Barbara Sabitzer. "Mirror Neurons for Education." Paper presented at Seventh International Technology, Education, and Development Conference, Valencia, Spain, 2013.

14. Streisand, Barbra. "Streisand's Fine Instrument and Classic Instinct." By Anthony Tommasini. *New York Times*, September 24, 2009. https://www.nytimes.com/2009/09/27/arts/music/27tomm.html.

15. Goldman, Jonathan, and Andi Goldman. *Chakra Frequencies: Tantra of Sound*, Destiny Books, 2011.

16. Hunt, Valerie V. *Infinite Mind: Science of the Human Vibrations of Consciousness*, Malibu Publishing, 1996.

17. The end of Streisand's interpretation of "Make Our Garden Grow" from Candide is one of many examples of these sustained belts.

18. Hemsley, Thomas. "Breath." In *Singing and Imagination: A Human Approach to a Great Musical Tradition*, 100–1. New York: Oxford University Press, 1998.

19. Schultz, Johannes H., and Wolfgang Luthe. "Special Formulae." In *Autogenic Therapy: Autogenic Methods*, 176. 1969.

20. Zarate, Jean M. "The Neural Control of Singing." *Frontiers in Human Neuroscience* 7 (2013).

21. "Concepts Within Taoism." BBC. Accessed July 27, 2021. https://www.bbc.co.uk/religion/religions/taoism/beliefs/concepts.shtml.

22. Pert, Candace. "Candace Pert on Molecules of Emotion." By Judith Hooper. *Omni Magazine*. Last modified November 22, 2017. https://omnimagazine.com/interview-candace-pert-molecules-emotion/.

Chapter Nine

A House with Four Rooms

Elizabeth Blades

> There is an Indian proverb, or axiom, that says that everyone is a house with four rooms: a physical, a mental, an emotional, and a spiritual room. Most of us tend to live in one room most of the time, but unless we go into every room every day, even if only to keep it aired, we are not a complete person.
>
> Rumer Godden, *A House with Four Rooms*[1]

The first time I read this quotation, I thought of CoreSinging and Meribeth's brilliance, courage, and passion for living an authentic life as a "complete person." As I wrote this chapter, I had a revelation: "core" is often associated with strength training, particularly the muscles of the torso. Looking up the definition in Merriam-Webster, it can also refer to the "central or most important part of something."[2] From my first career as a geologist, I think of the earth's core, below the mantle, composed mostly of iron and nickel. Meribeth never explained why she named her approach "CoreSinging"—she only defined what it was intended to offer: "An approach that encourages teachers to follow their intuition, curiosity, and natural abilities to further their own pedagogy and performance."[3]

I never thought to question why her approach has the name that it has . . . until now. Here are some of my thoughts: "Core" is an archaic form of *cuore*, the Italian word for "heart." Translating from Italian, it can also mean love, affection, generosity, courage, or center—all things that CoreSinging (or "heart singing") embodies. Thank you, Meribeth, from your place in the mystical beyond, for this realization.

Much like Meribeth, my own voice pedagogy career has encompassed science and academia in addition to mind, body, and awareness. In 1990, a family tragedy propelled me to enroll in a five-day spiritual healing course. I was the only voice teacher in a class of twenty-five individuals; others included registered nurses, psychologists, social workers, and Reiki practitioners.[4] The experience was eye-opening and compelled me to not only become a third-degree Reiki practitioner, but also advance my experience with kinesiology. These specialties drew me to Meribeth's CoreSinging approach to awareness, energy work, and intuition, which she first introduced in the fifth edition of *Dynamics of the Singing Voice*.

From 1992 to 1994, I chose *Dynamics of the Singing Voice* as the primary text for the Eastman School of Music voice pedagogy course I taught to vocal performance master's and doctoral candidates. In addition to revising the course curriculum, I was also permitted to choose the textbook with the caveat that it be approved by the voice faculty. While conducting research for my doctoral dissertation, I had read every book on voice, teaching voice, and voice science that was available at the time in Eastman's extensive Sibley Library.[5] One book stood out above the rest: *Dynamics of the Singing Voice* by Meribeth Bunch. Here was an extraordinary resource, unique in its approach and content.

A few years later, as a full-time professor at Heidelberg College (now University) in Tiffin, Ohio, I again chose *Dynamics of the Singing Voice* as the required text. In 1997, I was awarded a faculty grant to conduct research in the United Kingdom, interviewing prominent voice teachers and coaches. The International Congress of Voice Teachers (ICVT) met in London that summer, and I arranged to interview several pedagogues at that event. One can only imagine my delight and excitement in finally meeting Meribeth, who was exceedingly kind and gracious. With her permission, I recorded our conversation to share with my students—and she signed my well-worn book!

From that time on, our professional acquaintance grew into a deep friendship as a series of circumstances brought us together. We met again at the 2001 NATS conference, which was held in conjunction with the Voice Foundation symposium in Philadelphia, where Meribeth received the Van L. Lawrence Fellowship, sponsored jointly by the Voice Foundation and NATS. Meribeth also introduced me to Cynthia Vaughn in Philadelphia. In 2003, we dined together when I returned to London with a group of Heidelberg honors program students. Meribeth and I met once again at the 2007 Pan-European Voice Conference in Grönigen, the Netherlands, where we attended one another's lectures and workshops as well as social events.

In 2010, Meribeth invited me to apply for the first CoreSinging teacher certification training offered in the United States. I was accepted and joined five other teachers for a life-altering week at Cynthia's Magnolia Music Studio in Fort Collins, Colorado. The timing was serendipitous. Even though I had achieved much success in my career, after thirty years of teaching I felt burned out, stale, and exhausted. After the course, I wrote enthusiastically to Meribeth, "Then came CoreSinging and, suddenly, it's such a blast again! Everyone is having a terrific time singing . . . and I'm smiling, feeling so creative and inspired as their teacher."[6] The CoreSinging training was a transformative infusion of creativity, mind expansion, and permission to trust in my higher self.

After my CoreSinging certification training, our friendship continued, both in person and via Skype. In 2011, we were both included in the Indiana University "master teachers" week. At the 2012 NATS conference in Orlando, she invited me to some informal gatherings where I had the opportunity to engage in discussion and answer questions about CoreSinging.

When Meribeth moved from France to San Diego in 2016 to be closer to family, we could at last schedule frequent FaceTime video chats. That fall, I joined the voice faculty at Shenandoah University Conservatory. Among my courses was a voice class for instrumental music majors, and *The Singing Book* by Meribeth Dayme and Cynthia Vaughn was the required text.[7] Early in the semester, my students had the great opportunity to ask questions of the authors in a Zoom meeting. The following year, Rowman and Littlefield agreed to publish a second edition of my book, *A Spectrum of Voices: Prominent American Voice Teachers Discuss the Teaching of Singing*.[8] In addition to the first edition teachers, I invited six "new" pedagogues to be contributors. Of course, Meribeth was one of them.

The last time I saw Meribeth in person was in Las Vegas at the 2018 NATS national conference. In addition to spending a great deal of time together during the day, we also shared a hotel room. My fondest memory of that time was long talks we had over coffee at 4:00 a.m. Pacific Daylight Time (7:00 a.m. for my Eastern body clock) before the conference events resumed later that morning. That year, Meribeth and I were also invited to be contributing authors for *So You Want to Sing with Awareness: A Guide for Performers*.[9] Meribeth's chapter in this collection would be her last publication. At what was to be our final FaceTime video chat, she was distressed about the sudden onset of vocal hoarseness and anticipated further tests in the hospital with her neurologist. We closed off with promises to "catch up soon."

And then she was gone. So many grieved as a family whose matriarch was suddenly taken; I found some comfort in one of my classmate's observations that "now she is part of the energy of which she so often spoke."

INTEGRATING CORESINGING PRINCIPLES

How I sing and how I teach others intertwines with my chosen lifestyle and personal philosophy. These commingle and coalesce with training, experience, trial and error, strong mentorship and—yes—lessons in what *not* to do. For me, CoreSinging principles unify the disparate and inform, inspire, and transcend the ordinary while anchoring my own vocal performance and my teaching. The following describes several of the most important ways in which I have integrated CoreSinging principles into my pedagogy and practice.

Tune In, Tune Up, and Tune Out

In my book, *A Spectrum of Voices, Prominent American Voice Teachers Discuss the Teaching of Singing*, I organized the discussion in the first chapter according to the following guideline: "Describe your approach to teaching the following concepts of vocal technique: posture (alignment), breathing and breath support (*appoggio*), tonal resonance, diction, registration, unification, and tension mitigation."[10] In this chapter, CoreSinging principles and concepts—particularly the threefold guideline "tune in, tune up, and tune out"—offer a clear yet flexible "bucket" approach to working with singers.

Tune In

Meribeth used to say that "energy follows thought," and that "emotion is energy in motion." During our CoreSinging training, we would begin each morning with the qigong exercise Eight-Piece Brocades (*ba duan jin*). I continue to use these in my personal practice, and some of them I regularly teach to my students in both individual and class settings. I particularly like Lee Holden's ten-minute qigong routine, available on YouTube.[11] Yoga poses round out my tune-up routine. My favorites are "mountain," "warrior," and "rag doll," all of which encourage a sense of peace, tranquility, and tension release.[12]

Chakras can be a useful tool when "tuning in." In our 2010 CoreSinging training, Meribeth taught us to check chakras with muscle testing to find blockages or imbalances. I have since expanded with a tune-in exercise I call "breathing through the chakras." This warm-up uses oxygen as energy to clean and clear the seven main chakras, beginning with the first "root chakra" and steadily moving on upward to the seventh or "crown chakra." On each chakra, singers can choose to phonate on the pitch or vowel of their choice. Students and I have discovered that "toning through the chakras" is a liberating approach to warming up the voice without judgment or self-criticism.

Another favorite exercise that I use for tuning in is one derived from the Feldenkrais Method. Named for its discoverer—the physicist, engineer, and judo master Moshé Feldenkrais (1904–1984)—this method comprises two components: Awareness through Movement (ATM), which is a guided movement lesson, and Functional Integration (FI), a hands-on session with a practitioner. Basic tenets of the Feldenkrais Method are kinesthetic imagination as well as "control and letting go." These dovetail nicely with CoreSinging principles and concepts such as energy, balance, awareness, and performance preparation, especially for tension release and performance anxiety mitigation.

All my students learn the mini-ATM called "Releasing the Eyes." The eyes are a key component of the nervous system. Unless one is blind, we receive about 90 percent of our external sensory input from the eyes; thus, keeping the eyes released in turn relaxes our entire nervous system. When we are visually relaxed, we feel centered, and all the muscles in the head and jaw release as well. In addition, performance anxiety (also known as the fight-or-flight response) can be mitigated through this exercise.

Before beginning, keep in mind these rules and suggestions: First, ATM lessons are not "exercises"; Feldenkrais named them "lessons" because the body-mind-neuromuscular system is learning and reprogramming—how hard, how fast, or how much is not the point. Second, go slowly; do not hurry or become mechanical—stay mindful, because you want to *feel* what you are doing. Third, the exact number of repetitions are key, and *the pauses are as important as the actions*.

> Step 1: To begin, stand or sit forward in an armless chair. Put your hand (whichever you prefer) in front of you about one foot from your face with the palm toward your face. *Slowly* move your hand toward your face and then away to the full extension of the arm. At some point, as you move away from your face, turn your hand so your palm faces outward. Repeat this movement three or four times, following it with your eyes. Perform the movement gracefully, like a Balinese dancer. Put your hand down and pause for a moment with your eyes closed.
>
> Step 2: Again place your hand (you may switch hands at any time) a foot from your face, palm inward. Close your eyes. Move your hand toward your face slowly, then slowly move it away. Feel where you want to turn it, repeating the movement while you follow it with closed eyes. Repeat five or six times, going slowly and gently, with a sense of grace.

This is just a small portion of the full ATM lesson that Feldenkrais prescribes, but I have found that just these two steps can quickly and easily calm and quiet the stage nerves that often hit singers immediately before a performance.[13]

Tune Up

Creativity, curiosity, imagination, and intuition are at the heart of the CoreSinging approach. The familiar CoreSinging concepts can be a springboard for "thinking outside the box"—to which Meribeth would say, "There is no box!" What if you were an animal trying to communicate the text—how would you manage that? Pretend you are a violin or a harp, or any choice of instrument playing the song. How is that different? Find an emotion that is the opposite of what you are trying to express through your song; what changes? The possibilities are only limited by the student's imagination—give yourself permission to play, play, and play some more!

Tune Out

Meribeth's concept of "tuning out" is most helpful for managing performance anxiety. Instead of trying to block everything out when we were singing for other teachers in the CoreSinging training, Meribeth encouraged us to include everything as part of our performance. In Fort Collins, Colorado, that included freight trains that rumbled by frequently. The loud train whistles became part of our performance. One of the most fun tuning-out exercises was "Drawing the Song." We were encouraged to sing without criticism, judgment, or stopping—being grateful for our voices, whether performing for a real audience or an imagined audience of thousands.

Trust

Establishing trust between teacher and student is foundational to integrating CoreSinging principles. Every student I work with is unique, and for that reason every lesson I teach varies accordingly. While there is a familiar pattern—body, breath, phonation, articulation, emotion, and expression—I will always follow intuition and inner knowing as a trustworthy guide. I also share some of my favorite positive affirmations. Here are a few acronyms and quotations that I find useful:

1. FEAR = "false evidence appearing real." I first heard this acronym in 2014 in Boulder, Colorado, as an audience member for a taping of the television show *Beyond* with American author, producer, and clairvoyant James Van Praagh (b. 1958). As he described it, the egoic mind creates fear of the unknown and the future, which has no real substance.
2. EGO = "edging God out." The psychologist, motivational speaker, and spiritual author Wayne Dyer (1940–2015) is credited with creating this acronym. I personally heard him talk about this idea in a lecture

I attended in Denver, Colorado, in March of 2014. "Ego"—or mortal mind—is fearful, erroneous; God, or an "infinite being" (which Meribeth preferred to call "creator source") is love, truth, and "the way."
3. "Follow the watercourse way." Water is soft, yet powerful. Water always chooses the path of least resistance, ultimately to its goal—the ocean. Go with the flow.
4. "Worry is a form of prayer." Be careful what you ask for! Rather than concentrating your thoughts (intention) on what you fear, dread, or fret about—visualize the positive!
5. "Positive thoughts bring positive results." (See "worry," above.)
6. "It takes as much energy to say, 'I can' as it does to say, 'I can't.'" How true!
7. "This too shall pass." My mother's favorite saying. In even the very worst of times in life—when grief, devastation, worry, depression, and stress overwhelms—remember this: Five, ten, twenty, or fifty years from now—or, as my geologist timeframe kicks in, millions of years hence—none of it will matter. Life is a cycle and, as is often said, the only constant is change.

Proprioception through Meditation

Proprioception is "the reception of stimuli produced within an organism."[14] Whether it is an individual or a class, I introduce meditative practice by centering on the concept of proprioception then expanding upon that with a guided meditation I call "Going to the Beach." This exercise seeks to help students reach a state of consciousness while simultaneously experiencing deep relaxation. There is an old Quaker concept that refers to "peace at the center," and meditation can be a means to achieving this sense of inner calm.

Students are instructed to bring a yoga mat, beach towel, or blanket. They quietly stand in place, eyes closed, while I set the tone of peace and tranquility. Speaking in a calm, low voice, I draw their mental focus to various parts of the body without any movement or touch—e.g, "put your attention on your right kneecap, left hip, left big toe, etc." I begin by referring to external parts of the body where there is a clear and established sense of connection, but then move to more challenging areas, such as the "left earlobe, right ring finger, knuckle just below the nail, twelfth rib on the left side, etc."

Next, the students lie down on their backs while I ask them to visualize a beautiful beach—it may be an actual beach or one they imagine—on a perfect day. The first focal point is on their breathing, how the air comes in and then goes out, much like the movement of water at the edge of the beach. Attention is on the kinesthetic, moving and releasing any tension in various parts of the body.

Students overwhelmingly respond positively to this exercise. One young woman, when describing different parts of her body, expressed that it seemed like her body was "lighting up" as the various parts of the body were being listed ("left pinky, first knuckle, etc.") She described the sensations she was experiencing as "waves of energy." Another young man described the atmosphere in the room during this exercise as one of "innate calm" that was "both comforting and promising." "Going to the Beach" is a flexible exercise that can be easily practiced by anyone and in a variety of different situations.

FIVE SENSES: TAKING A "SLOW BREAK" EXERCISE

In addition to noticing our "internal orchestra"—breath, pulse, and so on—Meribeth invited the CoreSinging teachers to become aware of our "outer orchestra"—the sights, sounds, sensations, smells, and even tastes around us. The first morning of CoreSinging training in Fort Collins—when we were settled in our chairs, ready to take notes and learn—Meribeth instead directed us to go outside. She instructed us to find a quiet place to sit for fifteen minutes, allowing ourselves to notice our surroundings via the five senses. The city side street we were on was a very different environment than my mountain home, which was a log cabin on a one-lane dirt road surrounded by Ponderosa pine trees. I began to take in everything around me.

The first thing I noticed was the road noise coming from the busy thoroughfare nearby. I had to strain to hear the birds singing and my own breathing. Visually, it was quite lovely, with flowers, green deciduous trees, attractive homes, and Cynthia's professional studio entrance. A deep, cleansing breath made me feel calm and relaxed. I switched my focus and centered on what I could smell: a sweet floral scent, no doubt from a nearby locust tree, then the acrid smell of exhaust fumes from the traffic at the corner. Unfortunately, that was also strong enough to taste, so I walked a bit further down Magnolia Street. Here I found a more peaceful spot where I could feel fully aware, centered, and in balance with my surroundings.

Meribeth instilled in us the value of "slow breaks" such as these. Since having had that centering experience, I have assigned the "five senses" awareness exercise to my students—singers as well as instrumentalists. Many have commented that this process drastically improves their mood, lessens their anxiety, and helps them reconnect with the world around them.

FURTHER APPLICATION: BODY, MIND, AND MOVEMENT FOR MUSICIANS

I was about to board my plane from Dulles Airport to Stockholm, Sweden, for the 2017 ICVT conference when I received a text from the dean of faculty at Shenandoah University Conservatory asking if I would be interested in teaching a fall graduate course titled "Body Awareness for Musicians." (Of course I would!) In the true spirit of academic freedom, I was given free rein to approach it any way I liked. What a wonderful opportunity.

Upon return from Sweden, I devised the following course objectives:

1. To explore various modalities, including the Feldenkrais method, Alexander Technique, yoga, tai chi, and qigong.
2. To enhance physical and mental vitality in performance.
3. To facilitate greater sensitivity, mobility, movement efficiency, and expressivity with an emphasis on the body–mind connection, health, and joie de vivre.
4. To improve and enrich artistic and musical expression in performance.

My students were instrumental and vocal performance graduate students—both master's and doctoral candidates. I could not have had a more receptive, open-minded, perceptive group as "guinea pigs." During that September, I attended a four-day intensive training in Emotional Freedom Technique (EFT), also known as "tapping."[15] Clinical EFT uses acupressure and modern psychology to alleviate negative emotions as well as physical distress. Performance anxiety, or stage nerves, is a common, often debilitating condition of our art. Since the tenets of CoreSinging include focusing on positive energy, play, and self-development, I returned eager to share what I had learned and add that to their toolkit.

I also taught "Movement for Musicians" a required course for undergraduate instrumental performance majors. It was a wonderful learning experience, to which I added myofascial release and Dalcroze eurythmics. Through self-massage with a foam roller, the fascia tissue is released, which frees up muscle tension and adds to a focus on awareness, an essential component of CoreSinging. Dalcroze Eurhythmics combines music, body, mind, and movement, which I consider a natural extension of CoreSinging activities.

If any group desperately needed this course, it was these students! Weekly journal assignments afforded an opportunity for reflection and allowed the students to speak for themselves.

FINAL THOUGHT

As I was completing the second edition of *A Spectrum of Voices*, in which Meribeth was included, I asked her in a Messenger chat where she considered herself to be within pedagogical specialties: classical, commercial music, world music. After a moment, she wrote, "Meribeth has moved into a holistic, universal approach to teaching and singing. We're just going to need to find a way to say I've moved on."

Indeed she has.

NOTES

1. Rumer Godden, *A House with Four Rooms* (New York: William Morrow and Company, 1989), front matter.

2. https://www.merriam-webster.com/dictionary/core.

3. Meribeth Dayme, "The CoreSinging Approach," in *So You Want to Sing with Awareness*, ed. Matthew Hoch (Lanham, MD: Rowman & Littlefield, 2020), 123.

4. *Usui reiki ryoho* is an ancient hands-on healing art that intentionally channels *ki* energy to promote balance and well-being. The term Reiki is derived from two Japanese syllables, *rei* and *ki*, meaning "universal life energy." *Rei* represents the source of this energy and *ki*—also spelled "chi" in other contexts—represents the energy's movement within and around us. For more information, see Phylameana lila Desy, *The Everything Reiki Book: Channel Your Positive Energy to Reduce Stress, Promote Healing, and Enhance Your Quality of Life* (Avon, MA: Everything, 2004).

5. This dissertation was later published as a peer-reviewed article: Elizabeth Blades, *Journal of Research in Singing and Applied Pedagogy* 17, no. 2 (1994): 1–87.

6. Personal correspondence with Meribeth Dayme, June 2010.

7. Meribeth Dayme and Cynthia Vaughn, *The Singing Book*, third ed. (New York: W. W. Norton & Company, 2014).

8. Elizabeth L. Blades, *A Spectrum of Voices: Prominent American Voice Teachers Discuss the Teaching of Singing*, second ed. (Lanham, MD: Rowman & Littlefield, 2017).

9. Meribeth Dayme, "The CoreSinging Approach," in *So You Want to Sing with Awareness: A Guide for Performers*, ed. Matthew Hoch (Lanham, MD: Rowman & Littlefield, 2020), 123–42; Elizabeth L. Blades and Samuel H. Nelson, "The Feldenkrais Method," in *So You Want to Sing with Awareness: A Guide for Performers*, ed. Matthew Hoch (Lanham, MD: Rowman & Littlefield, 2020), 25–47.

10. Blades, *A Spectrum of Voices*, xiii.

11. https://www.youtube.com/watch?v=YpG7xCkiq0A.

12. For a more thorough explanation of these yoga positions and others, see Linda Lister, "Yoga for Singers," in *So You Want to Sing with Awareness*, ed. Matthew Hoch (Lanham, MD: Rowman & Littlefield, 2020), 49–73.

13. For a less abridged version of "Releasing the Eyes," please see Elizabeth L. Blades, "The Feldenkrais Method," in *So You Want to Sing with Awareness*, ed. Matthew Hoch (Lanham, MD: Rowman & Littlefield, 2020), 44–45.

14. https://www.merriam-webster.com/dictionary/proprioception.

15. Emotional Freedom Technique (EFT), aka "tapping," is based on the principles of both ancient acupressure and modern psychology. EFT seeks to calm the nervous system, restoring the balance of energy in the body and rewiring the brain to respond in healthy ways. For more information, see Nick Ortner, *The Tapping Solution: A Revolutionary System for Stress-Free Living* (Carlsbad, CA: Hay House, 2013).

Chapter Ten

Using CoreSinging with Children, Tweens, and Teens

Aimee Woods

I was introduced to CoreSinging in 2010, when Cynthia Vaughn hosted Meribeth Dayme and a group of teachers at Magnolia Music Studio in Fort Collins. One year later, I was given the opportunity to host a second workshop with Meribeth in 2011. These were life-changing experiences. I am not sure I understood at the time how much CoreSinging would enhance my teaching, but I could go on and on about all the ways that the CoreSinging perspective on energy, balance, and readiness changed my own performance practices. In this short chapter, I will focus on an area where I saw the clearest benefit of the CoreSinging approach: in my work with teens, tweens, and children.

WORKING WITH CHILDREN

I have been a private instructor in the northern Colorado region since 2004. In addition, I currently serve as the music director for a large children's theater and am the owner of a multi-teacher music studio in Fort Collins, Colorado. I love working with young people in a variety of ways—through individual lessons, theater camps, and other performance settings. Most of the children I work with regularly are ten years old or younger.

Immediately after my training with Meribeth, I began integrating CoreSinging principles into my teaching. My favorite tools for working with children involve giving them access to complex concepts through play. I ask them to move and make noise in a variety of ways that seem silly at first, but often lead to amazing results. Before I begin these playful exercises, I establish an important guideline with each student:

In my studio I avoid using the words "no," "can't," and "shouldn't."

These words must be replaced with achievable action statements. For example, in the past you might have gotten frustrated and thought, "I shouldn't stumble when singing!" In my studio, you would be encouraged to replace it with something like, "I will stay aware of my feet and floor space around me." Occasionally my students forget this rule, and that is OK. When this happens, I simply remind the student how amazing they are, and we jump right back into the music without hesitation.

Fluffy Stuff

Now it is playtime! I like using qigong movement to connect singers to their body. My favorite with children (and all ages really) is a stretch I simply call "fluffy stuff."[1] This exercise proceeds as follows:

1. Stand with your feet a little wider than the singer's stance (about a shoulder width apart).
2. Imagine a pile of "fluffy stuff" in front of you. This imaginary substance should be something that makes you happy and energized, like glitter or confetti.
3. Breathe in steadily over four slow beats, using both arms to scoop up your "fluffy stuff" and, tracing a line through your belly button to your nose, bring the "fluffy stuff" to the top of the head.
4. As you inhale, release or soften your knees.
5. Exhale and toss the "fluffy stuff" high into the air so it can fill your space with energy and sparkle!
6. Release at the end of the exhale, reset, and do the entire exercise again.
7. I have found that three or four repetitions of this exercise is ideal.

You may be asking yourself, "What does this exercise do?" So many things! It connects kids to their lower bodies, engages core muscles—the pelvic floor, abdominal core, a myriad of back muscles, and more—and connects them to the breath, which is the fuel for singing. The "fluffy stuff" exercise also connects the concept of breath to a positive mindset and intentional state of energy while giving the singer the opportunity to share that energy with their space.

Find Your Superpower

Have you ever found that some practice exercises can feel disconnected, cold, or just plain boring for young singers? When I see that a singer is disconnected from their singing choices (for any reason), I like to personalize

CoreSinging exercises to move awareness to different areas of the singing body—ribs, feet, spine, pelvic floor, and more. My favorite is one I call "find your superpower":

1. Find your feet and make sure they are rooted into the ground. (I tell them that I don't want them to fly away when their superpower comes in!)
2. Allow your shoulder blades to sink toward the floor. (Don't worry, they can't sink too far!)
3. Now you need to find your "superpower": Hold out your hands in front of you as if holding an invisible ball about the size of a softball (or somewhat similar size of your choice).
4. As you inhale, gather your power. Feel it stretch your ribs. As you exhale, fill your sphere with power by singing out on one sound. (This exercise seems most effective when you allow the kids to choose their own pitch, but you can zero in on a specific "trouble note" too.)
5. Repeat this procedure several times, focusing on whichever part of the body needs increased awareness: ribs, feet, spine, pelvic floor.
6. On a final repetition of the exercise, use your breath/voice/tone/energy to launch the "superpower sphere" through the wall!
7. Once they have found their superpower sound, I always ask them to finish in their favorite "superpose." (They all laugh and giggle and have a lot of fun doing this one.)

Why superpowers? Kids have wonderful imaginations. This exercise is great for accessing confidence in singing. After all, it is much easier to feel confident when you are imagining being a superhero! You can also use the superpower exercise to work on shaping the breath as they throw the sphere and extending their breath stamina as they sustain a note to follow the path of their amazing superpower. This exercise is especially effective if the young singer is willing to talk and make noises with you, even if that same individual is shy or resistant to singing in front of you or others.

Paint and Sing (Pantomiming)

While I love doing this exercise with a group, it is especially effective in individual lessons with younger singers. This exercise uses pantomiming—pretending to draw or paint while singing an ensemble piece or individual solo to connect the energy they feel on the inside to the expression on the outside. This one is especially useful to connect the technical aspects of music (like rhythm and intonation) to the concept of musical expression. You can do this with poster paper and markers or finger paints on old boxes. I have done both. With most groups of kids, I find it effective to ask everyone to simply imagine they have an invisible paint brush and a large canvas in front of them.

1. Breathe deep and exhale. Repeat this exercise, but this time blow the air over an invisible paintbrush.
2. As they exhale, say, "Look . . . your paintbrush is full of color!"
3. Then say, "Now, I want you to paint while you sing." Show them by doing it yourself. The kids will wave their arms about while they sing the song or section. It is silly and fun.
4. As they are getting the hang of it, ask them to lean in. Invite them to use more paint on the invisible canvas when they sing bigger sounds and less paint on quieter sounds.
5. Guide them to use their paint brushes as they make changes to their vocal line.

I am continually amazed at how quickly this exercise allows me to guide them to make musical choices that further their creative expression.

Sing the Colors

The following is a useful tool I learned directly from Meribeth during my training for CoreSinging. While I have modified the exercise, the concepts come from her.

1. Have the singers pick a color and "sing the color" as they sing a note or phrase. If they look doubtful, I add, "Avoid overthinking!"
2. Then we repeat the exercise. I ask them to imagine: "Your mouth is a spray paint can and your sound is the paint. Spray the walls with your color as you sing."
3. If the singers are having fun, I have them do the exercise a third time and ask them to adjust the colors (i.e., make their color more pastel, bolder, more solid, transparent, mix it with another color, etc.).

This exercise allows young singers to access changes in timbre, resonance, and to gain a new way to affect the sounds their instrument can create. This exercise is fun and can be learned quickly. Once children grasp the concept, this exercise can also be used as they are singing to find new and different sounds or free up a "stuck" musical phrase. I often say simple things like "OK, that was lovely! Let's keep going and add a [color quality—i.e., bright green, etc.] to the tone."

Remember that kids are hardwired for play. Play comes naturally to them. Work is boring, but play is fun! Therefore, it is relatively easy to get them to take risks with their music if it is done from a place of playfulness, and from that space of play they will be willing to explore ideas that they otherwise may not grasp.

WORKING WITH TEENS AND TWEENS

In my experience, the exercises mentioned previously were easily grasped by children. However, I generally struggled to access these same concepts with older teens and adults. This forced me to get creative with my singers over the age of ten. For purposes of clarity, when I use the phrase "teens and tweens" I am including singers who are eleven to seventeen years old. These young adults are a bit of a different animal than their younger singing compatriots. In addition to the clear changes that come as their bodies grow, there is also the sudden onset of heightened body awareness, doubt, self-judgment, and the emotional complexity that comes with transitions through middle school into high school. The tricks I used with young singers and with the youth theater camps did not work in these situations. However, going back to my CoreSinging toolbox I found some new tools to play with when working with these young preadults.

It is imperative that the first thing I do before working with teens and tweens—or really any age singer, individually or in a group—is to establish expectations. It is important that they feel like they are in a safe environment before play can begin. Outlining some basic ground rules for participation can be helpful. First, the singer has the right to stop an exercise at any time for any reason. They do not owe the teacher an explanation, but you should listen with an understanding ear to any feedback the singer chooses to share. Second, as long as it is safe to do so, the singer agrees to give the exercise at least one attempt before asking to switch exercises. There are also some rules for teachers. We should honor the singer's space and pause or change exercises if needed. Also, it is important for teachers not to engage in physical contact of any kind (even a touch on the arm) without the student's permission. This is for the student's safety as well as the teacher's. Once these basic rules are established, we are then ready to play with body movement, breath, and so much more.

"This Little Light"

When exploring breath awareness with teens and tweens, I often start by reminding the singer(s) that breath is something we work with throughout our entire singing experience. I love to deepen the awareness of breath with this exercise, which I learned during my second round of CoreSinging training. I have made modifications and now call it "This Little Light":

1. Sit with good posture to encourage optimal singing alignment on a chair or bench. (I have found stools are not useful in this exercise for many different reasons, but feel free to explore your options to find what works best with your students.)
2. Breathe naturally for a few breath cycles. Then take in a fuller, deeper breath and sigh out audibly. (It's OK to make a little noise!)
3. Visualize a light that can travel up and down the spine. This light is "light as a feather" and moves easily.
4. Breathe in again. Allow the light to rise through the interior of the spine.
5. Exhale. Allow the light to travel down the exterior of the spine.
6. Repeat this exercise several times.

You can also reverse the visual and have them play with taking the light up the exterior and down the interior. Each singer connects differently, so remember to be flexible in your implementation of this exercise.

"This Little Light" allows teen and tween singers to connect to their bodies on a deeper level, exploring sensations in the abdomen and pelvic floor while avoiding the temptation to overfocus on an uncomfortable body part or overthinking a particular breath management technique. An added benefit is that this exercise also teaches singers to find a calming breath, which can be especially useful if your singer experiences performance anxiety. Singers can use this exercise at any time to find a deeper breath connection and sense of calm.

The "Room Feedback Game"

While energy is a key component to CoreSinging, it is not an easy concept to explain or teach. There are many barriers to opening this conversation with singers and a strategy is needed when approaching a discussion of energy. I can hear Meribeth whispering, "Sometimes we don't need to share the details—just let them play and they will understand." Of course, she is right. How do you convey a sense of awareness without sharing too much information? By playing a game.

Using CoreSinging with Children, Tweens, and Teens 119

I structured this exercise after a drama game called "Detective." The "Room Feedback Game" uses muscle testing to show kids how their thoughts affect their own body and the performers around them, which I call "body feedback" or "room feedback." The exercise requires at least three participants, though you can certainly modify it for just two people.

1. Ask for two volunteers to play the performers. I remind them this is like a drama or improvisation game. The performers are instructed to wait in an outside room. (If you do not have a separate space, they can plug their ears and sing "la la la" while you are giving instructions to the rest of the group.)
2. The rest of the group are "observers" who have specific instructions to follow during each of the three rounds of the game: (a) in round 1, when the teacher says [color of choice], think of something you like about the volunteers; (b) in round 2, when the teacher says [animal of choice], everyone should think some negative thought about their chair—this keeps them from focusing negatively on themselves or others; (c) in round 3, when the teacher says [plant of choice], register a positive thought about the volunteers (again).
3. Bring the two performers back in. Ask them to stand comfortably in singers' alignment (i.e., noble posture). Then have them hold out their arm and remind them to stay strong while the teacher gently presses downward on their arms, making sure they stay strong and firm.
4. Round 1 begins. Communicate a color to the group (e.g., "blue"). Then distract the two performers by asking them if they like blue and ask them what their favorite color is. Then test their arms, pointing out how strong they are.
5. Round 2 is executed the same way, with distracting questions for the performers, followed by testing their arm strength. This time, with negative energy in the room, the strength of their arms always wilts. Let the room know this by saying something like, "Hmm . . . that is interesting."
6. Round 3 again goes like round 1, but this time with plants instead of colors. Test their arm strength again . . . it is always stronger! Be sure to point out how strong they are.
7. Pause to allow the singers to process what has happened. The brave may ask questions like, "What is happening?"

At the end of the game, I define energy as electrical energy generated by the body that is scientifically quantifiable. We talk about how our energy and thoughts can affect our bodies or how our stage mates can affect our energy too. This exercise almost always results in a robust discussion of how we use our energy, thoughts, and focus to strengthen ourselves and our stage partners.

Movement and Interpretive Dance While Singing

Our body is a complex mechanism. Sometimes, in an effort to understand information, singers have learned simplified concepts that unintentionally disconnect them from certain areas of their bodies. When this happens, I love to use dance and movement to help my teens and tweens reconnect. *NOTE: Since I am asking the singer to take risks, be vulnerable, and look silly, this is an exercise that is easier to use in a one-to-one lesson.*

The process looks something like this:

1. Ask the singer to take a moment and listen to the accompaniment of their song.
2. While playing the accompaniment or accompaniment track, have the singer move easily around the space. This may look like gentle walking, or it may look like swaying side to side.
3. Then, ask the singer to sing their song while they move. Some singers may need to spend a few lessons exploring this step to get comfortable with the sensation of moving and singing at the same time.
4. Once they seem to be connecting to the process, proceed to ask them to exaggerate their movements to make it more like a loose dance of the song. At this point the teens usually stop and give me "the look." You know the one I mean—it's the one that sarcastically seems to ask, "Are you serious right now?" I reply by gently encouraging them to play and remind them that this is not a performance, but rather an exploration of what their body and the music can do together.

What does this exploration of movement do for the teen or tween singer? Many things! They giggle, feel silly, and remember what it feels like to be playful. *This is so important and sometimes it is the only goal you need to achieve.* In the process of playing with this exercise, singers often find areas where their body reconnects to something they didn't even realize felt disconnected or stuck. Most important, this exercise gives teens and tweens a tool to reconnect their body to the music when they are practicing at home.

When encountering a singer who finds this tool especially effective, I eventually ask them to trust me enough to get even sillier. We then pantomime (one gesture for each word) while singing. This adds another complex layer of body awareness that helps immensely with expression and memorization. Ultimately, the goal with moving, dancing, and/or miming exercises is to give teens and tweens the opportunity to explore what it feels like to be intuitive with their bodies while singing.

Paint or Draw and Sing (the "Tween and Teen" edition)

As with younger children, I love to have my tween and teen singers explore painting or drawing while singing. I use large poster paper and markers for this. While teaching this exercise is somewhat similar to my approach when working with children, I like to add more depth and detail as the singers grow older and become more advanced.

1. Set up a large pad of poster paper on an easel or set up a large whiteboard on a wall. Provide a small selection of markers in a variety of colors
2. Allow the singer to select colors they would like to draw with. I like to have a marker for each hand, but they may only want to start with one marker. That is totally acceptable.
3. Ask the singer to sing their song and draw on the page. They should fill as much of the space with color as they can.
4. After they finish the first round, ask them to take a "sighing" breath and release any tension they may have.
5. Have them sing the song again and ask them what they would like to do this time. Perhaps phrase the question as, "What would you like to add and what would you like to avoid?"
6. Listen to them and acknowledge their response. Then, as they sing the song, instruct the singer to draw the music how they would like to sing it.
7. After they do this, ask them what changed. Discuss what they liked and repeat the exercise. If they answer that nothing changed, you can ask them to do it again. I instruct them to really exaggerate the changes with their voice by using the drawing tools.
8. Invite them to breathe and release any tension they may have acquired during the exercise.
9. Evaluate the results: good . . . bad . . . mediocre? What will they keep? What will they do differently the next time?

Drawing and painting while singing seems most useful with individual singers in one-to-one lessons. This exercise is a quick way to enhance a singer's mind–body connection. Remember that the singer may not always experience profound improvement over the course of a single exercise, and that is natural and fine. Remind them that even small improvements occasionally are still helpful and represent growth.

Singing the Colors (the "Tween and Teen" edition)

This exercise is so much fun with this age group! It starts the same as with younger children:

1. Have the singers pick a color and "sing the color" as they sing a note or phrase. If they look doubtful, I add "avoid overthinking!"
2. Then we repeat the exercise. I ask them to imagine: "Your mouth is a spray paint can and your sound is the paint. Spray the walls with your color as you sing."
3. If the singers are having fun, I have them do the exercise a third time and ask them to adjust the colors (i.e., make their color more pastel, bolder, more solid, transparent, mix it with another color, etc.).
4. Now, this new step for the "teen and tween" edition of this exercise is fun. Assign colors (as the teacher) and play with changing the colors as they sing. This further allows the singers to find new timbres and realize that there are many ways to affect the sounds they make—and myriad colors to explore!

WORKING WITH LARGE GROUPS OF MIXED AGES

Here's where I have gotten even more creative in my use of CoreSinging. I am a music director for a large community theater company where we produce a full musical every year that includes a blended cast of singers from children through senior adults. (My oldest performer was in their nineties!) At first, I wasn't sure if I could use CoreSinging ideas within the context of a musical theatre rehearsal. However, I was surprised to realize that all the tools that work so well with kids, teens, and tweens individually and in smaller groups, also could be applied—with a little creativity—to a larger group of mixed-age singers.

Many adults have forgotten how to be playful. This is a sad but true statement. It is therefore equally important that rehearsals involving adults begin with play, and I begin each musical theatre rehearsal this way. I call it "playtime," which it is, but it is also goal-oriented play. Did I detail that goal before starting? I didn't tell them that! Why spoil their play with overthinking?

In this setting I have found that many of the exercises I use in rehearsal are similar to what I do with individuals and small groups of young singers. With a wide range of ages in one group, I like qigong-style breath work in exercises like the pile of "fluffy stuff" and "This Little Light." I follow those up with at least one silly vocal warm-up that includes movement and awareness of the people around them. The following exercise, "Yes, with Guidelines," is one of my favorites, and I often finish with a connectivity exercise like "The Invisible Sphere."

Yes, with Guidelines

My favorite way to present ensemble warm-ups is to take a basic vocal exercise and add playful guidelines. I strongly encourage you to give the instructions for this activity one step at a time to avoid confusion. *Tip: It is OK if you need to remind the group, even the adults, to listen all the way to the end of the instructions at each step. The group attention may fluctuate depending on their level of distraction that day.*

1. Stand in your space with your arms raised out to your sides like you are making a "T" with your body. Move around until everyone has their own space and no one is touching another person. Now relax your arms.
2. Begin having them vocalize on a simple exercise like a five-note scale ascending and descending on a single vowel. I like using /o/.
3. Ask them to continue to sing and begin gently walking around the space. Important guideline: Singers must avoid coming in physical contact with anyone else in the room.
4. For an added challenge you can ask the singers to do this while they avoid looking into each other's eyes. You are helping engage peripheral vision and spatial awareness. I recommend you save this for your advanced groups.
5. Instruct them to continue to sing. The singers must now acknowledge each other while they sing. Remind them to still avoid any physical contact.
6. For an added challenge, ask the group to interact with each other in character!

This exercise often results in the singers enhancing their spatial awareness as well as connecting the energy of the singers into a common focus. Once they are comfortable and vocally warm you can do the same process with a song from the production. I like to use the show's finale or opening number as it usually involves the most singers.

The Invisible Sphere

This exercise focuses on connectivity and awareness. Discussing energy as used in CoreSinging with groups can be challenging. I often use terms like "ensemble awareness" to convey what I want them to focus toward and allow the exercise to do the work without much discourse.

1. Have the group stand in a circle. They do not need to touch but should be fairly close together.
2. Ask everyone to imagine that a large invisible/translucent sphere is floating in the middle of the circle. Use your body to show that the sphere is large enough to fit a person inside but floating slightly off the ground.
3. Tell them the sphere is empty and still.
4. Next, inform the singers that they will be singing shortly on a pitch of their choice. Yes, this will be chaotic. Yes, that is what we want. Create a sound wash.
5. Instruct the singers that when they sing, their voice will begin to fill the sphere with a color unique to them.
6. They may pick any color and the color is welcome to change at any time.
7. Once the sphere begins to fill with color it will begin to spin, slow at first but may change speed.
8. Now have them sing.
9. Explore what happens when you ask them to all sing the same pitch, a chord, or even a phrase from a song they are singing.
10. Explore what happens when you assign the same color to everyone. Or to groups.
11. Ask for volunteers to express what they noticed.

Invisible sphere is a great way to help ensembles tune in to each other and align energies. It is flexible as an exercise, so you can use it to also work on harmonies, unison, or simply to enhance the ensemble's connection to one another working toward an achievable common goal.

FINAL THOUGHTS

CoreSinging tools have revolutionized my music studio and musical theatre ensembles. By engaging in playful and connecting exercises, it has been possible to share many complex CoreSinging concepts while still having fun when I am working with young singers. I encourage you to focus on *play*. Remember that excessive explanations take up way too much time. Save those explanations for the singers who request more information and replace the time you would have spent explaining things with playful explorations of singing. Create a learning environment where learning feels like fun, and—most important of all—*enjoy* the process!

NOTE

1. This exercise is adapted from a traditional form of qigong known as Eight-Piece Brocades (*ba duan jin*). The first brocade is sometimes called "gathering the chi." Meribeth practiced qigong daily and taught the eight brocades to her CoreSinging students. There are many variations of this qigong form. Meribeth followed the teachings of qigong master Jesse Tsao (b. 1958), initially on video and eventually traveling to participate in his classes in person.

Chapter Eleven

Organized Fun

Trish Rooney

My initial contact with Meribeth Dayme was as a participant in my doctoral research. I was working on my dissertation, titled "The Understanding of Contemporary Vocal Pedagogy and the Teaching Methods of Internationally Acclaimed Vocal Coaches." After reading Meribeth's books, I was feeling ambitious and emailed her, asking if she would be available to participate. Fortunately for me, she kindly agreed. From the moment the interview began, I felt an immediate connection to her. Meribeth had such a powerful presence. I was drawn to her—not just because of her evident wisdom, wealth of knowledge, and incredible understanding of everything to do with the voice—but also because of her infectious energy, humor, openness, encouragement, and enthusiasm.

During our interview, Meribeth spoke about the concepts behind CoreSinging. The idea that the heart, soul, and spirit of your singing—infused into the learning process—can be done so easily and with so much fun really appealed to me. I began by taking some of her CoreSinging webinars in 2014 and later added some private lessons. My own singing gained much freedom, and quite quickly. At the time, I was working as the vocal coach for *The Voice of Ireland*, the Irish edition of the internationally televised reality singing competition. CoreSinging exercises were perfect for this endeavor, as they were quick and effective for getting results in performance. All the CoreSinging ideas—including tune in, tune up, and tune out; intention; focused practice; visualization; distraction exercises; exercises for connecting with the meaning of songs and lyrics; and fun ways of learning lyrics quickly (and testing how well you know them)—were invaluable for the contestants.

After the advanced CoreSinging training was completed, I kept in touch regularly with Meribeth on my progress with CoreSinging, and she suggested I hold an informal workshop with a group of my degree students and archive it on video (with their consent of course). This was loads of fun and after we were finished, Meribeth and I analyzed the video together. Her insight was enlightening, and since 2017 I have presented CoreSinging workshops at the Cork International Choral Festival, Society for Music Education in Ireland (SMEI) conferences, and other international platforms. Introducing CoreSinging to European audiences has been an honor, and I feel lucky to have had Meribeth as a mentor and friend.

MY PEDAGOGY: IMPLEMENTATION OF CORESINGING PRINCIPLES

Virtually all the CoreSinging exercises Meribeth taught me have been a success with my students, regardless of their age and experience. Whatever issues a student presents to me—whether in master classes, workshops, individual, or group classes—I find that CoreSinging concepts, principles, and exercises can be utilized with great success. Dynamic balance, 360-degree sound, the "stomping" exercise, moving with the music, and working with the breath are all regular features in my classes; however, "working with the text," "focused practice," and "fifteen ways to sing a scale" have been particularly fruitful. I will focus on these ideas in this chapter.

Working with Text: Rapping the Lyric

In my experience, younger performers pick songs for lots of reasons. They may not have thought much about why they selected what they did; more often, they simply like it. I recently taught a class at a summer camp that was for instrumentalists. The students comprised drummers, bassists, keyboard players, and guitarists. I thought it would be interesting to ask them all who they listen to, what their favorite songs were, and why. Most of them said that never listen to the lyrics; they had lots of reasons why they liked the song, but it was not because of the lyrics and story. These boys—mostly between the ages of thirteen and sixteen—primarily listened to rock and heavy metal. The purpose of my session was to help them connect to the story so their playing could be more sensitive and supportive of the lyric.

"Rapping the lyric" is one of my favorite CoreSinging exercises. In my experience, students have lots of fun with it and are surprised how difficult it is, even if they are confident they know the lyric well. This exercise is ideal for preparing for an upcoming performance; it is a fun distraction and an excellent test of how well they are connecting to the lyric and story. Rapping the lyric requires you to think quickly and stray from the original rhythmic pattern you have learned. It also makes you more aware of timing, phrasing, and rhythm. Once I have introduced this exercise, I take a step back and ask them to speak the lyric, encouraging them to use their natural everyday voice, speak a little slower, and pretend are telling a story to a friend over a cup of coffee.

Rapping the lyric opens up new possibilities for the performance of the song. Sometimes I see students singing back through the melody as they try to remember the words. There is no time for this with rap—the story must be known thoroughly up front so the student can deal with timing issues, punctuation, and phrasing, because it is easy to become distracted when singing it to a completely different track. (I have found the students enjoy using the backing track to *The Fresh Prince of Bel-Air* theme song.) Once they have been inspired by this rapping exercise, I then suggest singing the lyrics to the melody of a different song altogether. This is another wonderful challenge and also lots of fun. It is always evident that play and imagination are at work in this exercise.

The Importance of Focused Practice

The introduction to qigong during my CoreSinging training was fascinating. I discovered instant benefits from the qigong series of Eight-Piece Brocades (*ba duan jin*)[1] that included body movement, breath work, and meditation designed to enhance the function of qi by achieving focused and relaxed states.[2] Having incorporated qigong into my everyday life, I was impressed that it was applicable not only to singing, but also for general stress relief, mindfulness, and well-being. I went on a journey to discover more about qigong and tai chi and regularly introduce my students to these practices. I begin workshops with some simple qigong exercises to ensure that everyone is in harmony before we begin our exploration of CoreSinging concepts. I also encourage students to integrate some form of meditation and breath work into their daily routine.

Meribeth stressed the importance of having a clear intention and focus when practicing. This is so important for learning to occur and something I always discuss with my students. Although my background includes many years of experience as a performer and teacher, I struggled with nerves as a teenager and undergraduate student. I never really understood why, however, as I always practiced diligently and felt well prepared for performances. It wasn't until the end of my degree that I managed to overcome my performance anxiety. Having served on exam and audition panels for both second- and third-level singers for more than a decade, I have similarly observed students experiencing stress ahead of these exams. Material that was comfortable for them in class or at home seemed to go wrong on the day of evaluation. I regularly heard lyrics, high notes, scales, and sight reading suffer in exam situations.[3] It occurred to me after working with Meribeth that the cause could be from a variety of different things: a lack of centering, self-criticism, comparison to others, worry and negative thoughts, or poor practice strategies.

Meribeth believed you should never leave the practice room without performing, even if it is only a few lines of a song. Asking yourself what you want to go well or to happen during the performance—and even visualizing the dress rehearsals—can have beneficial outcomes. She related this to sports training. For Meribeth, "tune out" implies letting mental analysis go and just allowing yourself to sing with total involvement in the music. Once a performance before thousands of imaginary people—where there is no stopping to analyze or correct "mistakes"—becomes part of one's practice routine, the actual performance will feel and be quite different. I find that there are always a few students who don't believe in practicing performing and say they will do it on the gig. However, after explaining the benefits and the value of practicing performing, results usually can be seen quickly—especially when video is introduced.

We avoid practicing things we feel we are not good at. When students go to their practice rooms, they often end up singing or playing their favorite songs for the sake of comfort. If there are any bad habits or areas in need of improvement, this kind of practicing only reinforces mistakes you may be making and will not make challenging passages any better. Research has suggested that practice strategies may not always be implemented effectively.[4] Each musician requires strong metacognition skills to know what is effective for them, and effective practice can take many forms.[5] Lots of things count as practice—not just the time you spend in a room practicing your instrument. Keeping a journal and treating it like a diary is something Meribeth advocated, and I recommend this practice to all my students. Every time they sing or play, I encourage them to write down what they did—the kinds of warm-ups, exercises, or songs worked on (or listened to)—anything relating to the music. It is good to write down what you experienced during the practice session, as well as consider what still needs work and why. Were there different results the previous day, and if so, why this might be?

Keeping a diary like this helps students monitor progress and reveals certain habits and tendencies. Journaling helps them understand and know their own voices so that they can better focus future practice sessions and work specifically on what needs attention. It is important, especially early on, to show this journal to a teacher on a weekly basis so that they can guide the student, ensuring they are practicing as efficiently as possible. More important, this practice helps the singer take control of their own development and assume responsibility in their own practice routine.

Meribeth's golden rule of no self-criticism allowed is also extremely important to me. I regularly hear students say things like, "I'm terrible at sight-reading." They don't spend time practicing it, and once a year it becomes little more than a stressful moment at the end of an exam. Inevitably it doesn't go well, and they become convinced that they are bad at it. I encourage my students to be careful in their use of language. In my presence, I do not let them say things like "I'm not good at improvising," "I have poor technique," or "I can't belt" because the chances are something they think is difficult is simply unfamiliar. These things won't magically get better unless you work on them every day. Choosing your words carefully helps to reframe your everyday thinking patterns, especially if you are prone to experiencing negative thoughts about your singing or comparing yourself to other singers. Being grateful for your voice, letting go of any past insecurities, setting clear goals, and focusing on what you want to achieve is essential.

Years ago, I read a quotation from one of my favorite books that always stuck with me:

> The ancient Hawaiians used to believe that every child that is born is a perfect bowl of light. For each negative thought or action, a stone was placed in the bowl. If there were too many stones, the light eventually went out and the child would become like a stone. However, if at any time he got tired of being like a stone, all that was needed to change the situation was simply to turn the bowl upside down so that all the stones would fall out and the light would return.[6]

In sum, no one is allowed say "I can't" in my classes.

I have created a simple worksheet and practice plan below inspired by CoreSinging that can be adapted by students at any level of experience. Following this guide can help develop technique, musicianship, stylistic awareness, and performance and simultaneously make practice sessions both effective and fun. Follow this blueprint to focus your mind and direct intention. Doing so will help you achieve the results you are aiming for as a musician.

PRACTICE GUIDE
Inspired By Dr. Meribeth Dayme

I have created a simple practice plan below inspired by Meribeth that can be adapted for all levels of experience.

Questions To Ask

- What are your goals as a musician?
- What do you want to improve specifically?
- How often do you practice?
- Are your practice sessions effective?
- How can you be sure you are using your time efficiently?

> Always have an intent.
>
> Focus your practice.
>
> Set your goals clearly.

Warm Ups & Technical Work

uhming and chewing, buzzing, SOVT's, scale work, sirens, blending exercises, agility exercises, belting exercises, mix exercises, range extension exercises

Picking Specific Things To Work On

isolating sections of music, sing a section acapella, speak the entire text of the song, rap the lyrics watch balance and alignment, practice specific scale/s video a performance of the song/scale/study/improv slow down the tempo making sure all intervals and pitching is secure, listen to different recordings and performances of the song, think about the differences between recordings/differences in live performances analyze voice qualities, Rhythmic inflections, copy a lick/run precisely

Video A Performance

How is the tuning?
How are the runs/licks?
How is my sound?
What do I want it to be?
How am I starting these notes?
What is the story?
Am I bringing that across?
If there was an audience, would I keep their interest?
Would they believe me?
What are my eyes doing?
How does this look visually?
What is good about my performance of this song?
Is it rhythmically and stylistically accurate?

Incorporate Qigong or other mindfulness techniques into your daily life and practice.

"Practice Guide" worksheet
Courtesy of the author

Fifteen Ways to Sing a Scale

Meribeth spoke about the value of not starting with the same thing every lesson and not beginning each lesson with something a student can get wrong. I have found that this strategy has always worked well in my classes. I usually start sessions with fun warm-ups and improvisations that work on call-and-response patterns, pentatonic scales, and blues improvisation. Traditionally, many music lessons begin with scales, which students can find difficult or boring. They sometimes treat them as a mindless, perfunctory "thing to do at the start of a lesson"—almost like learning your times tables by rote at school. Understanding the purpose of scales and applying that knowledge and skill does not always become musically integrated.

So why learn scales? For some, it will be to pass an element of an exam. For others, the object may be to acquire technique and perhaps extend the range of the voice. Going even deeper, some may observe that an additional ear training benefit may be acquired, with scales assisting in the pitching of notes. The CoreSinging challenge, however, is to keep the student engaged by teaching scales in an interesting and engaging way.

Rather than singing a scale the same way every time, Meribeth suggested trying to find fifteen ways to sing a scale. I loved this concept—there are so many musical benefits to this approach, and the idea can be implemented in a simple and fun manner and developed further to meet the individual skill level of each student. This leaves room for the teacher to find creative ways to develop aural skills, harmonic awareness, stylistic fluency, coordination, and vocal flexibility.

There are endless possibilities for any scale. Although I offer some specific ideas below, there are many variations that can be applied to each one. The extent to which musicians enjoy practice might be an important factor in its frequency.[7] Since many students are inclined to believe scales can be boring, finding ways to present them in an engaging way is important.

Exercise 1 is a great way to warm up the voice while working in some tongue twisters. This exercise is a major scale, but this exercise can be sung on any scale and replaced with whatever words the students or teacher might like. It also can be accompanied by chords if you are working with a group, and they can each sing a note of the chord and discover how it sounds, working on blending and tuning, inserting silly names—anything you can think of. I find this to be most effective with younger classes, but the idea can also be developed for older students. You can extend the scale, play with the rhythm, or add body percussion. Be as creative as possible—and have fun!

Exercise 1
Courtesy of the author

Exercise 2 is an interval exercise that focuses on pitch and interval accuracy. The rhythm is interesting and has a nice "drive" to it. Sing this scale on numbers (scale degrees) in any key or be creative and use it as a semioccluded vocal tract (SOVT) warm up. You can also add movement, explore different larynx positions and voice qualities, or play with tempo. Practicing with a metronome (and recording yourself, to hear your accuracy) is also highly beneficial.

Exercise 2
Courtesy of the author

Exercise 3 is a pattern in fourths. This is another useful interval exercise for pitch accuracy and flexibility. It can be simplified and shortened for younger students or extended and used throughout the entire range when working with a more advanced student. Once the pitches are secure, tempo can be increased with different articulations, vowels, consonants, or numbers sung.

Exercise 3
Courtesy of the author

Exercise 4 is a simple scale pattern ascending diatonically in thirds. This is another useful way of working on flexibility throughout the range while working on the scale (whatever the scale might be). Note that the entire exercise is not notated—this is so that the notes are encoded strongly by ear. The first bar is a sample ascending pattern, and bars 2 and 3 are examples of descending patterns.

Exercise 4
Courtesy of the author

Exercise 5 is an ascending diatonic triad pattern and is a variation of exercise 4. These are useful for flexibility and working through the range in whatever key suits the student and can help with the passaggio, blending, and range extension. Taking these at different tempos is also useful for developing control throughout the range. It is a useful exercise to sing when working on articulation or onsets. All these exercises can be used as SOVT exercises.

Exercise 5
Courtesy of the author

While I strongly believe singers should develop good sight-reading skills, using one's ear to naturally finish the sequence is an important skill to acquire as well. Memorization occurs in real time rather than after wrangling with the score. Encouraging students to come up with their own "endings" for these exercises (drawing from the appropriate pool of diatonic notes, of course) encourages creativity, expression, and melodicism rather than a pedantic devotion to a notated exercise (which is neither right nor wrong per se, as Meribeth would remind us).

As another example of a variation on a simple pattern, exercise 6 is similar to exercises 4 and 5 with the addition of a chromatic note. This variation helps to develop musicianship as well as a strong sense of rhythmic and harmonic awareness.

Exercise 6
Courtesy of the author

Exercise 7 plays with rhythm. Observe that the notes below are the same as above, but instead of grouping the notes in threes (like their harmonic grouping) they are now grouped rhythmically in groups of four sixteenth notes (or semiquavers). This creates accents in different places and completely alters the sound and feel of the exercise. This variation engages students in a new way, to keeping them alert, interested, and challenged.

Exercise 7
Courtesy of the author

Scales with bigger intervallic jumps like pentatonic scales can be more challenging. As one of the most common scales used in contemporary commercial music, it is good to integrate pentatonic patterns into practice sessions. In exercise 8, note that we are moving stepwise to the next available note in the scale as well as skipping some notes in this exercise, taking a small melodic fragment through to one full octave. This pattern can be sung in any key and extended to suit the level of the student. If a student needs to work on chest register or belt, these exercises can be used to work on range extension, incorporating cry, twang, or whatever ingredient is necessary to aid a particular student in their own stylistic and technical development. I like to include Meribeth's "stomping exercise" when working on this one as it engages the entire body and builds stamina while simultaneously working on musicality and language.[8]

Creating tracks to accompany the pattern is a useful addition to such an exercise. Simple tracks can easily be created in iReal Pro, Garageband, or Flip (to name just a few of the current crop of music-making apps). If you are not familiar with these tools, now is a great time to jump in—they are easy to use, powerful, and here to stay. Additionally, your students will love them!

Exercise 8
Courtesy of the author

The minor pentatonic scale is merely a "mode" of the major pentatonic scale with the same notes, just starting on different degrees of the scale. "Root centrism" means starting melodies or improvisations on the root of any given chord. It is good to avoid this as the singer develops as the note choices are basic and predictable. Try to sing both exercises (8 and 9) against C major and A minor and note how both exercises work against the respective chords and modalities (major and minor). For clarity, the minor pentatonic pattern is notated below in exercise 9. Different onsets, voice qualities, and rhythms can be added to any of these exercises.

Exercise 9
Courtesy of the author

Exercise 10 is a sample Christina Aguilera–esque pentatonic "fill." What follows is that melodic fragment taken through the entirety of the scale. This is a great exercise to work on fluency for runs or riffs throughout the range. Why not have fun and try to take on the persona of Christina Aguilera (or whatever artist you like) while singing these? Add movement or growl, or play with tongue position, larynx position, or registration choice—anything you can think of, really. When you practice in this way, you are not just working on scales but learning musical language and style as well as developing flexibility and technique. You are also more likely to really enjoy the process.

Exercise 10
Courtesy of the author

The blues scale is another important modality for contemporary singers to absorb. Artists like Beyoncé (b. 1981), Christina Aguilera (b. 1980), and Yebba (b. 1995) are examples of singers who are fluent with blues runs and "ad-libs." The blues scale also lends itself well to developing your own patterns. Fluency with blues improvisation is acquired both through listening to the genre as well as scalar practice. The blues (or any genre) cannot be acquired by diligent practice of its harmonic components alone.

At this juncture, however, it is appropriate to reflect on the difference between scales and melodies. Scales ascend and descend, in a linear fashion, up and down a given note set (exercise 11a). Melodies, however, use the aforementioned note sets, but also utilize different intervals (11b) and rhythms (11c). Remember, the real purpose of learning scales is to learn the sound of each note (or scale degree) and be able to preproduce at will, by ear, without referencing the scale per se. Thus, one can recognize the sound of a sixth or reproduce it without having to sing the scale and stop on the sixth scale degree. It is helpful to think of scales as "ladders" of pitches; at any time, one can "fly" to the desired pitch without having to "climb" there.

The following are a few exercises to help develop this technique. In addition to these written examples, there are of course many nuances and variations. Listening intently to an artist is vital; by incorporating elements such as style and rhythmic feel, the student will see that scalar knowledge is not merely a boring or pedantic part of music acquisition but a way to truly progress forward. The student will discover that paying close attention to rhythmic detail (rather than nuance of voice/tone color) will yield the surprising results. To achieve this, take eight bars of your favorite artist and record yourself singing along. When you can only hear one singer (and not two), you've accomplished the exercise.

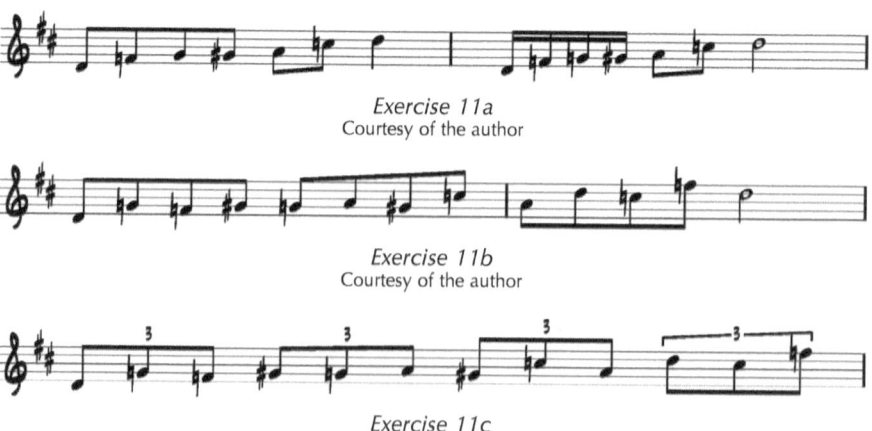

Exercise 11a
Courtesy of the author

Exercise 11b
Courtesy of the author

Exercise 11c
Courtesy of the author

As a "goal" of sorts, the culmination of the above might look like the following: The student hears a nice lick, run, or melodic fragment by their favorite artist. Utilizing the above, the student can pitch the notes correctly, diagnose the scale the notes came from and their harmonic function (i.e., number), and then take that pattern, singing it up and down through the scale. Changing a note here or there, altering the rhythm, or perhaps changing the tonality helps a student to avoid merely repeating a fragment, instead creating a truly original fragment of their own. This process of imitation, comprehension, and mastery—leading to innovation—is the fastest way for a musician to nurture their own original voice. This is a far more satisfying meal than merely passing the scalar requirements of a given exam. Finally, these exercises may be practiced over a drone and with a metronome, allowing the student to practice rhythm, pitching, harmonic awareness, style, and improvisation all at once.

Exercise 12 is a culmination of what we have been discussing so far. Sing the minor, pentatonic, and Dorian scales (on the pitch A) over the static chords below. Ensure that all degrees of the scale can be pitched at will by ear, without having to "get there" by singing up the scale from the root. Note the emotional resonance of the tensions, especially the ninth (B), eleventh (D) and thirteenth (F♯). While the root, third, and fifth are harmonically "in" (and we are accustomed to these sounds), these aforementioned tensions offer a slightly different emotional palette. When this step is mastered, one can then proceed to improvise in differing styles. Exercise 12 notates two different common grooves: lo-fi hip-hop and house. These differing styles (with widely differing tempi) will alter the type of lines sung, even though the actual notes are exactly the same.

Exercise 12
Courtesy of the author

Modal improvisation (exercise 13) is ideal for the more advanced singers who want to familiarize themselves with modes, harmony, and developing improvisation skills for CCM (and jazz in particular). The intended goal of these exercises is to give the student the tools they need to freely improvise within the tonality (i.e., the note set), thus using scales for the purpose they were originally intended—to create new melodies. These exercises are also useful for songwriters or singers who want to incorporate more interesting harmonic and melodic options into their musical toolbox. These exercises can be varied by creating different grooves to sing along with or utilizing different rhythms, phrasing, punctuation, voice qualities, syllables, tongue, or larynx positions—anything at all you can think of!

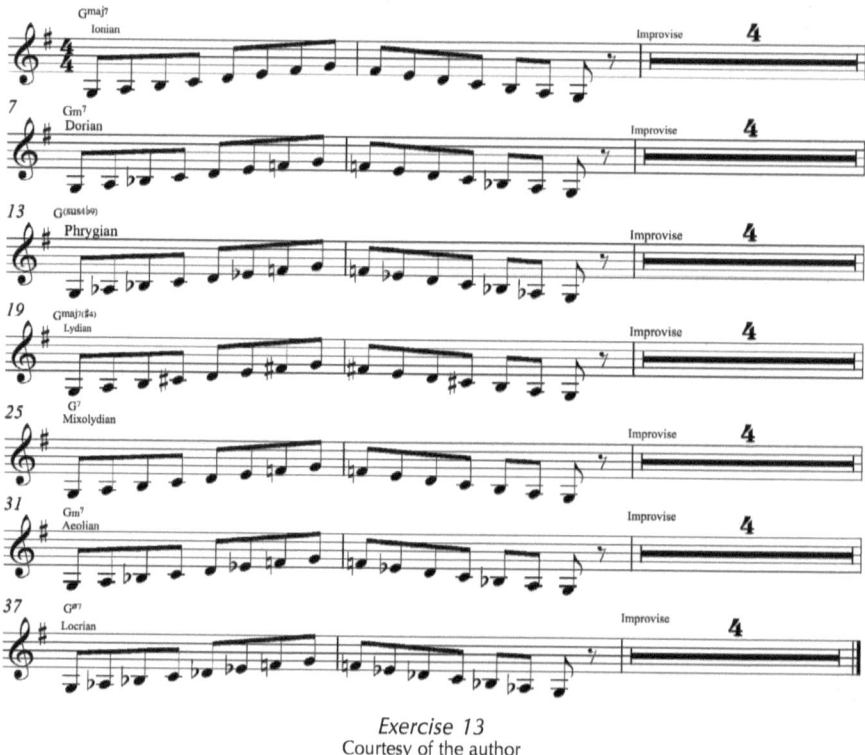

Exercise 13
Courtesy of the author

For students who are interested in learning something a bit more unusual or abstract, the whole-tone scale is a useful place to start. Whole-tone scales may sound a little strange at first, but singing them can be a great exercise to practice pitch accuracy. Exercise 14a is based on the whole-tone scale. Creating exercises like this along with a track or accompaniment is a helpful way of learning the scale and incorporating it into your practice routine. Listening to music that incorporates these scales is important as well so that the singer hears them in context; they are not learned in isolation from a piece of music. You can find this scale used in lots of places, such as "You Are the Sunshine of My Life" by Stevie Wonder (b. 1950) and the theme songs to *Sex and the City* and *Sabrina the Teenage Witch*.

Exercise 14a
Courtesy of the author

Exercise 14b is a whole-tone pattern ascending in major thirds and separated by whole steps. As already mentioned, melodies are usually not based on ascending and descending scales. Therefore, it is important to incorporate intervals to the scale patterns. This exercise can be used as an SOVT exercise. Feel free to play with rhythm and vary your onsets and voice qualities as you sing it. Exercise 14c are "half-whole" and "whole-half scales" (i.e., octatonic), which are useful scales for practicing musicianship and pitch accuracy.[9]

Exercise 14b
Courtesy of the author

Exercise 14c
Courtesy of the author

Exercise 15 is for professional-level singers who are looking to expand their knowledge and skill set. Sing G to G in key of C (i.e., G with a lowered seventh, or mixolydian), and then play the voicing shown below (with a G♯, or E7 altered). Hold that chord and sing the same notes. You'll probably try to ignore the chord, singing the same notes and clinging on to them through memory. To help yourself hear these notes as ones that are different (because they now have a different harmonic function), sing those notes slowly against the chord and encourage yourself to hear the root of the chord and to hear the function you are now playing. There is a big difference between singing the root of G and singing the raised ninth of E7, which can feel like a really "dark" note. Because it is a completely different experience, being able to shift between the two in your head is a useful exercise.

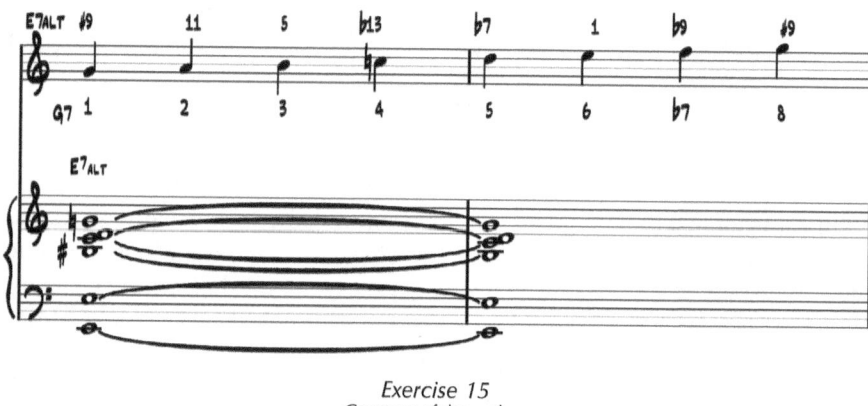

Exercise 15
Courtesy of the author

Now try singing some of the patterns previously discussed, taking them melodically up and down, playing with the rhythmic elements, and expanding upon the lyric. How you sing the melody—or how you sing any note for that matter—depends on the harmonic function of each note that you sing. For instance, the fifth may feel open and airy, the root strong and certain, and the third as indicative of a particular emotion. Regarding nonchord tones, the second is lighthearted, the fourth wants to resolve to the third, the sixth is good-natured and "twee," and the seventh is bittersweet. Of course, these are subjective reactions, but the important takeaway is that each of these notes has a unique emotional property.

FINAL THOUGHTS

Meribeth always asked me what I was taking away from our sessions and encouraged me to do the same at the end of my classes and workshops. I did this at the Cork International Choral Festival Workshops in 2018 and 2019 and the responses were wonderful. Participants included voice students, teachers, conductors, accompanists, and choir members from around the world. The feedback was so positive and clearly showed the effectiveness of the CoreSinging exercises and principles. The main themes that emerged from the sessions included the following:

1. Feeling motivated to practice in a mindful and more focused way
2. Becoming stronger and more confident performers
3. Having fun
4. Noticing immediate differences in the singers who performed
5. Feeling inspired
6. Having increased awareness of energy
7. Having a greater sense of balance and alignment
8. Positive thinking
9. Practical exercises and examples
10. Becoming more focused on performance

It is an honor to be a CoreSinging teacher who continues to give workshops and share Meribeth's wonderful approach with others. When I discovered CoreSinging, everything about it suited my personal philosophy and experiences as a musician. Meribeth was everything I believed a teacher should be—kind, encouraging, supportive, forward thinking, wise, and an expert in the field. I loved how Meribeth believed in finding new ways to look at old concepts, changing them so that they are more effective and exploring learning possibilities by going beyond one's own expectations. I am forever grateful to Meribeth for helping to shape me as a teacher and person.

NOTES

1. Jesse Tsao, "Qigong Essentials: Eight-Piece Brocades," https://www.taichi-healthways.com/Qigong-and-Other/qigong-essentials-8-piece-brocades.html.

2. Roger Jahnke et al., "A Comprehensive Review of Health Benefits of Qigong and Tai Chi." *American Journal of Health Promotion* 24, no. 6 (July 2010): e1–e25.

3. I loved when Meribeth told me that "we don't *hit* notes . . . we *sing* notes—and notes are parts of phrases . . . They are not a *particular* note." Helping students reframe how they think about this common source of stress was so useful.

4. K. Anders Ericsson et al., "The Role of Deliberate Practice in the Acquisition of Expert Performance," *Psychological Review* 100, no. 3 (July 1993): 363–406.

5. Susan Hallam, "The Development of Expertise in Young Musicians: Strategy Use, Knowledge Acquisition and Individual Diversity," *Music Education Research* 3, no. 1 (March 2001): 7–23; Siw Nielsen, "Learning Strategies in Instrumental Music Practice," *British Journal of Music Education* 16, no. 3 (November 1999): 275–91; Siw Nielsen, "Self-Regulating Learning Strategies in Instrumental Music Practice," *Music Education Research* 3, no. 2 (September 2001): 155–67.

6. Koko Willis and Pali Jae Lee, *Tales from the Night Rainbow* (Honoulu: Night Rainbow Publishing Company, 1990), 18.

7. Susan Hallam et al., "The Development of Practising Strategies in Young People," *Psychology of Music* 40, no. 5 (August 2012): 652–80.

8. The "stomping exercise" involves stomping your feet like a bold child throwing a tantrum. All your effort is channeled into stomping your feet into the ground, as if you are marching furiously. Meribeth recommended adding strong hand claps as well. In my experience, the stomping exercise is great for working on chest register or belt, and I also find that it works well for increasing breath capacity and dealing with nerves. The stomping exercise also helps students find projection, power, clarity, and freedom.

9. For those singers who want to delve further into interesting scales, a good place to start is Nicolas Slonimsky's *Thesaurus of Scales and Melodic Patterns* (New York: Scribner's, 2021).

Part III

SELECTED WRITINGS

Meribeth Dayme:
A Biographical Sketch

Susanne Bunch Hill

Meribeth Bunch, my sister, was born on April 20, 1938, in Aulander, a small town in northeastern North Carolina. Because of the seven-year age difference between us, I filled the role of her pesky little sister . . . and she ignored me as much as possible! Nevertheless, I still got to know her well and have many fond memories of her. The following paragraphs are some of my recollections of Meribeth's early years.

I was eleven years old when Meribeth left home for college. She did not spend much time at home after that, spending her summers as a camp counselor and performing in summer theater. Our dad was a pharmacist and owned Bunch Pharmacy in Aulander. From Aulander the family moved to Carolina Beach near Wilmington and our dad bought and ran Carolina Beach Drug Company. We lived at Carolina Beach, right on the ocean shore, until 1946 when Meribeth was eight. Our parents decided that the beach was not a good place for girls to grow up. There was a small permanent community there with a lot of tourists during the summer months, and it was an off-duty hangout for soldiers stationed at Camp Lejeune and Fort Bragg. Our parents thought it was too rough, so Dad sold the drugstore at Carolina Beach and founded Bunch Drugs in Goldsboro, another small town in eastern North Carolina about ninety miles from Wilmington. We kept our house at the beach and spent summers there. Goldsboro and summers at the beach are where Meribeth grew up and lived throughout her childhood and teenage years.

Meribeth loved sports. One of my earliest memories is the day Meribeth broke her arm playing football with the neighborhood boys when she was about eleven. I don't remember if she was throwing or catching the pass, but she fell and broke her left arm. She remained an avid sports fan her entire life and especially loved football, basketball, and tennis. Our family were big UNC fans because our mother grew up in Chapel Hill and our dad went

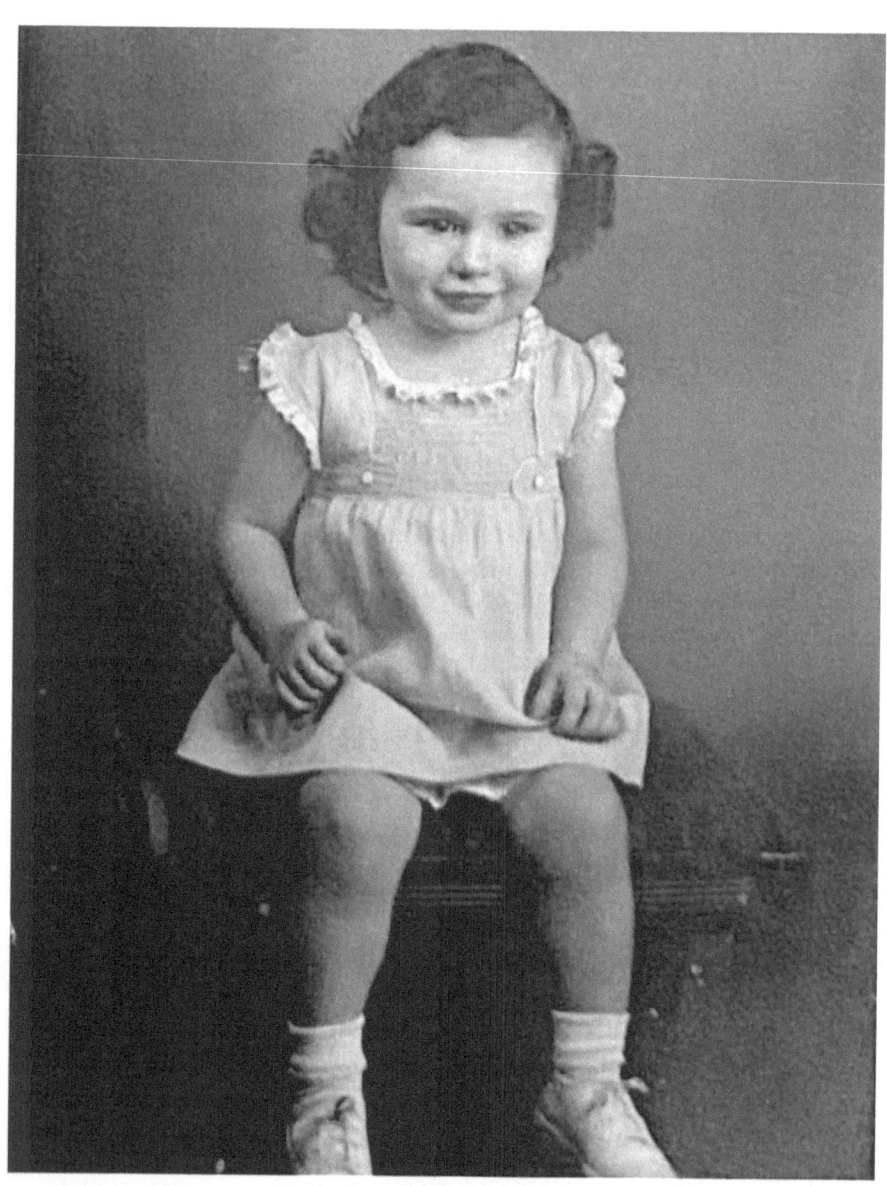
Meribeth as a toddler (circa 1940)
Courtesy of the editors

to school at University of North Carolina. We never missed watching or listening to UNC football and basketball. Meribeth loved college and professional football and basketball. She had her favorite teams, which included the Seattle Seahawks and Golden State Warriors, and never missed watching them until the day she passed away. She would watch no matter the time of day or night—especially the tennis matches taking place in Europe. As an athlete herself, tennis was Meribeth's greatest love. She learned to play when she attended summer camp and played competitively throughout her life. She won many tournaments over the years and broke her arm (a second time!) playing tennis in her seventies in France. Meribeth instilled this love of tennis in her niece (my oldest daughter), who is now playing league tennis, a feat largely attributable to "Aunt Meribeth."

Summer camp was also an important part of Meribeth's childhood. She attended Camp Seafarer in Arapahoe, an all-girls camp in the mountains of North Carolina for several summers from about the age of ten. In her teens she was crushed when our parents were no longer able to afford to send her to camp. I now treasure the brochures for Camp Junaluska that she saved from the late 1940s and early 1950s. The camp offered horseback riding, hiking, swimming, canoeing, badminton, tennis, target shooting, archery, ping pong, and volleyball in addition to arts and crafts, dance, and dramatics. I think that Meribeth always considered her days at camp some of the best days of her life. As a young adult, she worked as a counselor at a camp in North Carolina for several summers and loved working with the children there.

And then of course, there was music. Meribeth started piano lessons when she was about seven. Our piano teacher was the mayor's wife, and she was the only teacher in the small town where we lived. The teacher was good enough for Meribeth to realize that she loved music. Meribeth started voice lessons in high school and knew at that point that she wanted a career in voice and music. She sang solos in church and gave a recital her senior year of high school. Our high school also had wonderful glee club and drama teachers, both of whom were unusual talents for such a small town. She graduated from Goldsboro High School in 1956.

After high school, Meribeth attended Salem College, a women's liberal arts college in Winston-Salem, North Carolina that has always had an excellent music school. She had wonderful teachers at Salem and many opportunities there. Meribeth remained close to several of the music faculty, especially her lifelong voice teacher, Joan Jacobowski, who, at the time of this book's publication, is in her nineties and still singing. Joan was one of the first people I notified when Meribeth passed away. Meribeth also served as the choir director at one of the local Moravian Churches while in college, and she sang solos at church, with the Salem College choral ensemble, and gave multiple solo recitals.

After graduating from college in 1960, Meribeth attended Union Theological Seminary in New York City, where she received a master's degree in sacred music. Meribeth taught at Wilson College in Chambersburg, Pennsylvania, for several years before attending the University of Southern California to earn her PhD under the renowned voice scientist William Vennard.

In addition to these biographical details, there are several other things that I remember (or was told) about Meribeth. First, I think it's important to mention that Meribeth's earliest introduction to the arts was dance. She started dance lessons when she was very young while we lived at the beach, and she loved it. I don't recall her taking dance classes during high school or college, but I know she took lessons at the Royal Academy of Dance while she lived in London. This was not just about the love of dance but also about what dance could do for you as a singer. Movement and posture were of course an important part of her vocal work and pedagogical beliefs.

There are a few other things about my sister that I would like to mention—things that won't surprise anyone who knew her. From a very young age Meribeth was independent, strong-willed, and determined. (I think this may be why my parents waited seven years before they had another child!) One story in particular was frequently retold. Once when Meribeth was about three years old she was all dressed up, getting ready to attend a wedding with the family. Our mother had painstakingly styled Meribeth's hair in long "Shirley Temple" curls. While our mother was not looking, however, Meribeth decided to cut off half of her curls! She had more will and determination than anyone I know. And for those of us who knew her, this never changed. Only Meribeth would fly to France (without telling any of us) to get a puppy when she was eighty years old and could barely walk.

Meribeth was a lifelong dog lover. We had cocker spaniels growing up, and Meribeth got a dog immediately after graduate school during her first teaching job at Wilson College. It was a black Labrador mix and she named him "Tigger" after a character in her favorite children's book, *Winnie the Pooh*. Tigger went everywhere with Meribeth and lived a long and happy life. Meribeth got her first Coton de Tuléar puppy, "Sky," soon after moving to France. Thinking that Sky needed a companion, she then acquired "Chip" (another Coton) a couple of years later. Sky and Chip moved with Meribeth from France to California in 2016 and Sky died shortly thereafter at age thirteen. Meribeth really wanted another female Coton, so she returned to France in 2018 to get "Muppet." These dogs were her faithful companions for many years and were her family as much as the rest of us. Her main concern, when

"Sky and Chip" in France (2015)
Courtesy of the editors

learning that she did not have long to live, was making sure that her dogs—as well as her lifelong work—were going to be well taken care of.

Meribeth was always curious about everything and knew a lot about many things because she read and kept up on everything. She was also adventurous, never afraid to try or do anything. She went to Europe by herself to live, she traveled all over the world (including to India to work with Mother Teresa), reinvented herself too many times to count, and never gave up! And, perhaps most important, she was gifted and creative. In addition to being brilliant in her musical work, Meribeth wrote beautiful poetry—such as "Spring Birthday Walk," included in this book—which we found while going through her things after her death. She loved nature and was an excellent photographer. I have several albums of beautiful photographs of many of the places she traveled. During her last few years in France, she even took painting lessons. She had hoped to continue art lessons in the United States, but was not able to accomplish this goal due to her health. She sold some of her paintings and I own several others that I treasure.

Last but not least, Meribeth wanted to make a difference in the world. She wanted to be the best that she could be, and she loved teaching and sharing

Original charcoal drawing by Meribeth Dayme (ca. 2013)
Courtesy of the editors

her knowledge and experience with others. She was an amazing person, and she indeed made a difference for so many people in the voice world as well as others who knew her. Our family extends the deepest thanks to Cynthia Vaughn and Matthew Hoch for putting together this book and ensuring that her legacy is preserved. It is our hope that Meribeth's work will continue to inspire future generations.

Susanne Bunch Hill
Carlsbad, California
September 2021

Spring Birthday Walk
(unpublished 1986 poem)

```
           Spring Birthday Walk

April 20, 1938 - Birth

April 20, 1986 - Spring Rain - soft, gentle, warm
                             - quenching the thirst of new growth
                             - washing my face, clearing my eyes
                               and awakening me to renewed life.

               Buds - some reticent--appearing to seek permission
                                     to emerge.
                    - some visibly evolving in the rain.
                    - some bursting with anticipation.

               Light green leaves - young, tender, happy to be here.
                                              faces of
               Blooms - joyful, colourful, many shapes and varieties,
                        and the delicate aura of love.

               A Bird with a worm in its beak(nourishment) -
                    - who eyes me and says:
                              "You also have a worm!"
                              "Do you know it?"
                    - I reply:
                              "Yes, I do have a worm. It has
                               taken me some time to realise that
                               it is mine."

               Me - calm, peaceful, clear, love emerging.

               Rebirth.....
```

Meribeth
April 20, 1986

"Spring Birthday Walk" (unpublished poem by Meribeth Dayme)
Courtesy of the editors

The Little Book about Singing
A Guide for Those Who Want to Get Ahead Fast

Meribeth Dayme

2006

INTRODUCTION

"The Little Book about Singing" is full of basic knowledge to help you in your quest to sing better. It will help you whether you want to develop a career, sing in a choir, or sing for the pleasure for family, friends, or just in the shower. I believe that the body wants to sing; we just manage to get in the way most of the time. What follows on these pages are some simple concepts that will help you have a better voice and a healthy vocal instrument. What style you prefer is up to you—this book covers an efficient vocal technique that will help you achieve optimum voice quality, basic performance skills, and vocal health. This book does not replace a good teacher; its role is to serve as your advisor and coach when you do not have access to a teacher, or when you prefer to do something on your own.

First a few facts:

- Professional singers make it look and sound easy—well, most of them.
- They had to work hard to make it look and/or sound that way.
- Most singers begin by copying the faults of their idols.
- The most prevalent vocal fault in the world is misalignment of the head during singing and speaking. This is true for every style of singing.
- Making a recording will not necessarily make you rich.

Now that we have either confirmed or dispensed with a few of your preconceptions, let's talk about what you can do to sing better. Before we do that, there is a quiz to help you know more about your own goals in singing.

SECTION 1: WHAT'S YOUR SINGING-IQ?

Answer all the following questions with "true" or "false":

1. I want to sing because I must.
2. I want to sing because I love music.
3. I want to sing because I want to become famous.
4. I want to be famous, and if I need to sing to do it, then so be it.
5. I want to get it exactly right every time.
6. I don't mind taking a risk in performance.
7. My voice is the most important part of my singing.
8. I let my emotions rule my singing.
9. I get hoarse each time I sing.
10. My throat hurts when I sing.
11. Singing off pitch or out of tune is OK as long as I communicate.
12. My posture contributes to the quality of my voice.
13. Studying singing is only for "classical" singers.
14. Learning to read music is only for classical singing.
15. Good singers can't act, or don't need to act.
16. I don't have to worry about my sound, the microphone and sound engineer take care of that.
17. The text is secondary to my sound.
18. I get so nervous before a performance that I have to take something to get through the event.
19. Regular physical exercise is not important for singers.
20. I don't know anything about the voice, I just sing.

Point values for each answer:

	True	False		True	False
1.	+10	−10	11.	−7	+7
2.	+7	−7	12.	+7	−7
3.	−8	+8	13.	−7	+7
4.	−10	+10	14.	−6	+6
5.	−5	+5	15.	−5	+5
6.	+6	−6	16.	−10	+10
7.	−6	+6	17.	−7	+7
8.	−5	+5	18.	−8	+8
9.	−10	+10	19.	−10	+10
10.	−10	+10	20.	−6	+6

Lowest score possible = −150   Highest = +150

YOUR RESULTS

S-IQ of 125 or higher

You sound like a well informed, or possibly a well-trained singer already. Follow your passion and see how far you can go!

S-IQ between 75 and 125

You need to think about changing some of your perceptions about singing and get some training. Don't quit; persevere until you know what you really want to do.

S-IQ between 25 and 75

You definitely need to read this book, rethink your interest in singing, learn more about singing, and retake this quiz. Right now you are best singing for family and friends, or in a group.

S-IQ below 25 (between −150 and +25)

A singing career may not be for you. However, paying attention to the information in this book, observing excellent singers of all styles, taking some lessons, and enjoying singing for yourself are all advised. Your best singing at the moment is probably in the bath, shower, or car.

DISCUSSION OF THE S-IQ QUIZ

1. I want to sing because I must!

Nearly all singers who make it professionally are driven to sing and have an unremitting determination, passion, and focus. That is what keeps them working hard, and persevering no matter what obstacles they face. Look at what singers have to go through to win any of the reality shows such as *American Idol*, *Star Academy*, or *The X-Factor*; first, to get on the show, and then to win it. While there may be fame and wealth at the end of the road, it is not a guarantee. Indeed, sometimes singers become what we might call plastic throwaways for the sake of the entertainment industry—which is incredibly fickle. Determination, drive, patience, guts, musical talent and presence, or something compelling about your performance, are all needed on an ongoing basis for success in the performing arts industry.

2. I want to sing because I love music.

Love of music is a good start; however, love of something does not ensure a career. What is it you love about music, and how and why do you want to perform in public? Many people love music and are incredibly knowledgeable about it, but they make their living doing something else. Music furnishes them the sanity and satisfaction that keep them whole. These are the people who make up the audiences that support public performance and they are extremely valuable. Those who share their love of music by becoming teachers and healers are also providing the world with a valuable service.

3. I want to sing because I want to become famous.

We see so many "famous" people who are thrown at us by the media who encourage our curiosity to know more and more about them. What a lot of people want is the perceived glamour, wealth, and idyllic lifestyles that the famous seem to have. On the other hand, what many famous people see are never-ending camera lenses, reporters, and devotees prying into their homes, lives, and even thoughts, if they could. Do you really want that? Think about it. Your life is a gift, do you want to give it away to a well-meaning public just to be famous? To sing because you must is one thing; to sing to be famous is putting the emphasis on an "uninformed syllable."

4. I want to be famous, and if I need to sing to do it, then so be it.

If you want to famous, I'm sure you will be. But for what reason; and what is it you will be giving in return for this fame? There may be a high price to pay. So many young people just want to be famous for the sake of it, without realizing that most famous people have some skill they have honed. As the old saying goes: "Be careful what you ask for because you may get it, and then be unhappy."

5. I want to get it exactly right every time.

Accuracy is important, but not to the detriment of musicality, presence, and spontaneity in performance. It takes more than one or two small errors to produce a failed performance. Some of the most famous performers in the world will admit to making quite a number of what they consider errors in a performance—and yet the audience may never know it, so their appreciation is not dulled. The audience is there for entertainment, not to look for your errors. Sometimes it is necessary to improvise on the spot, and needing to get it right will prevent this from happening. The need to get it right every time can come from several sources: the self-critic, someone in your life who told you that if it wasn't exactly right that it was terrible, or one of the outdated teachers who bully pupils into doing well by constantly berating them. You do not need any of these things or people in your artistic life.

6. I don't mind taking a risk in performance.

Taking a risk does not mean walking on stage without adequate preparation such as knowing the music and the words. It means daring to be totally committed to the present and the performance where your intuition and spontaneity can carry the moment.

7. My voice is the most important part of my singing.

Of course your voice is important. However it is known that the voice comprises about 35–40 percent of your communication. So without your body, presence, and imagination you do not have enough for an excellent and compelling performance.

8. I let my emotions rule my singing.

When you pay attention to the text and meaning you want to give to your performance, the emotion will be there. Many singers substitute excess physical movement and exaggerated facial expression for emotion. These things simply get in the way of the voice and diminish the vocal quality. Exaggeration of movement and expression on your part will make it difficult for the audience to get involved or share the emotion of the song. They will be too attracted to your physical excess to become involved in the song. After all, they came to be part of it.

9. I get hoarse each time I sing.

Hoarseness means the membrane covering the vocal folds (cords) becomes swollen and allows excess air to escape with the sound. This can signal a number of problems: singing for too long at a time, singing loudly and forcefully, singing in smoke-filled rooms over time, singing with too much tension, or environmental allergies that affect the respiratory tract.

10. **My throat hurts when I sing.**

This is an indication of poor vocal technique and tension. Find a good teacher. To sing with pain is putting you in real danger of developing vocal pathology such as nodules.

11. **Singing off pitch or out of tune is OK as long as I communicate.**

Judging from a lot of singing today, this would appear to be true. However, it is not. Even well-known singers with raspy voices can sing with true pitch. If you sing off pitch deliberately for effect, that is one thing; however, it is not possible to have real vocal presence when you sing off pitch all the time.

12. **My posture contributes to the quality of my voice.**

It certainly does! Your vocal instrument, you, needs to be physically balanced so it can respond to your technique and imagination. Even though you may be in many different physical positions during performance, it is important to "set up your instrument" first. Give it a chance to develop efficient vocal reflexes before distorting it. No instrumentalist would play with a distorted instrument, and it is not to your advantage to do so, either. If nothing else, your ears need to be aligned with the points of your shoulders so your vocal tract is in optimal position to respond to your vocal demands and give you a chance to sing with your best quality.

13. **Studying singing is only for "classical" singers.**

Everyone needs good vocal coordination of physical balance, breath, and phonation. This keeps singers vocally healthy and prolongs careers. Studying with a teacher who can help you achieve a healthy vocal technique is important. Do your own research on teachers in your area. If a teacher specializes in classical singing and you are interested in pop or rock, then that teacher may not be for you. Find someone who suits your needs.

14. **Learning to read music is only for classical singing.**

Learning to read music is necessary for any performer. Professional musicians and singers are expected to learn quickly and come to practice or sessions prepared. If you have to have someone teach you the notes and rhythm, you are at a big disadvantage, and it will take you too long to learn your music. It is difficult to focus on performance when you are busy trying to remember the notes or rhythm. This leads to loss of confidence and vocal insecurity.

15. **Good singers can't act, or don't need to act.**

While this is true in many cases, you do not want it to be true of you. Compelling performance requires heightened awareness and a wonderful imagination. This feeds your vocal quality and enables complete communication on stage. When singers neglect areas such as acting and mime as part of their training, they run the risk of diminished communication on stage and keeping their audience from sharing the moment.

16. **I don't have to worry about my sound; the microphone and sound engineer take care of that.**

Wouldn't it be nice for the microphone and sound engineer to have that much ability to give you the voice you want? Sadly, whatever you put into the microphone is what is amplified. The microphone is a tool to help you be heard by a large audience, record a CD, or play with the sounds you make. The engineer can do some amazing things, but the final responsibility for your sound is you.

17. **The text is secondary to my sound.**

This is true when you are vocalizing and not using words. Why sing words if the audience cannot understand them? While you want the best possible sound, the words demand equal emphasis and help you achieve the sounds you want. Expressive text is the result of your imagination and emotional experience and gives credence to your performance.

18. **I get so nervous before a performance that I have to take something to get through the event.**

If you get this nervous, why are you performing? When performers get this anxious, I have to question their practice habits, learning style, or teaching. If you fear you will not be perfect, relax. You will not be perfect. God does not give performances. We are human and an audience prefers to see a human in front of them. Of course, you want to sing as well as you can. However, unreal expectations set up an impossible task. There are many mind/body techniques like meditation, visualization, and EFT (explained later) that can change those nerves into a positive energy for performance. Taking medication or other drugs only masks the symptom and does not solve the problem. Look into some other ways of dealing with your nerves.

19. Regular physical exercise is not important for singers.

Your energy and health are vital to your voice and your performance. Singing in public takes stamina—much like the athlete who competes in front of thousands of people. It is not easy for the professional singer to get enough exercise when he has late nights, constant travel, and long practice sessions. Ten minutes of appropriate exercise twice a day is better than nothing. Surely you can find ten minutes and the discipline to use them well. Exercise is part of your general well being and vocal health.

20. I don't know anything about the voice, I just sing.

Singers need to be well informed about their instrument without being analytical to a fault. It has been said that a little knowledge is a dangerous thing. On the other hand, no knowledge is also a dangerous thing for performers. Instrumentalists learn a lot about their instruments. This helps them in emergencies and in situations where no technician is available to help. The same is true for singers. A little knowledge can go a long way toward stopping panic when something goes wrong. When you are an informed singer you do not have to rely on others all the time to tell you what or how you are doing.

SECTION 2: TUNING YOUR INSTRUMENT

Your instrument is well tuned when you can coordinate the physical balance, the breath, the voicing (phonation), and text with a minimum of effort. When the coordination is there, it feels easy. The world is full of singers who use too much muscular effort and ruin their sound in the process. Don't forget that emotion, eyes, imagination, and mental focus affect the physical aspects.

WHAT IS PHYSICAL BALANCE FOR SINGING?

Good physical balance includes the following:

1. **Feet firmly on the floor**

Feel as the pores of the soles of your feet are in touch with the floor —even if you are wearing high heels. This will keep you grounded and help your voice to be stronger.

2. **Head and ears poised directly over the shoulders**

When the vocal tract (throat and larynx) is in optimum position for singing, the head (not the chin) is up, eyes looking outward, and the ears are in a direct line with the point of the shoulder (along the line of a seam in your shirt or jacket). Feel as if the back of your head is pushed up from the center of your upper back. The mistake most singers make is trying to tilt the head back to get this alignment. Look in a mirror and do not allow your head to tip backward or the chin to reach out or up. During performance this is usually the first area to go out of balance. So many performers are so eager to reach the audience that they try to do it with the head and not the voice. In doing so, the voice is put under strain and it is difficult to coordinate the rest of the body. The same problem occurs when the performer pokes the head forward toward the mike or looks like he or she is drinking the microphone. Pay attention to this. It is important.

3. The head is free and not held rigid

Your head must be free to move easily during breathing and singing. Not even the loudest singer who belts needs a rigid head and neck. This is a sure way to vocal abuse. Many singers become rigid at the intake of breath and at the onset of sound. Don't do this! Check your head by very gently moving it from side to side—as if saying no. Remember that head movement does not make sound or words.

4. The face looks natural

Ideally, your face matches the expression of your text or message. A distorted face, or jaw movement, is not necessary for singing.

5. Shoulders out (not back) and slightly down

Your shoulders do not need to be pulled backward as that tenses the upper back. Ideally they go out to the sides with the muscles in the back and the front released. Shoulders are not needed to sing. However, many singers substitute use of the shoulders for emotions that could more easily come from abdominal support. When shoulders are used, they interfere with the vibration of the larynx and breathing.

6. Ribs over hips

The ribs are centered over the hips in line with the shoulders and ears. If you have too much curvature of the back you will notice that it is difficult to have the ribs in line. However, by thinking of breathing into the lower back ribs, you can help the ribs move into a more efficient posture.

7. Knees slightly relaxed

The knees must be released, not bent, and not locked. Locked knees create tension in the lower back and make it difficult to breathe easily.

Good physical balance is the key to an efficient vocal production and gives your body a chance to respond reflexively. When you are in balance, the body is able to sing with little effort. Singing with poor balance means that all the muscles in the body have to work overtime to compensate for what you are doing, and the sound is compromised. Instrumentalists would not dream of playing a distorted instrument, but too many singers seem to specialize in it.

BREATHING IS NOT COMPLICATED

Breathe in by allowing the back ribs to move outward and breathe out by contracting the lower abdominal muscles. Feel as if the lower abdominal muscles are moving in and upward toward the lower back ribs as you exhale. This will give you the support you need for singing. Breathing is so much easier and more efficient if your posture is good.

Information about breathing is complicated by all the mythology surrounding its role in singing. What is important for any singer is that the vocal mechanism function efficiently and serve the best interests of the body and the song.

Every singer needs to breathe efficiently, even if you are singing short phrases. Learn how to breathe by using lower back rib movement. It is not necessary to have a huge abdominal forward bulge to breathe correctly. Using the lower back ribs will cause a balanced breathing action that will enable you to dance and sing without disturbing your breathing. More important, it will allow you to breathe without huge shoulder and chest movement that interferes with the larynx and tightens the neck.

There is no sound heard with correct breathing. When the back is working, the head and neck are free, onset of sound is clear and easy, and the audience is not aware of any noisy breaths. Gasping for breath is only effective if the song calls for that kind of interpretation. Otherwise, you stifle your voice, run out of air, and make a lot of noise into a microphone.

High breathing will inhibit your sound because it traps the larynx in the neck. In some teaching about belt-voice, high breathing is taught in order to stabilize the larynx. However if you concentrate on the collarbone as an anchor for the larynx you can achieve belt without so much tension in the upper chest and neck.

WHAT HAPPENS IN YOUR LARYNX DURING SINGING?

The vocal folds (cords) are basically a buzzer. There are two muscular folds housed in the larynx that sits on top of the windpipe (trachea). When air moves through the space between and underneath the vocal folds, they come together and begin to vibrate. The pitch you wish to sing determines the number of vibrations per second. This will all happen easily and without problems if the larynx is undisturbed or not displaced in the neck by tension or excess muscular action.

Cracks in the voice or sound occur when you are trying to sing too heavily, with excess tension, displacement of the head, or the perception that you need a heavy, big voice.

Some vibrato is normal in the easily produced voice. Excessive vibrato is often due to excess tension and pressure. A wobble, or slow vibrato, is due to such things as lack of energy, poor vocal coordination, or a fatigued voice.

RESONANCE

The open spaces in the throat and sometimes the nose contribute resonance to your voice. The vibration of the vocal folds is amplified in the open spaces of the vocal tract (throat). As this area of the throat is also used for chewing and swallowing, it is highly mobile and can take many shapes. The shape of the vocal tract determines vocal quality. The vowels we make are shaped mainly by the position of the tongue. When the tongue changes positions, the shape of the vocal tract alters and different vowel sounds are produced. This happens in overtone chanting as well.

Movements of the soft palate, the tongue, and of the larynx up and down determine the shape of the vocal tract. The whole head and neck area is complex with many interrelationships that affect each other. The best way to work with this is to remember your alignment, a gently loose head, neck, and jaw.

As the vocal tract is closely associated with the face, jaw, and lips, any undue distortion in those areas can change the resonance pattern and diminish your vocal quality. A good rule to follow is: look normal.

Nasal sounds are created when the soft palate is lowered and air escapes through the nose. Consonants like *m* and *n* are nasal. However, a consistent nasal sound that is not deliberate means that the soft palate is not raised sufficiently to keep air out of the nose when you sing.

The vocal tract responds magnificently to your imagination. Know your text and be able to create a complete scene with thorough knowledge of all the characters, the setting, clothing, and such things as air quality in very specific detail. The more you can do this, the better your voice will respond. Your audience will as well.

ARTICULATION

Words are important and your audience wants to understand them. Flexible lips and tongue and a relaxed jaw that is loosely suspended from the head will give you the physical structure for efficient articulation.

As mentioned above, vowels are made by the tongue and are a resonance phenomenon. What you need to remember about vowels is: first, sound is sustained on vowels and not consonants. So when you want to sing more smoothly or legato, you need to linger on the vowel.

Consonants are made with the movements of the tongue against the hard and soft palates and the teeth, and movements of the lips. Some consonants have voice sounds such as *m, n, l, v,* and *d*; *m* and *n* are also nasal, and the rest are mainly noises without use of sustained sound.

The more muscular effort you make to articulate words, the more distorted they will be. The most common causes of articulation problems are a tight jaw, a jaw that protrudes on pronunciation of a consonant or vowel, over opening the mouth so much that the tongue will not reach the palate or teeth to be able to make the consonant. Tense lips, lips that are over working, and chewing the sound by closing the mouth or moving the tongue while sustaining a vowel will all distort the vocal quality and words.

Above all, allow your face to look normal and express the message without distortion.

SUMMARY

The keys to easy, reflexive vocal mechanics are: balanced alignment, freedom of the body, silent breathing that does not interfere with the vocal mechanism, and an imagination that gives it energy. Excessive muscular activity such as noisy breathing, moving around on stage, and sloppy enunciation of the words will only keep you from achieving vocal presence or good communication. When singers find their vocal balance and coordination, the comment is: "This is so easy." Yes!

SECTION 3: FIVE THINGS TO INCLUDE IN EVERY PRACTICE

1. Create a plan for each practice or each studio session

A planned practice is an efficient practice. Whether you have fifteen minutes or more than an hour, think about how to best use your time before you begin. Set achievable goals for each time period. Yes, there are some days when nothing works. On those days take a walk, listen to some of your favorite artists, or just chill out.

Of course you can have a practice labeled "sing your heart out for the next half hour." You are encouraged to sing one song that way at the end of rehearsal every day. When you are working in the studio, take time to be ready rather than waste valuable and expensive time. Make a video of your practice and rehearsals. While you may not want to review all of it, it is the best way to see for yourself how you are meeting your own criteria.

2. Warm up! Physically and vocally

No athlete would think of going into a practice or a match without warming up. Your vocal folds are muscles, and like the rest of the body need to be warmed up to work efficiently. Stretches, slow sustained movements, yoga, and tai chi exercises are helpful before you begin to sing. They work well with gentle humming or improvised sound as well.

Vocal warm ups can include improvised sounds, lip trills (raspberries), and tongue trills done like a siren or using scales. It is better to begin with no set patterns and then move into scales or phrases of your songs. By starting with improvisation and random patterns, you will be under no pressure to get it "right" and become tense in the process.

3. Say and mime your words (with your hands) like a ham actor or actress

This applies to everything you sing—even the songs with a lot of repeated or seemingly inane text. You have to find a reason to sing that song for the audience and entice them to want to hear it. Playing and experimenting with many different ways of expressing the words will help solidify your interpretation and become convincing in your communication. Miming as you sing will also give added imagination and meaning to your text.

4. Improvise around the tune and words of your song

Play with your music, improvise, use nonsense syllables, and then gradually interchange these with the actual music and text. While accuracy is important in structured songs (as opposed to improvisation), you also need the flexibility and fun of playful practice.

5. Sing your song as if it were a live performance at least once before you leave the practice session

While it may seem difficult to emulate live performance in the practice room or your lesson, it is imperative for quality presentation. If you sing with a microphone, practice with a microphone. Leave nothing to chance where performance is concerned. Unexpected things may happen, so it is best to be prepared in the best way possible.

SECTION 4: THE BASICS OF VOCAL HEALTH

Your voice is a part of your body and needs to be treated with the same regard as any other aspect of your health. Therefore normal health issues like adequate sleep, good nutrition, and fitness are all part of a singer's responsibility as well. Performers need the same attention to the details of their health as athletes. A good athlete would rarely stay out several nights in a row or spend the evening at a big party the night before a match. Singers can learn a lot from athletes; peak performance is the same for both. While classical singers are aware of this and conscientious about their health, those in the huge population of contemporary commercial music (or CCM, formerly known as nonclassical) seem to think they can live by different rules. When your voice is your means of making a living, it becomes seriously important to keep it healthy.

Quiet time, stillness, and visualization are important for your mental health and for being clear about your performance. This is the best way to handle negative anxiety and nervousness and turn them into positive excitement and focus. Techniques for this are suggested in section 6.

Attention to vocal technique and adequate rehearsal are part of vocal health. When your physical vocal instrument is balanced and aligned, you are not likely to have too many vocal problems of physical origin.

Physical and vocal warm-ups will allow your muscles to get ready to work without a huge shock. To start off singing something vocally difficult without an adequate warm up is asking to have a performance that is shaky. You need confidence in your voice when you are in front of an audience.

COMMON PROBLEMS SINGERS FACE

Note: when in doubt about a vocal problem, see your doctor or an ear, nose, and throat specialist doctor.

Colds and respiratory diseases

These are difficult for singers because they can cause the mucus membranes covering the vocal folds to swell. This causes the raspy, breathy sound that you hear. There is also a tendency to cough and this irritates the vocal folds because it causes vocal folds to open under excess pressure. When this happens, it is best not to sing much because you can cause further damage and vocal fatigue. People who have to sing with these conditions stay silent during the day and warm up gently before a performance. Warm up with gentle hums and within an easy range first. If the voice is OK with that, extend the range, by using tongue trills and raspberries. Silence during the day means no talking— not even to your best friend.

Hoarseness

This is a general catchall term for any swelling of the vocal folds. The causes can range from allergies to things like smoke, respiratory problems, substance abuse, drinking too much alcohol, talking or singing too much, or singing with poor vocal technique. When you are hoarse, go easy on your voice. Become aware of when you are hoarse, for example, after a rehearsal or practice. If you have some hoarseness after singing or a late, loud party, it will normally go away the next day. When the problem does not go away, you are advised to see a doctor.

Laryngitis

Laryngitis is an acute inflammation of the area of the vocal folds. The more inflamed and swollen the vocal folds, the less voice you have. Do not sing or speak with laryngitis. You will only cause more serious problems. The causes of laryngitis range from infections, both viral and bacterial, to vocal abuse. In any case, see a professional.

Vocal Nodules

Nodules are small lumps on the edges of the vocal folds caused by vocal abuse. They begin as bruises and then progress to harder lumps. Vocal abuse such as yelling, screaming, singing with poor technique over time all put added strain on a very delicate mechanism. Basically you are beating the vocal folds together and battering them. The nodules prevent a clean vocal fold contact and the escaping air creates a breathy, fuzzy vocal quality. Nodules can go away of their own accord with a corrected singing technique, therapy, and attention to vocal health. When they are large, doctors often advise having the nodules removed surgically. However, a word of warning: nodules return when you do not change your habits.

What you can do to help yourself:

- Keep your throat hydrated by drinking plenty of water
- Get adequate rest
- Make physical fitness part of your daily routine

- Do not smoke anything.
- Stay away from smoky atmospheres
- Get rid of your self-critic
- Practice mind/body techniques
- Visualize positive outcomes
- Practice in several short segments a day rather than long ones
- Plan your practice time by having a mixture of repertoire
- Use a video camera for rehearsal and performance—you need to know how you performed

Your vocal health is critical to your performance. Singers are not called back when they cancel performances all the time. If you are an aspiring singer, then taking care of your voice is part of your vocal training and education.

SECTION 5: PRESENCE IN PERFORMANCE

You can have it all, voice, presence, and compelling performance. To achieve it you need the following: physical presence, including balanced alignment, eyes that see, vocal presence, a huge amount of imagination behind the text (even a mundane, repetitive text), and a video camera. Vocal presence means that your technique is coordinated with your physical presence and your imagination. The visible, vocal, and textual elements of your performance will all be saying the same thing. You will be able to see for yourself whether you meet these criteria when you replay your video.

Note: Today, there is a tendency to substitute hyperactivity for presence. The activity during performance is ideally matched to the message you want to convey. Hyperactivity is a kind of facade that masks the voice and message, and makes the singer appear to be insincere.

Your physical and vocal presence relate to the space you occupy with your body and your sound. Treat your space as a portable energy home with the audience as your guests. In essence, imagine yourself as the point in the middle of a circle or sphere with your audience all around you. Presence is multidimensional. When you have this, your body and voice will respond by occupying the whole room, arena, or concert hall, and you will have a special timeless quality to your sound. The emphasis only on what is in front of you, rather than the space surrounding you, will prevent you from being centered in body and in voice.

PHYSICAL PRESENCE

In studies on communication, it has been shown that more than 50 percent of your message is what the audience sees. When the visible elements do not match the text, it confuses the message, and your audience can leave without appreciating or understanding your performance. A powerful physical presence includes the means to command the attention of the audience by your posture, facial expression, eyes that see your audience, and your complete focus on the message. These elements can to be built into any singing technique from the very beginning.

Filling space demands a body language that is confident and aligned. Any physical shrinkage on your part will diminish your stage presence. It is difficult to fill any space with eyes that are doing anything but seeing. Staring at spots on the wall, choosing one person to see, downcast eyes, and closed eyes all diminish your space and prevent the audience from taking part in your performance. The way you use your eyes and good physical balance are essential elements of presence.

Using your peripheral vision helps the audience to feel a part of the song, and increases the presence in the sound enormously. Peripheral vision is that expanded visual awareness that enables you to see almost 180 degrees while still looking in one direction. Closing your eyes on stage is about the same as trying to sing with the curtains closed. Closing your eyes as a sign of emotion indicates a singer who is very involved with his/her own feelings and not caring whether the audience participates or not. Remember: they came to take part.

MENTAL PRESENCE

Complete awareness without internal dialogue is an indication of mental presence. The human mind can move incredibly fast, especially in performance situations. The last thing you need is an inner dialogue interfering with the message you want to deliver. Performing with an inner radio or a self-critic talking while you are singing divides your focus, encourages mistakes, and takes away your confidence.

VOCAL PRESENCE

Vocal presence is that timeless quality achieved by the balance of well-coordinated technique and total dedication to the moment. It is like being "in the zone" while singing. Singers often describe this as "being sung" rather than singing. It is possible in any style. This element is missing in the vast majority of singers today.

Role of the Microphone

Vocal presence is what you put into your voice; your microphone, or the sound engineer does not produce it. What you put into the mike is what it magnifies. So be aware that the responsibility for vocal quality is yours. Having said that, you can be very creative with sound and the use of a microphone. There are two things that you must be careful about: the position of the mike and the choice of different types of microphones at your disposal. Never trust the mike setup for a performance; always test it beforehand.

Sound engineers are known for adding presence to sound in a recording studio. However, tech treatment cannot compensate for something lacking in the voice. Perhaps this is why some singers cannot handle live performance today. The doctored studio sound cannot be replicated on stage and creates a problem in live performance where the audience expects to hear exactly what they heard on the recording.

In summary, singers who have physical and vocal presence have the mysterious X factor, and audiences love them. These singers exhibit: freedom, flexibility, spontaneity of response (to the whole person within), and imagination.

SECTION 6: YOUR VOICE TOOL BAG

PITCH PIPE

A pitch pipe is a must and will enable you to practice anywhere without a piano or musical instrument. Practice in the correct key! Your muscles need to know the pitches you plan to use for performance. Practicing in one key and performing in another is taking unnecessary risk—unless you are improvising.

VIDEO CAMERA

You need to know for yourself how you sound, how you look, and how well you are communicating. Taking the word of others regarding your performance is a start; however, you are the final judge, and you are the one who knows how you want to come across. Therefore, a video camera is a required part of your tool bag.

MIND/BODY TOOLS

Included in every performer's tool bag are ways of focusing and stilling the mind and nerves. Professional athletes have used personal coaches to help them learn mind/body techniques to improve technical skills, positive thinking, and mental and emotional focus. The use of these tools has taken performers to new levels of achievement. A few are listed below.

- Meditation—a way of focusing the mind by using sound, mantras, or silence. The effect is to bring you into present awareness and leave behind the inner talk and radio that often play negative recordings when we are about to perform.
- Visualization—involves the use of imagery and imagination to see what you want to happen. This can be used to visualize vocal technique, memorizing words, seeing yourself on stage or in an audition feeling comfortable and able to do your best, or any other aspect you feel needs work.
- Emotional Freedom Technique (EFT)—a technique that combines affirmations and tapping on the ends of acupuncture meridians to eliminate emotional blockages that keep us from achieving what we want. There is a lot of free information on the website: www.emofree.com.

NLP (neurolinguistic programming)—initially developed from observation of excellent communicators and analyzing what made them so good. It has evolved into a leading system for intrapersonal and interpersonal communication, with practitioners specializing in everything from business to personal performance in sport and the performing arts.

Alexander Technique—was developed by an Australian actor who kept losing his voice. The technique teaches people to be aware of the relationship of mind and body, and to recreate natural as opposed to habitual postural and mental reflexes.

Eastern practices such as yoga and tai chi—essentially moving meditations that take total physical and mental concentration. These are incredibly valuable for singers.

SHORT, EFFECTIVE VOCAL WARM-UP

Know how to warm up your voice in almost any circumstance. Any number of things can happen at the last minute to cheat you of planned warm-up time. You can always do gentle stretches while humming and/or singing parts of your song. You can even do tongue and lip trills into your coat if you do not want to be heard. To get energy slap your breastbone (sternum), the inside of each wrist, and the inside of each ankle several times. Then sit quietly and focus until time to sing.

AUDITION MATERIAL

Be ready to sing for anyone at anytime. If you are, you will have a tremendous advantage over many singers. Nothing is worse than being asked to sing and dithering over what you might sing. By the time you do sing, if you do, you have delayed so long that your self-critic has probably taken over as boss. Have at least five or six songs that you can perform at the drop of a hat—with or without accompaniment.

Auditions are performances. If you think of them as anything else, you are doing yourself a disservice. Always sing what you sing best. To sing something hard and do it poorly just to show off is going to lose you the role/part every time. Always audition with something you can sing easily and give a real performance. While you may not get that part, you will impress the judges and they will remember you for future consideration. *Always keep your tool bag with you.*

SECTION 7: SINGING WITH SPIRIT

I had an opportunity to meet a famous healer and Christian mystic named Stylianos Atteshhilis (1912–1995), aka Daskalos, who lived on Cyprus. Each of us there was given a chance to ask him a question. Since I was a singer, I asked him to talk about singing. His short reply was: "Oh, that's easy. Just tune into the archangels, their language is vibration and sound, and singing is how they communicate."

While it is not a requirement that every song be tuned to the archangels, the statement above indicates that there is a musical healer in every singer. It is the responsibility of every singer to bring his or her best self and honest communicator to the art of singing. The vibrations of your singing can contribute to the healing of everyone in the audience, or anyone who hears your recordings. How you use your voice, and the subliminal message that you give, is vital to a better world today. So think carefully about why and how you sing. While you may think it is your own personal self-expression, there is a lot coming through you that comes from higher (or lower) energies. Make a commitment to heal with your voice. The world needs it badly.

Creating Confidence

How to Develop Your Personal Power and Presence

Meribeth Dayme
1999, rev. 2006

INTRODUCTION

Going with the flow today means that it is necessary to live in the chaos that looks set to remain with us for some time to come. How well and how comfortably we live with this is a sign of our inner strength, self-esteem, and confidence. Most of us maintain the hope that we will find a way to control chaos only to find ourselves squarely in the middle of a whirlwind. Those without confidence and an inner source of strength to deal with chaos are soon left behind, discouraged, or stressed out. It does not have to be so. With appropriate tools everyone is capable of developing a physical, mental, and spiritual presence, which in turn leads to increased confidence, understanding, and the effective and integral use of personal power.

Personal power, as discussed in this book, implies the following:

a. having an innate sense of yourself that is not dependent on what you think other people think,
b. the ability and confidence to find out or ask what you need to know to do your job or task well,
c. the ability to listen to comments and criticism and pursue them positively until a way is found to resolve the situation with integrity and without emotional attachment to the outcome,
d. and finally, to take care of your own needs. In doing so, you are far better able to maintain your energy and sense of self-worth and you will be free to share and to give others what they may need at the time.

Very few people have personal power imbued as a gift from birth. We grow up with an infinite variety of perceptions, belief systems, and misconceptions about ourselves and others. As we grow and mix with others socially and at work, these patterns and attitudes manifest themselves and can easily throw us into turmoil because we are not centered. We are at odds with the working atmosphere and ourselves, and stress is the inevitable result.

The business community has begun to recognize employee stress and to make strides to help. Counselors, massage therapists, other personal therapies, even gyms are being added to the working environment. However these are cosmetic unless that environment is pleasant, energizing, and supportive—even fun.

Over the past thirty-five years I have had the privilege of working with executives, managers, and sales staff in large and small businesses, charities, university students and faculty, and those in the performing arts. In my capacity as a consultant I have noted a number of patterns that present themselves in the professional arena:

1. **We make hard work of work.**

There is a perception that "one must behave differently at work." We leave a comfortable home environment where we speak and interact easily and naturally, where we are natural hosts and hostesses dealing with others sensitively and with an awareness of what is happening around us. However, in a situation that we think is professional or work related we resort to a behavior based on perceptions about business, inadequate role models, some from academic, military, or dictatorial home environments, and lack of training in basic communication skills. We fall into the trap of playing a role rather than being ourselves and then try to create something artificial to match our perceptions of how we "should" be. This results in staff and professionals who are tired, stressed, and lacking in self-esteem and confidence because there is no inner power. It has been given away to those people perceived to be strong, superior to, or to be in control of their lives in some way.

When perceptions are distorted, it is easy to lose the ability to be ourselves and stand up for our own values. We become mentally and emotionally occupied with our own perceptions of what we think others are thinking of us and lose clarity of focus. Situations are replayed in the mind while we shrink into the nearest chair or the woodwork to go over what we would like to have said and done. Personal power has been given away and the groundwork for an atmosphere of distrust and secret grievances has been laid.

2. **Basic communication and rapport skills can be taught and have been neglected.**

While companies are beginning to train management levels in this area—very little is being done about it at staff levels. Few staff are given adequate communication skills training at induction. It is either assumed that those skills are in place already or that they are reserved for management development programs. Companies including such training at induction provide adequate communication tools with which to interact effectively and thereby enable their staff to interact with the public at an advantage.

3. **Being "me" is an important starting point for good communication skills.**

In my work with people in business, I have found that when people leave home, they perceive the need to play a role, or be something "other." It is very difficult to put a group of people playing roles together and, at the same time, create an effective and efficient work force. Our perceptions are often skewed. How we look and act, and how we *think* we look and act, are very different.

4. **The words "mentor"—or facilitator, perhaps—are more appropriate than manager.**

I've often said to managers: "If you want to know how you behave, look at those under you because they will behave like you." "They want your job and see your example as one to follow." Those people, in any walk of life, who are nurtured as human beings thrive and are helped to gain in confidence and self-esteem. Managers who nurture create future executives who will do the same.

5. **Staff are asked to change without being given any specific tools with which to implement the change.**

During periodic assessments staff hear such general comments as: "Your teamwork needs improving," "You need to be better at communication." I believe that each person does her best with the personal tools she has at any given time. Until we know what needs to be altered and specifically *how* to do it, it is virtually impossible to implement the change. A person with reasonable self-esteem will have the presence of mind to ask questions or do some detective work to produce specific ways of sorting out the problem.

Questions that elicit useful responses are best. For example: "Tell me, what area of my teamwork is a problem?"; "in regard to my communication—is it my words, my attitudes, my expression, etc., that need attention?" Having the presence of mind to ask questions when seeming criticism is being thrown your way creates difficulties for vulnerable staff. Many people are too mortified to ask and are left to their own devices to sort out the problem.

6. **When you want to reach someone quickly show him or her a relevant picture.**

Most of the books written for the business community are full of words, are very serious, and tend to have few or no pictures or cartoons. Studies have shown that the majority of the population store their information in mental pictures. The old adage: "A picture is worth a thousand words" is still true.

7. **Presentations tend to be based on models of school essays or theses which are meant to be read—not spoken.**

This is interesting because more than 75 percent of communication is considered to be nonverbal. As we move into the twenty-first century, professional men and women need specific and practical tools for communication skills and personal development. These tools can be made more accessible by being presented in a light, readable, user-friendly manner with pertinent illustrations.

Objectives:

1. To offer guidelines for developing a positive personal presence that contribute to a healthy, vibrant person and ultimately a positive climate in which to work.
2. To treat communication and presentation skills as basic to presence and confidence and therefore firmly placed at the heart of personal growth rather than peripheral to it.
3. To offer appropriate tools and language for individuals to find a way to strengthen or regain their personal power and confidence in a variety of situations.

SECTION 1: COMMUNICATION

Learning to communicate effectively is a lifelong process. Often it is a combination of trial and error and learning the hard way. This process contributes—sometimes positively and at other times negatively—to perceptions of ourselves, and others. Patterns and habits of communication develop from childhood and are carried well into adulthood and old age. These habits are so subconscious that much of the time we have no realistic idea of how we are perceived by others.

People communicate in the best way they know and do not realize when and how they are failing to convey their intended message. When it is understood that the message is not clear, it is not a matter of blaming the past or making excuses; rather, it involves the maturity to recognize and change the elements of your communication that are not serving you well for those that are more effective. It is a matter of saying or thinking: "No matter what has happened in the past, do I want this pattern or behavior now"? "It is my choice to behave, react, respond differently and now I choose to do it another way." "Past is past; I cannot go on behaving the way I have in the past and expect anything other than the responses I evoked in the past." There is a saying: "When you think the way you have always thought, you will act the way you have always acted and you will get what you have always got."

COMMUNICATION DEFINED

The word, communication, in itself tells a story. It is derived from the Latin word *communis* meaning common. Some other words derived from this root are community, communion, and communitarian. We communicate by creating common ground with those to whom we speak. When that is established a sense of community is begun and then followed by something greater than the whole; a spirit of community, which by some might be termed a kind of communion. The result of community spirit is the fostering and nurturing of people who cooperate, form effective teams, become friends, and can be called communitarians.

Developing a sense of community is important in the day-to-day running of a business. This is difficult when business executives today are in so many meetings that there is barely time for deskwork. These sessions consist of everything from one-to-one discussions to committee meetings. It might be said that a typical executive day consists of wall-to-wall people, talking, brainstorming, organizing, and facilitating. Those with good communication skills and an understanding of the importance of the business community soon develop a rapport with their colleagues. This fosters and creates a pleasant atmosphere where support and a sense of ease and cooperation are predominant. The result is good team building and focus on the projects and aims of the day rather than personal issues that arise because there is a perceived lack of support or dialogue. There are several common scenarios that are prevalent:

The first, "ideal" scenario is a give-give situation where each person is dedicated to fulfilling his role as defined by the project. Each team member is fully focused on giving his or her best to the goals of the project. Here the attention and language used is project-oriented and based on fulfilling what is needed to accomplish it. In this situation there are likely to be dialogues like the following:

A. "I am feeling pushed and would like some help with this report."
B. "What's the biggest problem? Do you need secretarial help or another mind/brain to help you think through it?"
A. "I would like an additional mind on this."
B. "OK, I will ask Sue if she would be willing to help and get back to you today."

Rather than a commonly encountered situation like the one below:

B. "Why isn't that report in yet? Are you sure you are up to this job?"
A. "I'm sorry, if Joe had got his work in on time, I might have finished it by now."

Note that the first conversation is open and honest rather than using excuses or blame. However in the second conversation there are two negative factors at play. Firstly, the question is accusative and finger-pointing. It is difficult not to be threatened by this approach. No matter what the reason, the report is not done. It is important to acknowledge that fact. Then the conversation is directed toward the report and not anyone's shortcomings. Secondly, apportioning blame does nothing toward getting the report done. How can the project go ahead if A is busy putting blame on someone else? When the focus of the conversation is related to the project itself, you are better able to avoid personal issues and less likely to create the need for excuses. Every time someone feels the need to make excuses, his or her confidence levels sink a little.

The second scenario is the "energy drainer." Practically everyone can tell you about knowing someone who, when in their presence, seems to makes them feel tired. These people are unknowingly draining the energy that you are unwittingly giving away.

Often these "drainers" are the poor-me types—the ones that seem to need constant bolstering. Working with such people can be time consuming. However, it is important for the project or job that they pull their own weight and feel valued as team members. Ideally, you will find some area of the project where they feel they can contribute what they do best with confidence. When this is not the case, you may have to consider placing this person in another area. It is useful to have an armory of questions such as: "Where, in this project/job, do you feel you most comfortable in using your skills?" "Would you like help writing the report?" "Could I ask you to be in charge of . . . ?" (This does not have to be a major job—just a small responsibility.) Finally if the person is unable take any responsibility for themselves, you have a problem and you will have to give them an assignment. If they do not like it, they have only themselves to blame. You have done your best.

The third scenario—the "unwelcome giver"—is very familiar in business today. This involves the "giver" who does not ask, but rather sees another's needs and orders change or presents an "unwanted gift." Anyone who has ever taught or been a boss will recognize this. It is difficult not to help when you perceive another person's need or when you are particularly enthusiastic about something. However, when that person has not asked for what you are offering or there has been no prior consultation, they may be offended by being given it. It may make them feel inadequate. When the ground for the offering is not carefully prepared the following perceptions may be encountered:

Giver: "I give him everything and he is never grateful." "He has had so many chances to make changes and has not taken any of them."

Receiver: "My boss never understands me." "She asks me to go on courses at the most inconvenient times." "I do not know why I need to learn more about . . . " "No one has said I was lacking in that area."

Rather than issuing what is perceived to be an order, spend time piquing the employee's interest and helping her to see and appreciate her own needs. Ideally, the "gift" is then presented after it has been requested. By approaching others' perceived needs carefully with sensitivity and understanding you gain their trust and are better able to have open and honest discussions with them.

Asking appropriate questions allows others to tell you what they want and need and is vitally important for an effective and efficient working team. This enables everyone to take responsibility for themselves. Such sensitivity to another human being is critical to developing a good working relationship and contributes greatly to that person's sense of confidence and self-esteem. It is too easy to think that the quickest way forward is to issue an order—yes, in conditions of war this may be important. However, in the professional environment, dedication and loyalty come from a different set of techniques and values.

BALANCED COMMUNICATION—BODY, VOICE, WORDS

If you have ever wondered how other people misinterpret your message—here is the answer. Your message is out of balance. When your body, voice, and words do not agree completely, it causes doubt in the mind of the listener. No matter how well intended your words, when your voice, unintentional habits—or even clothes are not in balance with the message, your words are going to be lacking conviction.

Research has shown that the impression you make on others is composed of three areas: (1) that which is visible, your face and eyes, gestures, physical habits, clothes, and so on; (2) your voice—the quality, tone, pitch, rhythm, and speed; and (3) the actual words.[1] This study also found that words are only 7 percent of the communication, voice is 38 percent, and the visual aspects are 55 percent. Obviously, these figures relate to person-to-person communication. Imagine the importance of the voice when talking on the phone.

The study found that words are only 7 percent of the communication, voice is 38 percent and the visual aspects are 55 percent. Obviously these figures relate to person-to-person communication. Imagine the additional importance of the voice when talking on the phone.

When my clients are first confronted with the statistics relating to this, they moan and offer many different reasons why the statistics are really different—until they see themselves on video. Then the realization sinks in. Their perceptions and the reality are different. They then work in a much more efficient way to convey their messages. What seemed to them to be over the top was more effective and their old pattern was then judged by themselves to be lacking in conviction.

While it is easy to become caught up in these figures, the important concept here is *balance*. This does not mean that you need to cut out 93 percent of your words (some might), but rather, what you say has to look and sound like the words you are using. For example, to say you do not want to do something with a smile on your face, sends a double message and creates a question in the mind of the listener—no matter how much you think you mean the words. The rationale for the smile might be something like "I did not want to offend him." This is a problem of faulty perception and creates doubts in the mind of the listener.

Another example seen in presentations relates to using the hands. Too often a presenter has been told to keep her hands quiet and stop waving them about. However, most of us use our hands quite naturally and expressively in casual, comfortable situations—when we do not think we are giving a presentation. In presentations people tend to develop a twitch or a movement pattern that replaces the natural use of their hands. In other words, they will twitch at the moment they would normally have used their hands for expressive purposes—or at times when they want to emphasize a word. These movements rarely have anything to do with the meaning of the words and interfere with the clarity of the message. This issue will be discussed in detail in a later section.

A final example relates to voice quality. It is not uncommon to hear someone asking others to be calm or confident with a voice that is full of tension and is of poor quality. Something does not fit. That person has no idea that his voice sounds harsh or is offensive. How the voice is heard inside our heads and how it sounds to the listener is very different. Anyone who hears his voice on tape for the first time will attest to that. Tensions and erroneous perceptions of the quality in the voice again unintentionally confuse the message.

Interestingly, most people spend about 98 percent of their time conscientiously working on the words—not realizing the importance of preparing voice and body. Add a few nerves to that lack of complete preparation and you have a lost message. You can never assume that it is the responsibility of the listener to get your message. It is your job to make it as easy as possible for anyone hearing you. The more difficult it is for your audience, the more of the message is lost.

It is easy to assume that the burden of responsibility is on the listener to absorb everything. This is largely because our learning styles have been dictated by schooling that insists on our taking in copious amounts of material—often presented badly.

Business and social situations are not the same as our days in school. People do not need to have to work hard to listen and get the message. When we speak, we must command attention by the clarity of our visual signals, voice, emotional honesty, and text of our messages. It is the responsibility of each of us to help people listen by giving out such congruent signals. Balancing the message means we have to be self-aware, sensitive to the response of others, willing to change faulty perceptions of ourselves and others, and able to listen without an ongoing internal conversation.

THE TWO MOST IMPORTANT CONCEPTS IN PERSONAL COMMUNICATION

I Want to Be Here

The most important aspect of any communication lies in one critically important attitude. It is simply this: *I want to be here!* The implication of this statement is enormous. It means being fully present with mind and body fully attentive to what is going on. When you want to be here you consider what you are doing at the moment to be the most important thing there is.

Think about it: there is no other place you can be except where you are at this minute. Wishing and hoping that you were somewhere else simply takes your mind and attention away from the present moment. There are whole committee meetings where most of the members are mentally on holiday. Virtually nothing is accomplished and another meeting is called to finish the work. Functioning in the present is the only way to accomplish the task at hand—and it is certainly the only way for you to be heard by another person.

Being completely "here" is the first step to speaking, to listening, and to developing a recognizable sense of presence.

Acknowledging Others

When you want to be where you are, you will also want to be aware of those around you. The second most important concept in communication is acknowledging other people. I have never met a person who did not need acknowledgment. We all need it. It is part of human validation and the nourishment process.

CASE STUDY

While teaching a customer service course in a large company, I found that the young, shy staff did not like asking "Can I help you?" My response was to give them a list of ways to acknowledge customers differently. Speaking or a greeting of some sort is the most obvious way to recognize someone. However, for those who are shy or those who have been taught not to speak to strangers, this can be difficult. There are a number of alternatives: smile, think the positive greeting you might have spoken, or make a friendly gesture or nod of the head that will let them know they have been seen. I have seen customers and other staff seemingly ignored by someone talking on the phone. Even when you are busy, the other person needs to know that you realize they are there. Many staff are unknowingly rude to customers when they do not acknowledge their presence because they are not ready to wait on them.

No one likes being ignored or feeling like they have been overlooked. The easiest way to acknowledge another person is to see them and let them know they have been seen.

Another area of acknowledgment that is neglected or not understood is how we honor the people around us in a professional or social context. People must be honored for what they do best and for their preferences, not for what we think they should be doing or thinking. Too often it is easy to dismiss what someone else desires because we ourselves do not think it is necessary. How are we to know that?

CASE STUDY

James, a young executive, felt his boss was asking him to do something he thought was unnecessary. His boss wanted a listed summary of his activities. James did not think it was necessary because he saw no need for it. He felt his boss was just being overly exacting. When I asked James what his boss's strengths were, he listed an ability with detail as one of them. Yet that ability was being partly denied him by James. I asked James if he had the information his boss wanted. He said yes, it was on his computer. I then asked if his secretary had access to that information. Again the answer was yes. The next question was: "Do you feel comfortable asking her to compile these details for a once a week meeting with your boss?" The answer was yes.

Once James understood that he was continually denying one of the strengths of his boss, he realized why his relationship with him was poor. We need to find a way to bypass our own opinions and judgments so that we are able to acknowledge the strengths of other people. Unless we can do that, they will feel uncomfortable and unappreciated for what they do well. This form of acknowledgment is vital for any kind of relationship.

SUMMARY

Your appreciation for your friends and colleagues will show in your recognition and acknowledgment of them. When you determine to want to be where you are at all times, you will begin to enjoy everything and everyone in your space. It then becomes easy to establish the common ground necessary for good communication.

SECTION 2: THE SELF-CRITIC, SABOTEUR OF CHANGE

THE EVOLUTION OF THE SELF-CRITIC

Your own criticism is the great saboteur of change. The biggest obstacle to personal growth, communication, and certainly presentation of all kinds, is the self-critic. It is like an alien that takes us over, determines the words we use, the actions we take, and contributes to a general state of fear or panic.

We come by it naturally. Many methods of education use criticism as a tool for teaching. All of us have grown up with this method, as have the generations before us. The result is generations of people who have an internal radio that constantly tells them how bad they are at what they do, destroys self-respect and confidence, and creates critics who do the same to everyone else.

The origins of the self-critic stem from a common set of vocabulary used since time immemorial and ingrained in us from parents, teachers, and friends. (This is not about blame; it is about a long tradition. None of these people deliberately set about to cause the problem. It was the only way they knew.) There are three pairs of these words. They are:

Right—Wrong
Should—Ought
Control—Hold

Think about it. When someone tells you that you have to get something "right," your first reaction is to become tense or to worry. When we think we have to get something right, we are put at a disadvantage immediately and begin to doubt our own ability to do it.

Even in role-plays, telling someone that they have done something wrong causes them to go pale. Kinesiology tests and studies in psychoneuro-immunology (PNI) suggest that using these words causes a temporary depletion of the immune system.

Once we have been told we have to get it right or that we have got it wrong our defense mechanisms begin to respond by creating excuses or internalizing the criticism. Those who have leveled the criticism begin to tell us what we should or ought to have done. Our minds do the same. Now we have a double-barreled situation where the rights and wrongs and the shoulds and oughts are competing for our thinking time. When the words should and ought are used, a person can feel talked at or preached to.

Once we have been chastised because something was not right and told what we should have done, we begin to think of ways to control the situation. That is where the defensiveness, denials, and blame begin. We want to hold on and control what is happening and what is being said. Soon this internal dialogue of criticism, judgment, and blame begins to take over situations in which we are concerned or deem important. In doing so we stifle spontaneity, creativity, and intuition—the very things we need most. While most people admire these qualities in others, they are reticent to let go of control long enough to find out what being spontaneous, creative, and intuitive are like. It seems too risky. Sometimes we have to lose control to gain freedom.

This is particularly true in presentations, interviews, competitive sport, and performance. Sportsmen and women will attest to the times when their bodies were shut out because of too much mental discussion. This made them stiff and unable to respond to the situation. When this inner conversation with the self-critic is present, you exhibit a stilted, monotonous voice, a rigid body, and eyes that are not seeing. In other words the person speaking or performing is not present—only the self-critic.

I had a long talk with my self-critic and we made two agreements. The first one is: my self-critic may not talk to me while I am talking or writing. We can confer afterward when necessary. The second, and more difficult is: my self-critic may not give its opinion unless I ask for it. Sometimes I have to mentally put it in a box outside the door so it will stop interfering.

Of course there are times when it is appropriate to analyze what we are doing. Then the self-critic can be invited to help. Any analysis while something is in progress stops the process dead or slows it to a stuttering crawl. Creativity and change need a mind that is free of vocabulary such as right/wrong, should/ought, and control/hold. This vocabulary is what the rampant self-critic uses to become stagnant.

EXERCISES

1. Go through any recent material you have written and change the words right/wrong, should/ought, and control/hold to less dictatorial and finger-pointing vocabulary. An example: "We have got to get this contract right." Change to: "It is important to do quality work on this contract."

2. Test yourself by going a whole day without using the above words in conversation. What happens? What other words and phrases can you use instead?

SECTION 3: CREATING A POSITIVE PRESENCE—AN OVERVIEW

Presence is obtainable. It is a matter of knowing what it is and working at it. Often presence is confused with the term charisma. A person with charisma has achieved a special way of being that seems to permeate both him or herself and the room. Some people are born with it and for others it is the end product of dedicated inner personal and spiritual work. Presence has to do with a sense of space and how to use it. Anyone with a desire to change and a little imagination can achieve presence.

CASE STUDY

In my seminars I ask the question: "How much space are you occupying at this moment?" The majority reply with something like: "just around my chair," "a direct line to you," or "as far as the person sitting next to me." I then ask the group to ascertain the amount of space I am occupying. Without hesitation, the response is: the whole room. The next question is: "How do you know?" Answers I get to this question include: something about your posture, you are standing and we are sitting, you are in charge of this seminar, and so on. They know when someone is commanding space, yet cannot quite discern the specific reasons why.

DEVELOPING PERSONAL SPACE

Why do you take notice when some people enter a room? How is it that you know when friends are happy or sad without speaking to them? How do you know which days not to disturb the boss? These are things we sense or feel—often without knowing the reason intellectually.

Your personal space is your energy field—a portable "home," if you wish—and is comprised of many facets. If those around us can discern it, it must be more than just imagination. A person's presence and that individual's use of personal space has a number of visible and invisible factors which contribute to the whole picture.

The obvious indicators of a person's presence are posture, energy and health, the eyes, the voice, and levels of awareness and sensitivity. The seemingly invisible factors such as attitudes, thoughts, and imagination contribute equally. In the end, the whole is greater than the sum of its parts. However, by looking at the parts we can begin to analyze presence and then create ways of gaining it.

YOUR POSTURE—IS IT STATIC OR DYNAMIC?

Physical alignment and posture contribute enormously to presence and are crucial to commanding space. Balanced alignment and good posture help us to look energetic and healthy and contribute to voice quality and the kind of image we convey.

Postural bad habits begin early. However they are correctable as long as you are willing to cope with feeling strange for a week or two. (As you know, change always creates a feeling of not being in our habitual comfort zone.) It is important to remember that the body is full of atoms that vibrate. Therefore posture is dynamic, not static. Unfortunately, the word itself tends to be perceived as something rigid or fixed. It would be preferable for you to think of yourself being as flexible, mobile, and physically responsive as a cat. When we think of ourselves as having such a dynamic flexibility it brings energy and flow to body, voice, and image. Those with this kind of energy have sparkling, alive eyes, look healthy and vibrant, and appear to be a person you would like to know better.

YOUR EYES—DO THEY LOOK OR REALLY SEE?

Nothing is more attractive than a person with shining, sparkling, fully present eyes. Such eyes are an indication of the expansiveness of your space and interest in "being here." Eyes with a light in them show life, energy, awareness, and a reflection of a physically, mentally, and spiritually healthy person. Your eyes hold the key to a large amount of information about you. They have served as a basis for diagnosis of physical and mental problems by different therapies and systems of medicine for centuries. Sayings like "the eyes are the mirror of the soul" permeate the literature. Many love affairs have begun because of being drawn to someone's eyes and many poems have been written to this effect.

It is easy to ascertain the presence of a person by the eyes. When you have eyes that are seeing, you are fully present in the moment ready to listen or respond. Eyes that reflect thinking, feeling, or inner listening are not seeing but appear to be defocused or roaming inwardly. This can happen when we are thinking about something, looking for an answer, or preoccupied with our own internal dialogues and feelings. For example: watch a speaker who is self-conscious. No doubt the eyes are not really present in the room and neither is the message because it has been forgotten. It is obvious that the speaker is thinking of themselves rather than what is being discussed. When you are "self-centered," you prevent yourself from being fully present and it is most apparent in your eyes.

The most widely used—and abused—term related to using the eyes is: eye contact. Rarely is this concept defined adequately. Most of us have been left to our own devices when figuring out how to do it. Too often eye contact becomes "eyeball" gazing and it is extremely uncomfortable for all parties.

Many presenters have been taught to choose one member of an audience to whom to direct their message. This kind of attention creates a number of problems—especially for the poor person picked to be *the* one. The "one" chosen has to remain glued to the speaker—he or she cannot escape this constant gaze. Secondly, the rest of the audience is then neglected, and nine times out of ten they feel left out of the talk or conversation. The presenter who uses such a technique limits the scope of his or her presence considerably.

How you see people is extremely important to the way you are perceived by them and is an indication of the way you are managing your personal space. When you use 180 degree or a wide peripheral vision to see another person, they know they have been seen and you have given them a very powerful form of acknowledgment. No one likes to feel ignored. Having tunnel vision when around people, whether it is simply a bad habit or deliberate, can be interpreted as being cold, aloof, and uncaring toward your fellow human beings. Everyone needs acknowledgment and the simple gesture of seeing them is the easiest way to show it.

Seeing and looking are two different things. Looking tends to be a bit tunnel visioned. Seeing involves the use of our peripheral vision—the vision that we use when we do not want to miss anything that is happening. Classroom teachers use this all the time. They want to know what children all over the whole room are doing. They have been accused of having eyes in the back of their heads. You need that same vision and awareness in order to know how your audience is responding, whether they are asleep or need a change of pace or energy. This kind of visual awareness is important and keeps you present.

Peripheral vision involves using a broad scope of seeing and involves using 180 degree vision. Most of us are physically capable of achieving nearly 180 degrees of vision. You can test this for yourself by extending your arms to the front with your hands touching. While looking straight ahead, move your arms slowly apart keeping them at shoulder level. Note the point where you can no longer see both hands. It is probably close to 180 degrees. Without moving your head you can see the ceiling, the floor, everything within the 180 degrees in detail. You are seeing in the context of the whole.

When you look at another person this way, you see that person and most of the adjacent surroundings at the same time. This is very different to intently glaring into their eyes and being unaware of what else may be in your space. Instead you are visually aware of the whole scene and your eyes portray a softer, less aggressive look, as if the eyes are placed further back in the skull.

Those who glare tend to look as if their eyeballs are bulging. Such a gaze is intimidating and uncomfortable.

AWARENESS

Once you begin to see with a wider vision, your sensitivity is heightened. You are alert to your audience, yourself, and your environment and well on your way to 360-degree awareness. This heightened awareness increases your sensitivity to those around you, sounds, colors, smells, and the quality of the air. You are alert and kept in the present by the millions of antennae around your body that constantly feed you information.

POTENT INVISIBLE ASPECTS

Sometimes it is the invisible rather than the visible attributes of a person that define them more precisely. The obvious aspects of presence have been introduced above. However what is sensed and felt about a person contribute equally to personal space and presence. You may think that these factors are difficult to define, change, or improve. However it is precisely these areas that we redefine continually as we pursue inner growth and development. These include such things as thought patterns, attitudes, belief systems, our sense of imagination, play, and our ability to change our inner processes to adapt to current situations. Such factors are critical to personal survival today.

THOUGHTS

Learning to live with overly active internal conversations is not easy. However such overactivity puts invisible busy signs on us and inhibits our presence. Your thought patterns are more visible than you think (just ask someone who knows you well). There are many meditation and mind-control courses and systems that devote themselves full time to teaching people to practice a modicum of control over their thought processes.

An inner stillness is requisite to making clear, informed decisions about every part of your life. Thoughts are much like the chatter of a very active internal radio. When we are occupied completely in our own minds, it is virtually impossible to be observant or listen. Being fully present demands a mind that has space to see, listen, and observe. Needed answers can be found with a quiet mind.

The person who has mainly positive thoughts is much easier to be around than someone who is occupied with ongoing internal critical conversation. The positive person fills his or her space with a pleasant atmosphere. Most of us like to be around such people. On the other hand, when you have an overabundance of negative thoughts, you give out a prickly atmosphere and quickly send people away or make them wonder why they came to see you in the first place.

ATTITUDES

Thought patterns that are reinforced over a long period of time become the attitudes and belief systems with which we lead our lives. We grow up with attitudes derived from the positive and negative experience gained from family, cultural and educational environments, and the "school of hard knocks." Being objective is easy to talk about, difficult to achieve. We all carry a full suitcase of attitudes and preconceived ideas of how we need to function in a variety of situations.

Having a positive attitude is not only an asset, it expands your presence. For anyone to have a comfortable space for themselves and others, a positive attitude is essential. Those who do not have this and insist on being continual pessimists drag down the energy of everyone around them. Having a positive attitude does not mean that nothing negative ever happens. It simply means that you have the energy and ability to deal with negativity or unpleasantness in a mature, responsible manner.

"I Want to Be Here" is an example of a positive attitude. By living this statement you create an atmosphere that encourages openness, sharing, honest discourse—and most of all an expanded and compelling energy field. On a subconscious level, others are generally aware of your attitude. It affects them and the rest of the environment. Think of it this way—if you put a drop of red paint into a whole bucket of white paint, it will still come out pink. It is the same with thoughts—they can turn the atmosphere blue!

IMAGINATION

Preconceived ideas about work often cause us to ignore our most creative and imaginative thoughts. The most neglected gift we have is that of our imagination. It is the aspect we tend to deem unimportant at work and leave at home with the children. Whatever happened to the statement: "All work and no play makes Johnny a dull boy"? Ask yourself why work, by definition, can be considered dull or boring? We spend most of the hours of our adult lives doing what we call work. What miserable human beings we can be without using our imaginative and creative resources in our professions—no matter how serious the responsibility. Who said that we could not mix work and pleasure? If you have perceived these two things to be incompatible, ask yourself why and do at least one imaginative thing immediately. Imagination stimulates creativity, curiosity, and a sense of play. Those who can enjoy this aspect of themselves are more likely to be able to laugh with others and at themselves, are happy in their jobs, and succeed in achieving desired goals with ease.

VISUALIZATION

Imagination taken one step further becomes visualization. It is an extremely potent tool. Visualization is your ability to picture yourself in or project yourself into a situation. It is a way of creating your space, programming positive thoughts, creating confidence in a variety of situations, and in general, programming your mind and body to achieve what you want.

Many top sports personalities speak of this kind of training as being critical to their performance. Just as they see themselves winning, having stamina, and doing well, you can do the same in your personal and professional life. It is a good way to prepare for important presentations, meetings, interviews, and public performance. Musicians are learning to use this to enable them to be more confident and to use their nervous energy in a positive way while performing.

Visualization is your way of creating an environment where you are able to do your best. It has nothing to do with having power or the advantage over another person. For example: in an interview situation, you desire to do your best—and you also wish to explore the situation and get to know the other people. In the final analysis, you may not want the position. However, you need the presence of mind to discover whether this is the place for you. By visualizing yourself being at ease and asking appropriate questions you will create that possibility in your mind and it is likely to happen. In some ways it is similar to programming your computer. When you are busy visualizing yourself being nervous, inept, and hoping to do well, you are setting yourself up for a possible negative outcome. You want to create an atmosphere in which you have options as to how you behave and react rather than becoming caught up in old patterns that are unhelpful.

GENETIC AND CULTURAL FACTORS

In the best of all worlds, we retain the positive aspects of what we inherit genetically and culturally. These can include a disposition toward longevity and good health, a good physical structure, a pleasant voice, or such things as regional and family speech patterns. They are all to be honored and savored as part of your unique inheritance.

THE UNIQUE SELF

You may give this part of yourself many names—persona, soul, and so forth. I describe this part as your core—the spirit that lives in you that no one else has. It is the very thing that makes you human.

SUMMARY—THE EXPANDED HUMAN

Your space is an energy field that can be expanded and contracted at will. You are in charge of it. You can choose to want to be where you are, stand tall, acknowledge those around you, see rather than look, think positive thoughts about someone, use your imagination, and visualize yourself being able to do these things. It is possible to do this at anytime and anywhere. When you are brave enough to do these things as part of daily life, the atmosphere in which you work changes—becoming more congenial, comfortable, and less stressed. Negotiations and difficult decisions are treated differently with the focus directed toward the task at hand rather than personal issues.

It took a long time for me to realize the term "human being" was not one word and that the second word was a verb. "Being" creates a comfortable home that can expand at will to accommodate a variety of physical, mental, and emotional states. Think of this home as one that is portable and expandable and it goes everywhere with you. It is much like your house. However, it is your personal space that can include what and whomever you choose.

Our behavior changes when we feel at home. For example: when friends or strangers have been invited into your home you become the gracious host or hostess, you are aware of the needs of your guests, or if there is anyone who looks as if your attention is required, you introduce people who do not know anyone, know who needs a refill of food or drink, what is happening in other parts of the house—a child that needs attending or something happening in the kitchen. In other words, you have optimum awareness and are on top of the situation in every way and are at your natural best. You are comfortable and in command of your space.

An understanding of your personal space, the ingredients, and tools for making it work for you will give you the ability to create a comfortable home for yourself and those around you. Fear, worry, and faulty perception cause this portable home to shrink and atrophy. What follows are some ways of becoming aware of these tools and of developing a positive and meaningful presence.

OBSERVATIONS AND EXERCISES

Most of the exercises in this book are designed with busy people in mind. They can be done in three minutes! Having read this section, begin to observe yourself and those around you more carefully. Notice the following:

- Your own physical awareness of expansiveness.
- Are there others around you who seem to have presence?
- What are their qualities?
- At what times and in what situations are you most at home?
- At what times are you most comfortable? Why?
- What happens to the body when someone is happy, sad, at ease, uncomfortable?
- Do people shrink noticeably when around senior executives or others who are perceived to be very important?
- How many people in your working environment see others around them?
- What are the general awareness levels around you?
- Are you aware of the times when you are fully present? For example, when you walk through the office is your internal dialogue such that you barely notice those in your path—or at the sides?

EXERCISES

1. *180-degree vision*

   (a) Extend your arms straight out in front of you, palms touching.
   (b) While keeping your eyes straight ahead slowly open your arms out to the side. Notice where your peripheral vision stops. Note how much you can see without moving your eyes.
   (c) While looking straight ahead, describe the detail you see in front, on the sides, upward, and downward.
   (d) Practice this (without the arms) while walking somewhere in the office, down the street, and so on.

2. *Awareness*

   You can do this when you first arrive at work:
   (a) Sit quietly with both feet flat on the floor.
   (b) Spend three minutes making a list of the following:
       Sounds you hear, temperature, air flow in the room, smells, colors, the feel of your desk, the general mood, the location of other people, are they seated or moving about.
   (c) Become aware of the area outside the room. What things do you sense from that direction?

SECTION 4: VISIBILITY AND IMAGE: THE PHYSICAL AND MENTAL YOU

The physical characteristics of a confident person include a balanced, easy posture, seeing eyes, and a pleasant, freely produced voice. As stated earlier, 55 percent of personal communication is that which is visible while a person is talking. In this section posture and alignment, which form a large part of the visible aspects, will be discussed in relation to health, image, and voice.

A NOTE ABOUT CONFIDENCE

The characteristics above are the outward manifestations of confidence. All of these things are changeable and you do not need confidence to make the changes. You need only good guidance and teaching and the willingness to improve yourself.

Confidence is an end product. You do not have to wait for the confidence to do something. Confidence is gained as part of the process of doing it. The discussion that follows includes tools for developing confidence. Sometimes it takes courage to use those tools and to live with a change of habits. Do not confuse courage with confidence. Most of us have courage even when we think we do not have confidence.

PHYSICAL ALIGNMENT AND ITS RELATIONSHIP TO HEALTH, ENERGY, IMAGE, AND VOICE

Like many of us, you have no doubt been told to stand up straight, get your shoulders back, and not to slump—in many instances to no avail. Such directions seem strange and rigid and do not fit with our self-concepts. Furthermore, it is virtually impossible to correct posture on the basis of verbal instructions. Physical alignment and posture relate to our kinesthetic awareness of our position in time and space. We have to *feel* changes in alignment. Verbal directions for posture are simply not as helpful. People will do their best to follow such directions. However, since few of us know the feeling of straight it is an exercise in futility.

CASE STUDY

In my seminars, after we have discussed good posture, I ask the group to tell a volunteer how to stand. The result is a very strange-looking person. We all have a good laugh and then there is no problem understanding the physical and sensory nature of where we are in time and space.

Anytime we begin to change our habits it causes havoc with the internal message systems for a short time. This is why how we feel and how we look are not the same. For example, if you have tendency to lean to your right and someone comes along and straightens you, you will feel as if you are leaning to the left. However, on looking in the mirror, you will see that you are straight. For this reason, when making any physical alterations in posture or stance, it is wise to use a mirror. You will not be convinced until you see it for yourself. The most useful tool is the video camera because you will see yourself more objectively.

GOOD POSTURE DEFINED

Researchers are agreed generally on the basic elements of a physical alignment that is efficient, uses gravity to an advantage and causes the least stress on the body in standing, sitting, and moving. When you are properly aligned, a plumb line can be dropped beside you that will fall through the center of the ear, the point of the shoulder, the highest point of your hip, just behind the knee cap, and just in front of the ankle. Your weight is balanced evenly between the heels and balls of the feet. When sitting, the only difference is that the knees are bent. The line from the head to the hips remains the same.

When any of these points deviate from the line, the body will have to work hard against gravity to keep you balanced. For example: when someone habitually pushes the head forward, the bottom will move out to balance it. The people who pull their chins inward usually protrude the chest or belly to equalize the balance. Such imbalances cause your muscles to have to do an immense amount of extra work which puts an excess strain on the whole postural system. Over time, these imbalances become bad habits which you think feel comfortable and you label them "natural." Your physical computer (brain) is now programmed to automatically use the bad habit of choice. Now when you begin to change these, you feel "unnatural." It is easy to confuse the word natural with the word habitual in such circumstances. However it hinders our progress when we think that changing a bad habit is "unnatural."

The quickest way to change your posture is to be physically shown (ways to seek help with physical alignment and movement include the Alexander Technique, Feldenkrais, Pilates, yoga, and good dance classes). This involves someone else moving your body until the alignment is correct and balanced. Because this new alignment is different to your old habit, it will feel strange—just like any change. Remember, you will need to see yourself to be convinced that you do not look as weird as you feel.

Your body is comprised of a dynamic, vibrating mass of atoms. Therefore posture is also dynamic rather than a static, held position. By giving each of these atoms space to vibrate, we become "expanded humans." This enables you to be well balanced with gravitational forces, increases the space between joints, allows flexibility and ease of movement and muscle action, and eases breathing. Being static or fixed leads to rigidity and stiffness, creates discomfort and pain, and makes you look uneasy.

Physical rigidity creates potential health problems, slows spontaneity, and makes thinking difficult. When working on your posture, make sure you get up, move around, and shake your arms and shoulders. It is easy to try to hold on to any new position or feeling. Basically we have to recreate it all the time. Staying loose is important and is not to be confused with the concept that many people have regarding being casual. Balanced alignment will allow you to look and feel lighter and taller and to move easily.

"CASUAL" AND "RELAXED" DEFINED

The first reaction of many people who have had their posture corrected is to think they now look formal rather than relaxed. Muscles do only two things: they contract to shorten and move a joint or they relax or let go. When muscles relax, your joints move further apart creating more space and allowing expansion of your body. In other words, relaxing is the opposite to what many people think. The casual and relaxed posture that most people exhibit in reality is more like a collapsed heap. In my seminars, we often have to redefine the word relaxed, as used by most people, to collapsed—certainly where posture is concerned. If you could see an X-ray of your skeleton during your "relaxed" posture, you would see vertebrae that were pushed onto each other creating a lot of pressure on the vertebral disc and the joint itself. Over time with such pressure, the discs begin to erode or collapse and infringe on the spinal nerves. This degeneration leads to all kinds of pain.

HEALTH AND ENERGY

Physical alignment is linked inexorably to good health. We deny this with excuses such as "that is just the way I am" or "it is natural for me." We forget the years of habits that have contributed to our current way of behaving. The folly of this response only sinks in when the body demands to be heard in the form of discomfort and pain.

When you are in a good, balanced alignment there is space between joints for mobility, the vertebrae are balanced on each other, there is room in the chest to breathe more easily, and the internal organs are easily mobile and not cramped. Any other way of being is going to create problems given enough time. The most common problems have to do with the back.

Back pain is the most common cause of days missed from work. While we can blame the chairs, long hours of sitting, we are still responsible and have a choice in the way we sit. It can seem like too much effort at first. However after sitting properly for even a week, you will begin to notice that it becomes uncomfortable to sit poorly. Your body has begun to let you know.

When your chair is too high, sit forward and put your feet flat on the floor or a footrest. There is no rule that says you have to use the backs of chairs. Your back is capable of supporting itself; it does not need to lean on a chair. When you remain dynamic, your body will cope without a backrest. However, if you try to hold yourself up or fix a particular position, you will become stiff and your muscles will complain. A good chair will help but will not solve the problem necessarily. Ultimately it is up to you to sit properly lest your back take the strain. Going to a good osteopath or chiropractor can help sort you out. However, they are no substitute for the work you do on yourself.

Any joint that is not balanced will begin to show wear and tear. For example, people who have the habit of sitting with their feet twisted or the weight on the outside of the ankle will, over a period of time, begin to stretch the outside ligaments that stabilize the joint. The foot will begin to remember that pattern and on a microscopic level will begin to exhibit an uneven walking pattern. One day, that person will sprain her ankle because of a buildup of poor habits—not really an accident. When I ask for a show of hands as to who in my seminars has ankle problems, the ones sitting with the outsides of their feet on the floor raise their hands.

The same is true of any joint. The habits we have eventually distort the true natural alignment and we begin to have so-called accidents. Those people who cross their legs when sitting are pulling the pelvis out of line each time they do that. If they cross one leg the majority of the time, the pelvis and spine will be pulled in that direction. This causes the pelvis on one side to come forward and twists the spine in that direction. The muscles of the back adjust and over time there will be a scoliosis of the spine (a lateral S-shaped curve in the vertebral column), one hip will be higher and one leg slightly shorter. Now the walking pattern will change and again the body will have to work incredibly hard to keep its balance. Inattention to balance may work when we are teenagers, however, as we get older, the body will take its revenge. It is never too late to correct the problem but takes more effort after the habit is ingrained. However, you *can* teach an old dog new tricks when the old dog is willing to learn and the rewards are great enough.

Another area affected greatly by alignment is our breathing patterns. Breathing is a reflex action that occurs approximately 24,400 times a day. The efficiency of this act can be hindered enormously by the state of your posture. Our oxygen supply is very important to good health and having free unrestricted breathing. Because breath is vital to life, the body will take it in any way it can. It is our duty to make it easier by standing properly.

Adequate oxygenation of the blood is dependent on the efficiency of our breathing and contributes to our sense of well-being and energy. When you are in a sunken state of collapse, the chest is pulled down toward the abdomen and the contents of both areas are compacted. This makes it impossible for the diaphragm to do its work, the lungs do not have adequate space and breathing becomes shallower and shallower, gradually restricting the oxygen supply.

IMAGE

People with an air of ease about them have a radiant energy and look special. While image includes clothes and other factors, they become less significant when confronted with a radiant person. This is an image built from your physical, mental, and emotional ease. However, this radiance can be obscured by doing something that is outlandish or out of keeping with you as a person or the occasion. For example if you wear jeans to a black tie affair, you will be out of balance and out of keeping with the occasion. Your actions may be interpreted to mean that you do not respect your hosts or the situation. While you may stand tall, say brilliant things, and be a most interesting person, you will not be remembered for what you said or how interesting you were—only for your inappropriate dress. On the other hand, the best clothes in the world will not look good on a slumping body. Posture and physical alignment are vital to your impact.

It takes only minor physical changes to create an impression you do not intend. One of the most common postural faults is that of shortening the back of the neck and throwing the head back thereby causing the chin to lift upward. This creates a number of physical problems. First with the chin up in the air, you must look down your nose in order to see. This in turn causes the eye muscles that pull the eyes into that position to become stronger. When this fault is corrected by bringing the head into alignment, people sometimes feel like they are looking at the floor. They have to be made aware that eye movements are separate from the head and can be readjusted with the new head position.

This position of chin in the air is interpreted by others to mean "stuck up," haughty, proud, snooty. Most people exhibiting this postural pattern say to me: "People think I am being conceited when I'm not." As soon as the head is aligned, they are no longer accused of being that way.

BODY LANGUAGE

One of the most discussed areas associated with image is that of perceived body language. Looking at body language from a cultural perspective is fascinating. Using it as a tool for judgment and analysis creates a number of communication difficulties. How nice it would be if everyone saw and described the physical nature of a person without needing to add an interpretation. Such interpretation invites unnecessary judgment and hinders the process of communication.

When you are busy analyzing someone's body language, you are somewhere in your head and not fully present. You cannot listen to another person and analyze at the same time. They will not feel comfortable talking with you. Being there for another person means no judgment. How are we to know whether the twitch in the left shoulder is a nerve problem, an injury, or a strange habit? When we are occupied with trying to remember whether that twitch means the person is a thief, liar, or if this is a closed person because the arms are folded in front, we will never find out much about him or her. Accepting people as they are is primary to good communication skills.

A NOTE ABOUT HAIR

An audience will get many clues about you from your face and expressions. Therefore it is very important that your face, and especially your eyes, be seen. While you may feel comfortable with your hair hanging around or in your face, your audience may not. Hairstyles need to be planned carefully for any public appearance.

CASE STUDY

I was once speaking on a panel with a woman who was meticulous about her presentation and information. However she had given no thought to her looks, particularly her hair which was very long. She had pulled it behind her ear on her left side and allowed the right side to dangle and cover part of her face. She had a tendency to lean forward when talking to the audience so those on her right never saw her face because the long hair completely covered that side. Sadly, one half of her audience never saw any part of her face and missed some vital visual elements of her communication.

It is best to keep your hair well away from your eyes and eyebrows. Even pop singers who have hair falling in their faces block an important part of the visual aspects of their communication. For women there are a number of styles that prevent them being seen adequately. One current style is to have a long fringe or bangs that extend to the eyebrows. Again it is impossible to see part of the facial expression. All we see is a hairline that takes attention away from the eyes. It is important also to be aware of the effect of eyeglass frames. Image consultants often ask people to change frames so that more of the face is seen and that there are not too many distracting extras about the face.

Men with beards and certain types of moustaches can have problems as well. Hair that covers the lips or forms unusual shapes can look exaggerated from a platform or at a distance. Beards are best trimmed to the shape of the face. The outline of your lips must be clearly seen. Otherwise, from a distance the mouth looks like a piece of moving fur with teeth and can be quite distracting and comical for an audience. The moustache that curves downward gives the impression that the person never smiles. From a distance it looks like a magnified frown—no matter how much you smile.

VOICE

A good resonant voice is directly related to your alignment. Like any instrument, the voice must be put together properly. By maintaining a good alignment, its power source, vibrating mechanism, and resonator will be connected and able to function efficiently. No one would wish to play a bent cello or clarinet; however, many people walk around with bent voices and expect them to sound good. Talking on the phone particularly seems to bring out our worst postural habits. No wonder so many messages are garbled. The better you sit and stand, the clearer your voice. Section 5 is devoted to the further understanding of your voice and how to use it effectively. Therefore, suffice it to say that your voice cannot reach its potential without first correcting your alignment.

GUIDELINES FOR CHECKING AND CORRECTING POSTURE

- Posture is dynamic. The body is made of vibrating atoms. We are never meant to hold a position.
- Check alignment according to a dropped "plumb line." Ideally this line hangs from the top of the head, through the center of the ear, the point of the shoulder, the highest point of the hip bone, just behind the knee cap and barely in front of the ankle.
- Make sure the feet are placed firmly on the floor with a sense that every part of the foot is touching the floor. Feel as if you have Velcro on the soles of your feet.
- Balance your weight evenly between the heel and ball of the foot. You can test this by rising on your toes. If you have to shift your weight forward before rising, the weight is too far back.
- Even the smallest changes in weight distribution and spinal alignment will feel strange at first. Some muscles will be relaxing and others will be taking on new responsibilities. They may feel strange and even ache. It is very important to remember the dynamic nature of the body and allow yourself to move rather than remain stuck or try to hold a position.
- Posture is related directly to physical balance, energy, health, image, and voice. Changing your alignment affects every one of these areas.

EXERCISES

Wherever possible do these exercises in front of a mirror or use your video camera. Remember, change feels strange and different. For a while, use how you look as a guide rather than how you feel. There is a tendency to stiffen the knees when you are standing taller. Make sure they are very slightly bent because when you brace your knees, your bottom tends to protrude. Think of your joints as having very thick grease between each one—so thick that they cannot freeze into position but have to stay balanced and poised in relation to one another.

1. *Standing taller*

While facing a mirror, place the palm of your hand just above the crown (toward the back) of your head. Stretch the crown up to touch your hand. You will feel quite tall when you do this correctly. The back of your neck will be stretched and feel long. If you mistakenly place your hand at the very top and center of your head and stretch, your chin will rise. This is not what you want. Just placing a hand over the crown will remind most people to stand taller. You can do this at any time when you are standing or sitting. As a reminder to stand tall, place Post-it notes on your mirrors, your desk, especially by your phone, on top of presentation notes, or anywhere that your eyes will fall during the course of your day. This way you will not have to think of what you need to do, the reminders will do it for you. A week of doing this will begin to program your postural muscles to perform a different set of habits.

2. *Finding your balance*

You are centered when your weight is evenly balanced between the balls of your feet and your heels. Many people have their weight much too far back. You can test this by rising on your toes. If you first have to rock forward before you can rise, your weight is too far back. This would be very obvious if you were able to look at yourself sideways. To alter your balance, first plant your feet firmly as if you had Velcro on the bottom of your shoes. Become aware of the sensitivity of your feet and allow the whole foot to feel the floor (even with shoes on). Gently rock forward from the ankle joint until the weight is evenly distributed between the balls of your feet and your heels. Any adjustment other than at the ankles will alter your spine and cause you to lose your stretch.

3. *Giving every atom space*

Think of each of your atoms as needing its own private space. Allow your body to expand and stretch in all directions to accommodate this vision. As you walk from place to place feel you are getting taller with each step. Imagine that at the end of the day you will be taller than you were in the morning. Aim to be ten feet tall and six feet wide by the end of the day.

4. *Feeling of stretch for breathing*

Lie on the floor on your back, hands by your sides. Slowly stretch your fingers as far away from your shoulders as possible without allowing your arms to leave the floor. Now breathe in while mentally counting to eight, slide your arms along the floor until they are overhead. Breathe out to an eight count and slide your arms back to the starting position. This exercise will help you keep your chest expanded and encourage movement of your abdomen during breathing.

SECTION 5: IMPROVE YOUR VOICE

Even the most beautiful of people can be betrayed by an unpleasant or unsuitable voice. This was particularly evident when movies changed from silent to sound. Suddenly the most ravishing men and women became laughingstocks because no attention had been paid to their voices. The vocal 38 percent of communication took on massive importance.

The voice is one of the most deeply personal aspects of communication. Physically it lives inside of us and seems untouchable. Because the voice comes from the inside, we are fooled into thinking that we have no control of it. The sound is affected by emotions and tensions, mental and physical. For this reason the voice is considered to be the most difficult aspect of ourselves to change. This misconception is due mainly to faulty perceptions about our own sound and ignorance about how the voice works. Once you understand, you can choose whether you wish to make any changes or not. Change in this case means creating more variety in pitch, expression, tone, color, rhythm—all the things you do easily when you are comfortable, feeling at home, and not being self-conscious.

HOW THE VOICE WORKS: AN OVERVIEW

Your voice is like any other musical instrument in that it has a power supply (breath), a vibrator (the larynx), and a resonator (the throat or pharynx). The housing for this instrument is your body. Therefore the alignment of your body is the first step to connecting the parts of your instrument. The efficiency, quality, and depth of your sound depend on this connection. Sound is made by air moving up through the larynx causing the vocal cords (most accurately described as folds) to vibrate. These vibrations are then magnified and modified in the spaces of the throat, mouth, and nose, in the case of nasalized sounds. Actions of the lips, tongue, palate, and jaw provide the vowels and consonants of speech. Any distortion in the movement of these structures will have a direct effect on the quality of the voice.

Power Source

There is no sound without air to carry it. Your voice needs a steady, supported stream of air to function at its best. The more efficient your breathing patterns, the more effective will be your voice—and health. During a normal day we breathe approximately 24,400 times. Breath is responsible for maintaining the acid-base balance in the body and regulated by a subconscious body reflex system.

Air is crucial to life so the body will use any means necessary to breathe. However, basic to good voice use is an efficient system of air intake and release. Efficient, easy breathing is dependent upon physical alignment, lack of tension in the neck, throat, and mouth and the actual physical patterns we use to allow air in and out.

Most people become concerned about how they take air in. I suggest that you concern yourself with how you expel air first. This will allow the inhalation to become a reflex action and the support mechanism to function naturally. When we cry, cough, wail, groan, or sob or use what are sometimes referred to as primal sounds, the muscles of the abdomen and back of the waist engage. You can feel this when you put one hand on the lowest part of your abdomen (well below your belt) and one hand on your waistband toward the back and use any of the above sounds. You can also feel this abdominal pressure when you use the sounds *pshhhhh* forcefully or rolled r's—as if you are revving up an engine. At the end of this expulsion of air and sound, the abdomen will release to allow more air to enter. All this is done without any interference from the throat, lips, and tongue.

As you make these sounds you are using a strong abdominal muscle action to support the sound. Ideally this is what you will do in speaking as well. This action does not have to be forceful or punched; the abdominal muscles need to be engaged. This will give you a sense of being connected to your whole body and prevent you from substituting tensions in the chest or head and neck area. The ensuing sounds will have substance and there will be minimal wear and tear on your throat and larynx.

THE VIBRATOR OR SOUND SOURCE

Your larynx or structure of which your Adam's apple is a part, houses the vocal folds. The vocal folds are like two shelves made up of muscles, a small piece of cartilage and other elastic membranes and ligaments. They are located in the larynx, which sits at the top of the windpipe (trachea). These folds first act as a protector of your lungs by keeping out foreign matter, and secondly as your source of vocal sound.

You have probably had some experience with the protective aspect. Normally when you swallow, the vocal folds close tightly to prevent food from entering the lungs. However, if you have ever tried to talk and eat at the same time, you may have had the unpleasant experience of something going "down the wrong way." The resulting gagging is the protection action of the vocal folds at work. They are so sensitive that it takes something smaller than three microns in diameter to get through them.

When you wish to make sound, air comes from the lungs through the vocal folds. They close— or move closer together—and begin to vibrate. You can get an idea of how this works by blowing up a balloon and then stretching the mouth of it. The squeal that follows is distantly related to the way the vocal folds make sound.

The regulation of pitch and the heaviness or lightness of voice involve the action of the vocal folds. The pitch will rise when the folds are elongated and the voice becomes heavy when they are thickened.

Any tension in the neck around the larynx will inhibit the vibratory pattern of the folds. You may recognize this as some of the strangled sounds you and others produce when you are afraid. You know the situation—high chest breathing, neck tension, larynx high under your jaw—self-strangulation. Untrained speakers and singers often try to do it this way. It is important to maintain the emphasis in the abdominal area so that the chest and laryngeal areas can function easily and naturally with no effort.

The coordination of breath and vocal fold closure is important for the onset of the sound. When there is inadequate closure the sound is breathy. Usually this is caused by a combination of poor posture, faulty breathing, and a lack of energy. If the vocal folds are tightly closed, as in holding your breath, the beginning of the sound can become harsh and strident. This is caused by pressurized air held below the folds being emitted forcibly as you begin a word. Many people speak as if they are trying to hold on or save their air. This may come from old ideas of not having enough air or attempting to control the breath from the chest or neck. Such habits are abusive and over time can cause the voice to become hoarse or create more serious vocal disturbances.

THE RESONATOR

Aesthetically, the most important area of the voice is resonance. The quality of the voice is unique with every individual and is difficult to quantify. Your voice quality is determined by the shape of the throat (pharynx), general vocal and whole body coordination, and imagination. Very few people reach their potential and optimum quality when using their voices.

Anatomically, the resonating area of the voice is extremely complex. It is a soft, muscular, sleeve-like structure which is capable of assuming an infinite variety of shapes and formations. There are intimate connections with the jaw, tongue, lips, and larynx. Any distortion of movement in these areas strongly affects the movement and shapes of the vocal tract and resonating chambers. The muscular actions that give us our individual qualities come from the habits and patterns we develop, family background, and local and regional environments. Each of us will have slightly different and unique patterns.

Not only do various muscular patterns alter the quality of sound but the emotions play a very large role as well. You probably have noticed when a friend is feeling well or unwell just by the sound of the voice. Emotions can cause subconscious changes in the way you make sound and alter the quality.

Because the pharynx is a dual pathway for food and air, we sometimes speak by constricting these muscles as we do during swallowing. For food to move into the esophagus, muscles at the back of the throat have to contract to squeeze it downward. This constricts the throat and raises the larynx—the opposite of what we need for good voice. A number of people unwittingly speak in the swallowing position and produce tense, garbled sounds. For optimum voice quality and depth of sound, the throat/pharynx must be wide and released with a continuous free flow of air.

ARTICULATION

The formation of words is done by the actions of the articulators—the lips, tongue, teeth, and hard and soft palate, and the jaw. These structures help shape the resonator in such a way as to create the vowels and consonants needed for words. The vowels are shaped in the throat and mouth by various positions of the tongue, soft palate, and lips. Consonants are formed by the action of the tongue, palate, lips, teeth, and minimally the jaw.

Relaxed tongue and lips work far more efficiently and produce clear speech. Some people speak comfortably and easily on a one-to-one basis, however to ensure clarity when in front of a group, they exaggerate their articulation by distorting the movement of the lips and tongue. This is unnecessary and often is unsightly, abnormal looking, and affects the quality of the sound.

Efficient articulation for speech will involve minimal movement of the jaw. Ideally, it will be suspended, flexible, and free to respond to the need of the moment. Any undue tightness such as clenching of the teeth, jamming the jaw downward, or protrusion will affect the shape of the pharynx and soft palate, the movements of the tongue, and indirectly the larynx.

The speech patterns we develop derive from our parents, friends, local and national cultural practices initially, with additional patterns adopted for reasons of psychological and physical balance. These become a set of predominant muscular habits which shape the way vowels and consonants are made by each individual. This is sometimes called "accent" or regional dialect. There is nothing wrong with an accent as long as it is clear and free. When efficient habits of speech are balanced with good physical alignment, the articulation becomes easier and clearer. What appear to be heavy regional accents become understandable and much less distorted. Sometimes this is all that is needed to understand a previously garbled voice.

PHYSICAL HABITS THAT INTERFERE WITH VOICE AND MESSAGE

Voice quality, your message, and its underlying meaning are linked to facial expression and the physical habits you exhibit both consciously and unconsciously. What follows is a rogues' gallery of common habits that can lead to questions, doubts, or misinterpretation on the part of your audience.

1. Furrowed brows or wrinkled foreheads

Many people who are very serious tend to show this with excess tension around and above the eyes. Presenters with these habits can sound very intense when saying something very light or casual. When they do this the face and voice become hard and contradict the intended message.

2. Tense lips

This habit tends to make the speaker sound terse and have a rather reedy, white sound. The sound usually lacks warmth. Saying "I love you" with tense lips can look and sound funny.

3. Constant or fixed smile

This has the opposite effect of number one above. Someone with a fixed smile will never convince the other person of being serious or can be taken for a person who is not being truthful. Church choir sopranos have been known to look like this. The resulting voice quality is shallow and lacking in resonance.

4. The deadpan face

Someone who perceives control to be maintaining an expressionless face will find that everything else about him will be dull as well. It is very difficult to get anything other than a monotone voice from a person with this habit.

5. The tense tongue

It is common for speakers trying to make a bigger sound to create tension in the throat and especially in the tongue. The resulting sound can be guttural or garbled and the articulation muddy.

6. The anatomical neck

People who are exceedingly tense and use a lot of pressure to speak will often display clear outlines of the muscles and structure of the neck. This can be seen in many rock and pop singers. Sound under this kind of pressure is unpleasant to hear.

7. The "determined" jaw

A strong, overly firm or held jaw distorts voice quality immensely. It will give a person a look and sound of defiance.

In my seminars I have a crazy exercise in which I ask people to choose one sentence or phrase to be used throughout. They and their partners say this sentence using each of the habits outlined above. They are asked to make a note of how each example sounds and looks and their gut reactions to each habit demonstrated by their partners. There is always a great deal of laughter because some of the sentences seem so ridiculous done that way. However, there is also a general recognition that they all know someone who looks and sounds exactly like the exercises.

Stand in front of a mirror and try this for yourself. If nothing else you will have a good laugh. Record this session and you will find many changes in voice quality as your expression is altered. If you have any of these mannerisms or habits, speak or read in front of a mirror so you can change what you are doing. When you want to stop a habit, you can.

Your voice will work best when you are connected by an aligned, balanced body that powers and supports the voice with use of the muscles of the abdomen and back of the waist. This connection encourages the air to flow freely through vocal folds that are unimpeded by neck or chest tension. Absence of tension in the neck and jaw create a throat that is flexible and responsive. The shape of the throat and resonating areas will respond to the emotion, imagination, and intention of the speaker (or singer) and the articulation of words will be audible and clear.

The physically free and efficient functioning of the voice sets up the possibility for a beautiful, natural sound that is a true representation of you. Your connection to this sound enables you to let your imagination, intuition, and creativity trigger spontaneous interaction with the messages you are conveying. You are then ready to fill your personal space with sound—as if your voice is coming from every pore in your body (360-degree sound). There is no need to think of pointing or projecting your voice. Simply fill your space, which can be expanded to include as many people as you like.

CASE STUDY

A woman in a very senior position consulted me because she was told she could not be heard at meetings. This lady was powerful in her role and in her person. I was shocked learn that her voice was letting her down. During a consultation in her office I was seated directly across from her. There was nothing obviously wrong with her voice or her posture and her speech was clear. As we talked, I noticed that she seemed very withheld. So I asked her what would happen if I leaned forward into her space. Without hesitation she said she would move away from me immediately. I then asked her how far she felt her personal space extended. Her space was defined as being about one to two feet in front of her. She believed she needed to protect herself and felt extremely vulnerable in extending her space further. After some discussion and experimentation, she began to think of her space as much larger. When she did, her voice began to fill it. She realized that she had been talking to her own protective wall. As the wall fell away her voice began to fill the space. She no longer has a problem being heard at meetings.

BEING EXPRESSIVE

Words and language developed as a way of describing pictures and feelings. Words have an inherent meaning and expressive people convey it when they speak. Too often presenters go through the words without any consideration of the voice or expression—as if the information and words themselves were enough. Your voice reflects the extent of your energy, feelings, enthusiasm, and imagination. The energy comes from both the physical connection of your voice and your passion for your topic. The feelings from your perceptions, background, and sensitivity regarding the subject and your imagination will furnish the color and sparkle—or the twinkle in your eyes.

This is another area where our perception of what we are doing and the actual sound that is being produced is extremely misleading. In order to become better, many people have to go over the top by a huge amount just to look and sound normal or plausible. My clients only believe this when they have seen it for themselves on the video playback. Were they not to have this facility, 99 percent of them would simply not believe what was being told them by anyone. When they see it for themselves, there is instantaneous recognition of the need to change and self-permission to do more than they thought was ever needed.

Going over the top means taking what seems like a huge risk. This is one of those areas where courage is necessary. It is easier to do when the task involves something whimsical or imaginative. I use children's stories in my seminars. Often we get so involved that we are dissatisfied when there is not enough time to finish each story.

CHILDREN'S STORIES

Anytime you think you are exaggerating, it is best to use a video for feedback. Otherwise you will never go far enough because you will be convinced in your own mind that you have done it already. Here is a way to work on your expressiveness. Choose material such as a children's story or fable to read aloud. This exercise demands spontaneity. The more you think about it, the more difficult it is. Allow yourself to become completely involved in the story. If you feel embarrassed to do this exercise, close the door and ham it up in front of your mirror. Give yourself permission to be a fool or a clown momentarily. Read this three times—each time a little differently. Record yourself on video or tape recorder.

This exercise builds in the very things needed most in our conversation and presentation. By acting out the story or the company report, you develop a spontaneous rhythm and sensibility to the words, the pace is appropriate, pauses come naturally rather than being contrived, the pitch and color of the voice respond to your imagination and mental pictures. It stops the measured monosyllabic approach to what are perceived as formal presentations.

My clients have found this exercise to be of great benefit in changing their perceptions about their presentations. What they thought was over the top looked like a normal expressive human being to them. What they perceived to be expressive was dull, bland, and—basically—boring.

EXERCISES

1. Read two or three minutes of the text in the way you might read to children.

2. Read another two or three minutes of text making sure that you have given each of the characters an appropriate voice, that is, a bear or lion voice, or a little girl or boy voice, and so on. When no characters have dialogue, choose important or colorful words to emphasize.

3. The third time, read and act out the text at the same time. Pretend half of your audience is deaf and you must show them the story. This means that if the text reads "they walked down a very long road," you will demonstrate this with your hand at the same time by "walking" with your fingers down a long road. You will probably feel more like a ham actor. However, persist, because it is important. While you are busy carrying out this ridiculous exercise, your voice is gaining in color, giving each word its true meaning, and your pace fits the text rather than having the same pitch and rhythm throughout.

4. Now find several paragraphs of a company report, news article, advertisement, a business letter you have written or received, and read this in the same way as you did the final version of the children's story. Be careful because this is where your preconceptions of how you "ought" to be in a business setting will get in the way. Believe it or not, the words can be just as colorful. It is possible to demonstrate words like dichotomy, bottom line, procedure, large undertaking. Make sure that named people are shown to be in different places so that they will sound like different people. John Smith and Joe Martin are different and need to sound like it. People and grocery lists can sound the same when there is no vision of what the words mean in the mind of the speaker.

CASE STUDY

Sometimes when a client comes to me for voice work, I find that it is not really the voice itself that needs correcting but some other area that is affecting the voice. Rob came to me because he was interviewing for an important executive job and wanted to stand the best chance of getting it. When I asked him what he thought would hold him back, he shared the information that others felt he lacked "gravitas." His voice tended to be a bit high pitched and did not sound fully connected with his body so he was robbed of some of his resonance. I noticed as he sat he was constantly moving his feet and that they were never on the floor. I asked him to place both feet on the floor and keep them still. Suddenly his voice was deeper, he sounded far more serious and he began to sound like an executive. Just keeping the feet on the floor quieted his body enough for his voice to connect. We worked on other areas of his presentation but the voice was by far the most dramatic change. He got the job.

SUMMARY: WORKING WITH YOUR VOICE

You can improve almost any voice by balancing the physical alignment of the body. It is particularly important to make sure the head is positioned over the shoulders rather than poked forward or tilting backward. When a person is connected physically and well-grounded with feet firmly on the floor, the voice is much more resonant and pleasant.

Power and efficient use of breath come from supporting the sound from the lower abdominal area. We do this naturally when we laugh, cough, cry, or moan. Using any of these sounds can help you get a feel for what "support" means. Any physical tensions around the shoulder and neck will disengage the abdominal support and constrict the area around the larynx and throat.

It is best to treat the inhalation as a reflex of the exhalation. Breathe out using a *psst* or hiss until you are completely out of air. The reflex intake of air will usually be correct and cause the lower abdominal area to expand. At the onset of sound this area is then contracted to provide support.

Airflow is essential for quality of sound. "Saving" air creates tension at the level of the larynx and inhibits the sound.

Optimal voice quality comes from good alignment and free neck and throat areas. Any tensions around the neck, mouth, and jaw will cause a change in voice quality and a more strangled sound. Physical habits that indicate tension include: furrowed brows, glaring eyes, a deadpan face, tight lips, an exaggerated smile, any deviation of the jaw from a central position, a held jaw or clenched teeth, an overly opened mouth, raised shoulders, and clavicular breathing.

Color in the voice comes from free, uninhibited imagination while speaking (or singing) and presenting. This is enabled by the ability to picture everything that is being said. Every word has onomatopoetic qualities and we tend to forget this in business. Use of hands to help make the picture will often free the voice and allow much more expression.

Use of singing or singsong can help voices that are hesitant or brittle. A continuous sound has a kind of resonant hum that is always present. Singing a text will help the airflow as well as continuity of sound and phrasing.

EXERCISES TO IMPROVE VOICE AND EXPRESSION

1. *Breathing and support*

   a. To get a feeling for breathing without shoulder movement or chest tension do the following: Sit on a chair or stool, feet flat on the floor, and let your body fold over so that your chest is resting fully on your thighs, your arms and head hanging down loosely. Take in a big breath. Without chest and shoulder involvement on the in breath you will feel the action of your abdomen expanding against your thighs and your back expanding behind. This is the area that needs to be active when you are standing.

   b. While standing (or sitting in a chair) do the following: First check your alignment and make sure that your head is over your shoulders. Then stretch your arms over your head, without raising your shoulders, clasp your fingers and turn your palms toward the sky. While maintaining this stretch, using a hissing sound or the *pshhhhh*, let air out until you feel you have released your last drop. The reflex in-breath is likely to be felt and seen in the expansion of the abdominal wall and lower back ribs.

   c. Visualize an open pipe extending from your mouth to a place just above your pubic bone. Think of your breath as traveling both to and from that area without restriction anywhere in the pipeline.

   d. Place Post-it notes at your desk, on your telephone, in your car to remind you to breathe from the lower ribs in the back.

   e. When sitting, support your voice by feeling your tummy button moving toward the back of your chair as you speak.

2. *Releasing tension and freeing the neck*

When we become stressed, one of the first places to show it is the voice. There is a tendency for the breath to be high and for the throat to become a "bottle neck." The voice can become strident and harsh—not what we want when doing our best to communicate well. Release any tendency to hold in the neck area by gently and slowly moving your head from side to side while breathing and speaking (as if maintaining a continual "no-no" motion of your head). Make sure you do not stop the movement to take in air or to begin a sentence. Think of your head as being poised on top of a heavily greased joint. Most people tend to stop this motion to speak or breathe and cause momentary blockage of the speech mechanism. Watch yourself in a mirror to make sure you are not doing this. Either read or talk aloud to do this exercise. Use more air than you think you need. Your vocal folds will not vibrate easily without adequate air. Read a passage from a book or newspaper with an extremely breathy voice. Remember, what it sounds like in your head is not the same as it does to others.

3. *Increasing depth and resonance*

When you have done the previous exercises and gained more vocal freedom, you will find that already your voice is showing increased depth and resonance. The more centered you are, the more quality you will have in your sound. Imagine your voice as being at one with all the millions of atoms that vibrate in your body. This will give you and your voice a sense of depth without effort and will also fill the space around you.

4. *Articulation*

Efficient and flexible use of your tongue, lips and jaw are the keys to clear articulation. Again, if you have paid attention to the previous exercises, your articulation will be better without additional effort. Any exaggerated movements of the structures above will distort your diction. Commonly, when someone is asked to speak more clearly and distinctly, the response is to begin to exaggerate movements of the lips and jaw. This creates a comical look and strange sounds. A released jaw, no exaggerated movement, and flexible tongue and lips are the key to efficient articulation. Any book on diction will give you exercises for every vowel and consonant. This is not the purpose of this book. However, be aware of several potential problem areas:

   a. Look in a mirror to see that your tongue tip is in the front of your mouth when you pronounce s, z, and r. When the tongue deviates to one side, the diction is distorted and may sound like a speech impediment.
   b. Check to see that the consonants made by the lips—like f, v, b, and m—are made directly in front as well. It is a common habit in some cultures to distort these sounds.

5. *Expression*

Practice going over the top with everything you say—in private, of course. This kind of practice will plant seeds that you will use in your communication and presentations. Your natural reticence will stop you from going too far. So rest assured that you will use about 10 percent of what you have practiced. Gradually as you become braver you will get a feel for a good balance.

SECTION 6: LISTENING AND RAPPORT

LISTENING

When in doubt, listen. It is one of the best ways to establish rapport. Being a good listener takes patience and is a skill rarely taught. In the haste to "get to the bottom line," or to appear that we know it already (or to be perceived as precocious), we rush in with comments and questions, hardly waiting for the end of the sentence, much less the thought. When we are mentally impatient, we interrupt without hearing the other person finish his "paragraph." Our busy minds are like radios, chattering away, analyzing, comparing, and hearing very little. By remaining mentally quiet, silent, and listening long enough, most of our questions will be answered.

Leave the internal analysis and questions for later. Listening with an open, accepting mind creates an atmosphere of trust in which discussions and issues can be pursued in a rational and logical manner. Communicators who know how to do this create a situation in which others can be themselves.

The analogy of the computer is useful here. When listening, think of yourself as a blank computer screen. You have information and knowledge stored on your hard disc—the brain. To put new information in your computer you need a clean screen. There is no need to edit or analyze or judge the information as you write it down. This can be done later after you have had time to decide what is appropriate to store.

Trust your mind and knowledge. It is not going to go away for the short time you are listening to someone else. To attempt to listen at the same time as internally repeating or memorizing your question or statement is another form of internal sabotage. It is a great temptation to hold on to our own knowledge while at the same time trying to understand the information we are receiving.

Neither of you will communicate unless one of you hears the other person fully. It is important to accept that the other person is speaking his or her truth at that moment. Whether you agree or disagree is not the issue. By remaining quiet inside, you will be able to sort out the issue in a rational manner. This will allow the speaker the freedom to change his mind or alter his stance without losing face. You are then in a better position to respond from the vantage points of knowledge, logic, experience, and wisdom.

A good way to ensure that you are listening is to offer a brief literal summary of what you have heard rather than making assumptions which have to do with your perceptions, not necessarily the other person's statements. By summarizing you can check the accuracy of your understanding. At the same time this gives the other person a chance to hear what they have said fed back to them and allows the possibility of changing anything that is not accurate. If instead, you make an assumption, it can create the need for the other person to justify what they have said before they have finished a line of thought. Rather than using language such as, "I assume you mean/or want to do . . .," say "Tell me what you mean by that," "Will you tell me more about . . .," or "What would you like to do about it?"

Rather than directing conversations to yourself by saying I assume/presume, focus on getting information from the other person. Ask open questions like: "What excites you most about this project?" "What proved to be the most difficult problem in reaching this goal?" or "Tell me what you need from me." Such open questions can be followed by asking for more detailed and specific information.

These kinds of open question are useful in social situations as well. For example, when you know someone likes cars, ask, "If you could have any car you wanted, what would it be?" "What in particular do you like about that car?" You could substitute many different words for car— dress, kitchen, dog, house. Find out what interests others and help them enjoy it. Soon enough they will ask you about yourself.

In summary, the characteristics of skilled listeners are as follows:

- They are fully present and "want to be here."
- They listen with a quiet mind and body. (Remember that the words listen and silent are anagrams.)
- Judgment and analysis are momentarily suspended.
- The momentary truth of the other person is fully accepted.
- They summarize what they have heard and ask appropriate questions.
- They understand that their personal presence is their home and act as good hosts and hostesses.

ESTABLISHING RAPPORT

Wanting to be there, listening and genuine interest in the other person are ways to instant rapport. When we are fully there we will respond easily and comfortably to those around us. When you feel comfortable talking with someone, probably the rapport is established without your being conscious of it. However, it is helpful to have some fallback mechanisms when we feel ill at ease. "When in Rome, do as the Romans do" is worth remembering. Learning the nonverbal tools for building rapport can be extremely helpful in cultures other than your own. The tools of rapport have been developed over a number of years from the research and study of the characteristics of good communicators. This is true particularly in situations where we are self-conscious—such as meeting someone for the first time, dealing with awkward situations, needing to talk with other members of staff who hold different positions, or any other time when we may not be feeling well and are nervous for some reason.

People who are communicating easily tend to look (have the same body positions) and sound alike. They exhibit similar energies. This is true whether they are happy, sad, excited, or angry. You can observe this for yourself by becoming a people-watcher. Children are particularly interesting to watch. Those engaged in the same activity will look like a school of fish all moving in the same direction, then changing and all moving in another direction, looking like clones. Partners dining together will have the same physical pose and the movements of their bodies will move toward and away from each other in rhythm. Look around at a committee meeting. All those truly involved will look alike, either all sitting back or all sitting forward. When there is one who is completely different, you might question whether that person is "there." In fact, it would offer you an opportunity to ask that person what he thinks. That way, he would be pulled back into the group and its activities.

CASE STUDY

I once had a group of skeptics who did not believe this when we were discussing it in a seminar. However that evening at a birthday dinner I looked up to see that there were two people at either end of the table quietly talking to those close by. At each end of the table were groups that looked exactly alike: the same posture, positions of the arms and legs, etc. I asked them to freeze and then look. They were astounded.

Creating rapport is about momentarily putting yourself in the other person's shoes. It is easy to draw attention to yourself without thinking. For example, if your best friend comes in excited because she has just won the lottery, she will likely have an animated face, voice and body, high breathing, and an energetic, high-pitched voice. The ideal response to that is for you to say "that's wonderful" and react with the same energy in body, voice, and feeling. The worst response would be to fold your arms in disgust and say, "I never win anything." First share her joy. If you need to be disgusted, do it at home later.

CASE STUDY

In one seminar I had a woman who told me that when she saw herself looking like the person to whom she was speaking, she immediately changed. She deliberately created a mismatch of energies. According to other staff, she was unpopular and difficult to engage in team activity. No wonder! All her life, her perception was that she was supposed to be different. She had no idea that her lack of rapport was making communication difficult for her and those around her.

When rapport is discussed with those on my seminars, their first response is to think that learning about it constitutes a form of manipulation. It is not a manipulative tool—simply a way to become more observant and relate better when you are uncomfortable. Imitating someone by copying all their gestures and movements is not a responsible way to establish rapport. If you speak to someone who is copying and mimicking all of your movements and gestures, you have permission to do something outlandish. If they still copy you, find someone else with whom to talk. Rapport is established when you momentarily put yourself in that person's shoes. It is about matching energy.

Do not confuse energy with emotion. You can take on a similar energy without becoming involved in the emotion. You do not have to become angry when the other person is irate. You can match the tone, pitch, and energy of their voice and posture and use your words and logic. For example, when someone comes in angry and hot under the collar, the worst scenario is the one in which you go into ultra slow, measured mode and ask them to calm down. This is a mismatch. You are far better off using their energy, rate of speech, and pitch to say something like: "Let's sit down and talk about it." When you have an excitable person talking to a slow and deliberate person, one of them is going to become impatient or annoyed. Take the responsibility to match the other person. It will not be long before they begin to warm to your pace.

There are many ways to create "common ground" or rapport—some obvious and others very subtle. Because it is natural to be in rapport, people generally do not go around looking to see who is in rapport with them. Therefore you do not need to worry about using these techniques. You can choose to match posture, breathing patterns, voice, physical rhythms—but not the same way (that is mimicry)—and words.

MATCHING POSTURE AND RHYTHM

The easiest way to gain rapport is to adopt the same body posture. For example, if the person's right leg is crossed, you might cross yours. You mirror their position. Note: This means body position not exact imitation of movement habits such as twiddling the fingers or various twitches of feet and hands and so on. Because I worked on my posture so much, I never altered it when I was with other people. It was much later, when I had learned about rapport, that I found out that these people perceived me as being hard to reach. I was mismatching them because I was busy being an example of good posture. My misperception was a hindrance to my communication with those around me.

Another easy way to establish rapport is to pick up their rhythms or twitches very subtly in some other way. For example, when someone taps their fingers, you gently tap your toe to their rhythm in a manner which is not observable.

BREATH

Breathing in the same rhythm is subtle and very effective. (However, *not* if they have just run the four-minute mile!) Many therapists and healers breathe with their clients as a way of establishing contact. To observe the breathing pattern look at the area between the shoulders and neck or the chest (make sure it is with 180 degree vision or they will think you are staring).

VOICE

When we share someone's happiness or sadness we usually match their tone of voice without thinking about it. Sometimes we have to do this more consciously and deliberately match the tone, energy, and pitch of the other person's voice. It is not easy to do when you are in a hurry to get on with it. However, it is especially useful on the telephone where you cannot see the other person.

WORDS

Use similar words and phrases to the people with whom you are speaking. Be aware of words peculiar to their vocabulary and use them in your own way where it is appropriate. In other words, speak their language whenever possible.

As stated earlier, it is easy to direct conversation back to yourself unwittingly. When someone tells us about their situation we often interrupt to tell them about ours before they have had a chance to fully explain or complete a story. Yes, we all have friends or colleagues who go on and on without breathing. However, when they eventually take a breath, you can interrupt if necessary. Sympathize when it is needed, agree when it is reasonable. These are things you usually do with friends. In general support the person as a fellow human being.

Unconscious eye movements give us clues for verbal preferences. The brain stores information in pictures, sounds, and feelings. Eye movements give clues to which system is being used. While each of us uses all of these systems, one tends to predominate. In general, the majority of the population stores information in pictures. These people will use words and phrases like: "Let me put you in the picture." "How do you see this?" or "I see." This vocabulary will be a cue for you to use it because it is that person's preferred way of accessing and storing information. They will respond best when you address them in that mode. To ask people who are primarily visual how they *feel* about something is likely to illicit a blank stare or eyes that move in a number of directions as if searching their computers.

How do we tell which is the predominant method of accessing for each person? This takes careful observation. When you ask someone a question, watch the eyes. When they go up, right or left, or straight ahead, they are searching for a picture; eyes moving left or right on a horizontal axis signal sound or "auditory" mode; eyes down to the right, except in some left-handed people mean "kinesthetic" (feeling); eyes down to the left, except in some left-handed people, mean they are searching through verbal material for an appropriate answer or "internal dialogue."

A predominately auditory person will use vocabulary such as I hear you, how does this sound to you, does this ring any bells. The kinesthetic person will use words relating to sensing and feeling. All these people will respond best to vocabulary relating to their own storage systems. You can tell when you have confused them because their eyes will go through all the systems searching for an answer. That is a clue for you to rephrase or change the wording of your question or statement. It does not signify the other person's stupidity. The way we phrase questions is an important art and skill.

VALUES

Appreciating and listening for what a person values will furnish you important options in presenting information, ideas, or products. It is never a waste of time to explore what is dear to someone. Useful phrases for finding out what a person values include:

- "What characteristics would you like to see in . . . a director, manager, secretary, neighbor?"
- "Tell me what you like best in this type of service, product . . ."
- "If you could have anything you wanted for your organization, meeting, presentation, what would it be?"
- "Tell me what you would like instead." (Use this in response to a negative statement.)

EXERCISES RELATING TO LISTENING AND RAPPORT

1. *Listening*

Engage in a conversation where you do not use the word "I." Redirect the questions to what the other person has said without stating your opinion or experience but instead asking for his or hers.

2. *Rapport*

   a. Practice matching the following separately (you may choose a different one per day or week): posture and alignment, voice, and vocabulary.
   b. Become observant of the other person's eyes when you ask a question or during pauses when they are talking to you. Look for predominant tendencies of eye movements.
   c. Experiment with using vocabulary relating to visual, auditory, or kinesthetic characteristics. Observe the response you get. If you notice that a person looks up to find the answer, deliberately use an auditory or kinesthetic word and note the reaction.
   d. Whenever you ask a question, note the eyes of the other person (with 180-degree vision). Never stare at another person's eyes.

e. Experiment with asking others questions that ask for ideal solutions or positive responses. Pursue that line of questioning until you get specific positive answers that are possible.
f. Enjoy finding out about other people and what they think. It will change the way you communicate and relate to them.

SECTION 7: DEALING WITH "FEEDBACK" AND CRITICISM

One of the most important tools for developing confidence and personal power is your ability to deal with criticism or feedback, the positive description of criticism. Most of us deal with it by putting up some kind of verbal or mental defense where we try to justify what we have done to cause the criticism. This behavior causes us to turn off our listening ability, start an internal conversation, and begin a process of justification and/or blame. The issue becomes personal rather than one related to the job or project.

If you want to see someone shrink, criticize them. I have seen students do this even in a role play. The way we criticize and the way we use words is powerful—especially when they are directed negatively toward people. However, there are many in this world who do not know that and they think that criticism is the best way to teach. There is a long history of criticism in our society that has instilled the ability for us to criticize ourselves excessively and to extend it to those around us. How we deal with inner criticism, the self-critic, has a direct bearing on how we treat others. It might be useful for you to reread section two at this point.

ACCEPTING CRITICISM AND SUGGESTIONS

Not everyone knows how to criticize impartially and likely it will be directed to the person rather than toward the project or behavior. It is easy to take it as a personal affront, feel offended, and shrink or fight/argue.

Upon hearing criticism your first duty is to listen and hear out the other person fully. They need to know they have been heard. Once they have been heard you may then ask questions for clarification. Accept that this is their truth for the moment. Accuracy, as you perceive it, is not important at this stage. First you must acknowledge that there is a problem. The fact that the other person perceives a problem needs to be accepted by you.

Acknowledging that there is a problem does not in any way indicate that you accept blame. The focus is centered squarely on the issue, not the people involved. Play the role of detective and find out the exact nature of the problem and how the other person sees the resolution. Request specific details and ask for suggestions. Honor this person as a fellow human being—whether you like him or her or not.

By the time you have done all this, the atmosphere will have changed considerably and you will have a lot of information. When you choose to argue and not hear, it is likely that both of you will go away with the issue unresolved and feeling demeaned by the process.

GIVING CRITICISM OR FEEDBACK

Giving criticism is an art. It is easy to offer suggestions or criticism when the other person asks. They have opened the door for you and given you permission. However, your rapport skills, the words you choose and how you say them are extremely important. That person's strong points need to honored.

One suggestion is to ask the person for her own assessment of the situation. Likely she will have the answers already. What they are asking for is really some support from you. It is helpful to ask questions like: "If there were no constraints of any kind, how would you sort out the problem?" or "How can I/we help you to improve?" Once you have elicited a response, then give your own assessment of the issue or problem.

When you feel obligated to correct a situation where a person's behavior or work is a problem, it is a bit stickier. Ideally, you will be able to get them to see the problem by the way you approach it. However, this is not always possible and you have to tackle it head on. Talking these things over in a casual situation where you can build up a nice rapport is best. Boardroom or public bullying is not the way to generate self-esteem, quality work from your staff, or to win you any Brownie points. It creates stress at all levels.

Stay away from personal language, in other words, avoid words like "you" and "I" used in an accusing manner or as purely personal opinion. Here are some examples: "In this company it is better to wear . . ." "Is the project report complete as is?" "The information on . . . might be valuable to the report." Bear in mind that the person you are addressing is still a fellow human being and his or her strengths are to be honored.

Personal opinions are just that. You can choose to listen or not depending on your own preferences and the circumstance. The personal opinion of your CEO or director may be important. Listen. Ask appropriate questions and look at all your options. When people use words like "I do not like . . ." That is their prerogative. However you do not have to take it personally. It is a stated opinion and basically it is their problem. Arguing with personal opinion is a fruitless task. It is better to allow them their opinion. You can respond by saying that it is not true for you. Our personal truths and perceptions are varied and different. You do not have to rescue the world or attend to all of its issues. Consider the following scenarios:

A: I do not like John Doe.
B: I do not know him well enough to have an opinion. He is certainly good at selling.

A: I like your hair better short.
B: That's interesting. Thanks for telling me.

HONESTY WITH WISDOM

Some people might say the scenario above was an example of being honest. However the honesty in this case is an unsolicited personal opinion on the part of "A." "B" is remaining positive by not debating the issue or arguing. Anyone is entitled to personal opinion. However it has to be recognized as just that and not taken any further.

There are far more delicate and sensitive situations where it is necessary to be honest with another person. Redundancies, deaths, serious and life-threatening diseases are among the topics that arise in the professional arena. These situations are difficult for both parties. The seemingly easy, protective way out is to be brash, terse, do your best to show no feelings and say what has to be said quickly and remove yourself from the situation. In the long run this approach is an emotional disaster for both parties. Blatant honesty without wisdom can be extremely hurtful to the person on the other end of it and create a great deal of stress in the deliverer of the message. Sharing feelings is a way of creating rapport and gaining trust in this situation.

It is a skill to be able to say how you are feeling and empathize and be aware of the sensitivity of the other person at the same time. Honesty of fact and feelings are part of the message which must be appropriate, tactful, and wise.

The next time you feel the need to be honest ask yourself: if your honesty is purely a personal opinion; if your opinion has been solicited; whether the time is appropriate; or whether information is vital to the other person. After you have answered these questions you can choose to say something or remain silent. Sometimes it is wise to remain silent.

GIVING EFFECTIVE FEEDBACK IN GROUP SITUATIONS

Group situations provide many opportunities for feedback. If you are leading a meeting that includes your colleagues or staff there are a number of important issues which you might want to consider.

"Discovering" is a powerful learning experience; being told can be painful. An excellent manager has the ability to allow the staff member to discover for him or herself. Remember that the people with whom you are working are more vulnerable than they appear. It is easy to hurt people with careless comments or "throwaway remarks." These remarks are not meant to hurt; however, they can be perceived to do that by a vulnerable person in a sensitive situation. Unfortunately, where personal change is concerned comments are likely to be made more important than they are intended. Be aware of this and be willing to acknowledge the hurtfulness of the remark and apologize. It is not appropriate to be self-righteous in such circumstances.

First, give a person the opportunity to say how she thought her performance satisfied her own goals. Check to see if her feelings and fears distorted her perceptions of the performance. Remember that how we look and how we think we look are very different.

The most useful tool for self-discovery is the video. Even when a person is unwilling to acknowledge the need to change, he will see his behavior and compare it to those around him. Quite often he will then implement the changes gradually as his "secret." When someone is too self-conscious or afraid of making a change, the video can offer convincing evidence that the change does not look or sound strange or over the top. When no video is available, use mirroring or role-play to allow the person to see her actions or behavior.

Encourage positive and constructive responses from peers by setting an example in what you say, and the way you say it. Be ready to intervene to prevent a negative situation from arising. Address issues and problems with something positive to do in place of the unwanted action or behavior. Giving general directions like "stand up straighter" will often create confusion. Clear directions for change are essential. When you do not know how to do this yourself, send that person to someone who does.

The following can serve as personal guidelines for accepting and giving criticism:

- Listen without internal dialogue and remain in rapport with the other person.
- Use criticism and feedback as opportunities to learn more about yourself.
- First hear the other person out completely. Ask questions to bring out further specific information.
- Acknowledge the situation or problem. Others' perceptions are accurate as far as they know. Remain objective. Relate to the problem, not your emotions. Find a way to solve the situation rather than trying to change the other person.
- You can empathize with your critic without accepting the blame. A good way to resolve the situation is to acknowledge that there is a problem and clarify the issue by asking: "Tell me what you would like instead." or "Give me an example of what you would prefer."

- When giving criticism, find something positive to say. People need guidelines. Find the good teacher in yourself by providing examples of what you want and give clear instructions.

When you do not understand, ask for clarification. This saves a lot of time and misspent emotional energy.

SECTION 8: THE ART OF PRESENTATION

According to opinion polls, one of the things that strikes the most terror in men and women is to be asked to give a presentation. Most of the population become weak in the knees or self-conscious and suddenly feel the need to be perfect. In a millisecond their personal power is freely donated to an audience that is given credit for being able to see every wart, spot, or error. The self-critic becomes the one giving the presentation and we forget that it is OK to be human. The person who was at home in her personal space suddenly becomes a stranger who is self-monitoring and apprehensive. Audiences do not expect perfection or a god in front of them; they come to hear *your* message. They deserve an enthusiastic, energetic person who is dedicated to and congruent with his or her message.

In a skilled speaker, presentation is a continuation of good communication skills and is visually, vocally and verbally congruent. It is concerned with rendering a message that is far more important than you personally. Every time you become aware of yourself or wonder what your audience is thinking, the message has been forgotten. Everything you say and do must match that message or it will become distorted in the minds of your audience. Anything like self-consciousness, gestures that have nothing to do with the message, pacing without a purpose—all create conflicting information. Ideally the message and you are at one. When this happens, the speaker is spellbinding and captivating and the audience remembers.

WHAT MAKES A SPEAKER INTERESTING?

Spontaneity and complete dedication to the message play key parts in making someone interesting to hear. When we are "at home" we tend to be spontaneous and uncritical about how we talk. Appropriate gestures, words, a voice that responds to the meaning and varying rhythms are all part of our communication. These are the attributes most needed in any kind of talk from informal discussion with colleagues to boardroom presentations.

Faulty perceptions about what constitutes a presentation, and particularly a formal presentation, are at the root of 90 percent of the problems relating to speaking in public. This causes people to lose confidence and to rely on memorization or reading their texts. Both of these are deadly. When you memorize a text you become excessively aware of going off script. The self-critic then takes over and it becomes difficult to be involved with the message. It is virtually impossible to react or respond to the needs of the audience with a memorized script. Unless you are a fine actor or have been specially coached, reading a speech is a poor way of being interesting. My clients find this out for themselves when we do the children's story exercise.

So many clients have told me that they have given presentations where they did not want to be there. My first response is: "What makes you think the audience did not know that?" When the speaker is focused on the message so is the audience. When your mind is elsewhere so are the minds of your audience. It is your responsibility to make your audience want to hear more or to follow up on what you have said. They are not supposed to attend a course on listening first. You can stimulate them to pay attention.

BOREDOM FACTORS IN PRESENTATION

The listener that is not stimulated very quickly reverts to his own thought patterns and personal concerns. He is no longer there. Usually this person rationalizes that he can read your handout later. Anything about the presentation that establishes a repeated rhythmic pattern will put the audience to sleep—just as we use such patterns to go to sleep at night. In a way, it is just like counting sheep. Some of these patterns in a presentation are as follows: every speaker sounding the same and using the same techniques; hand patters that are tied to the rhythm of the words rather than the message; a controlled, monotonous voice; words that have no inherent rhythm or imagination behind them; slides that have too much information; and speakers who appear to be unenthusiastic about their topics. There are a number of boredom factors which contribute to sleepy audience syndrome.

THE "TELL THEM" TECHNIQUE

While it is helpful for people to know what you are going to talk about, to give it in the form of a grocery list is an insult to the intelligence of your audience. Originally the concept of "tell them what you are going to tell them, tell them and then tell them what you told them" was probably a reasonable way to organize a talk. However, like most ideas it has gradually become a kind of mechanized tool to create corporate or academic presentation clones. Nothing is worse than going to a business or scientific meeting where each presenter uses the same format, computer presentation templates, speech patterns, methods of delivery, and professional jargon. Anytime everything and everyone sounds the same and has similar rhythmic patterns, the audience will be lulled to sleep. People remember the presenters who are different. Paradoxically, those learning presentation skills are overly concerned with *not* being different.

READING YOUR TALK

There are a few top level directors of companies and politicians who are required to read public speeches as a matter of policy. The reason for this relates to media exposure and accuracy. Many of these directors are given coaching so that they can read as if they were speaking spontaneously. This takes rehearsal and practice.

For the rest of us who hurriedly scribble a presentation, discuss it only in our heads or count on a computer template for a quick way out, reading becomes a crutch. If you are not sure what it is like to be a recipient of the "read" presentation, have a colleague read part of a serious business paper to you. It is likely to have little or no spontaneity or normal speech quality in it.

Reading a presentation tends to inhibit the freedom and range of vocal expression, particularly when all the words and phrases are read at the same rhythm and pace. It becomes difficult to find the important points. Expressive reading is difficult without a great deal of rehearsal and planning. The children's story exercise in section 5 is a way to rehearse a talk that must be read. However, such talks are rarely as spontaneous or effective as those that leave room to maneuver. Reading passages, quotations or specific data where accuracy is critical is acceptable. However, such material is best printed so members of your audience can review it in their own time without distraction. If they are busy looking at it while you are talking, you have lost them.

AN EXCESS OF SPECIFIC INFORMATION

Managers, young teachers, and others tend to want to tell an audience everything they know, leaving no space for the listener to absorb the material. Even when the listener has a focused mind, it is difficult for him to take in the vast amounts of information contained in excessive data, lists, or complex graphs. This kind of presentation indicates that such a speaker is unsure of the message and therefore has tried to include everything he knows. Too much information causes indigestion, overwhelms the brain, and frustrates the listener. The result is the mental loss of your audience.

I like to think of information like a fuel gauge—really more like a full or empty stomach. When you are on empty, you are uncomfortable. However, when you are full, at that moment you never want to see food again. The same is true of verbal or information overload. The fill-factor is best at about 75–80 percent. That way your audience will have space to know whether they want more information or will want to go away and read your materials.

THE APOLOGETIC PRESENTER

You never need to apologize for being there or for giving a presentation. It is not part of your message and it sounds as if you are preparing the audience for a poor presentation. People are there to hear your message, not your excuses. We have far more expectations of ourselves than the audience does and it is usually the self-critic who is apologizing. The only time it is appropriate to apologize is when something unavoidable arises spontaneously during a talk.

UM'S AND ER'S

Extraneous sounds occur because the speaker has a warped sense of time and feels the need to fill in the gaps in sound. For the presenter time goes slowly and any silence can seem an age. It is OK to be silent. Your audience will not go away. Those silent periods, usually lasting seconds, give your audience time to catch a breath and allow your information to sink in.

Many years ago I was having a terrible time making sense of the class notes from one particular course. I had thought that the professor was boring but I had not analyzed the reason. The next class period I counted more than forty um's and er's in ten minutes. No wonder, my lecture notes were a mess. It was difficult to find the beginnings and endings of sentences because they were chopped up with so many extraneous sounds. I tried to imagine what a foreign student would make of this language.

Apparently the new computer voice recognition systems are not understanding these extraneous sounds and they are creating havoc with dictation. Who would have thought that computers would improve our ability to speak?

In summary, repeated patterns that have no variety quickly become boring. You need to take a personal risk to give a presentation that is truly you rather than some habit or pattern you have memorized or learned, consciously or unconsciously. If you do not want your audience to remember what you have said, why are you there?

APPROACHING PRESENTATION CREATIVELY

The creative approach to presentation offers variety, interest, and substance to the listener and the speaker. Passing on useful information is similar to teaching. An outstanding teacher will offer knowledge in a way that the students want to listen and to participate. This can take many forms—anything from straight delivery to brainstorms and syndicate groups, group art work—I've even heard of a company composing and singing their own opera in a seminar on communication skills. Know that you have many, many options and dare to risk some of them. Organizing your approach and thoughts on the basis of wide-ranging choice will enable you to mix and match ideas spontaneously in your presentation.

Presentations become dull and lacking in spontaneity when they are treated like an essay or a piece of literature rather than a talk. The oral presentation model is not intended to be the same as the written model. We do not talk the way we write. When we do, it often sounds wooden and stilted. Written models are generally patterned on intellectual essays, school reports, and/or scientific papers that are designed to be included in journals rather than given orally. It is not uncommon for written material given as an oral presentation to be repetitious, boring, and to run over the time allotted.

We do not write and speak the same way and it is important that the two approaches are not confused. Think back to times you have discussed a work-related subject with friends and colleagues in comfortable, casual circumstances. Were you at a loss for words or a way to describe the information? And, when they did not understand, probably you were able to describe issues in several different ways. However, the thought of giving a "presentation" immediately conjures up concerns and thoughts of inadequacy. How is it that you are not inadequate with friends and barely functional with a perceived audience? The key to spontaneity and creativity is feeling at home in whatever space you occupy. Whatever you do, do not sit down and start to write a presentation without first going through the process outlined below.

HOW TO PLAY WITH YOUR INFORMATION AND ORGANIZE YOUR MATERIAL

Broaden your perspective first before you narrow it. Each profession has its own set of in-house jargon and preferred definitions and unfortunate assumptions are made regarding audience understanding of these. The best way to alleviate this problem is to pretend you have never heard of your topic before. Look up the key word, and its original derivation, in a large dictionary and begin a mind-map of all the words that are given. Remember that this key word is your topic, not necessarily the title of your talk. Do not edit out any words or ideas at this point. Accept what you see. If you use a word like "management," be sure you look up the root word, "manage," as well. You may well come up with a few surprises and some thought-provoking definitions during this exercise.

After you have exhausted the dictionary definitions, think of all the associations, good, bad, or otherwise, you might have with your chosen word. Add these to your mind-map. Do not forget any sayings or phrases that come to mind. This part of the exercise is best done with a group because each person will have his own associations and memories. You might also ask your spouse, children, and colleagues what they think the word means. The diversity will astound you. The more you broaden your concept, the easier it is to come up with multiple ideas and options.

Now add any emotional words associated with your topic. While you may not think emotion is relevant to your topic, you will find that others have had pleasant or unpleasant experiences to share. In fact, many and varied emotions surround any topic.

At this point you will have a page full of words. If you wish to group them into major headings or topics, do so. You may have a subject that contains several modifying words, for example, "group financial management." Think of ways these words might modify your main topic. Include the most important of these words now. However do not start to plan your talk yet. Before beginning to work on your talk, there are some questions that need to be answered.

Ask yourself the following questions before preparing your presentation:

1. What one thing do I want my audience to remember?

The answer to this question can be a fact, a value, a concept, or the creation of trust or credibility for you or your company. Unless you have an answer, you will not have a focus for your presentation. This answer is informed also by your knowledge of your audience, who they are and why they are there.

2. How much can people remember?

You do not want to leave them with information overload and indigestion. If you have five minutes, one main point is all you can make. The maximum for any talk is five major headings—and still only one focus.

3. How clear are my data?

While you live with your data all the time, you cannot expect an audience to decipher it as quickly as you. Keep charts and graphs simple and key items well marked or colored. Anything complex needs to be put on a special handout.

4. How do I show my main point(s) on a slide or overhead?

Note: Remember that most people store information in pictures and are visual. Therefore a simple picture or a cartoon is very helpful. "A picture *is* worth a thousand words." Make sure that your important items can be seen a split second after a slide is shown. When your audience has to look to find or follow the information, they will not hear what you are saying. In other words, make points blatantly obvious.

5. Would a simple one-page handout be useful?

It is much easier to go away with one page than a wedge of paper—and far less daunting. Using your slides as handouts saves time but they are more likely to wind up in the trash. More will be said about this later.

6. What approach will I take?

This will be dependent on the size of the group, the topic, and the atmosphere you wish to create. There are numerous options available: discussion, brainstorm, syndicates. With a large group you can get them to interact with each other for a short time. I have seen it done with as many as eight hundred. For example: pose a question and give your audience three minutes to discuss it with those nearby. It will start them thinking and they will be ready to listen to your thoughts on the subject.

7. What are my personal options? Is it appropriate for me to stand? Or sit?

For small groups, I suggest that you sit. Be one of them. You will have a better rapport. You can get up to write on a flipchart or change a slide.

8. Do I want to use a lectern? Do I want to use a microphone?

Your comfort and ease during the presentation is important. Do not be afraid to ask for what you want.

Having answered these questions, you are now ready to begin to organize the ideas and text of your presentation. In fact, much of your work will have been done by following the process outlined above.

INTRODUCTION

Look at the words on your mind-map. Are there any stories, experiences, real life situations that would serve as a good introduction to your talk or meeting? The introduction serves only one purpose—to get your audience interested in hearing what else you have to say and to establish the focus on your issue or topic. Your introduction can be varied infinitely. It can be a story, incident from work or a short, one-word brainstorm that sets the stage for what comes next. You may choose on the day to change your introduction. When you have done the preparation above, you will be able to make the change easily.

The introduction is the time to create "common ground." You create common ground by relating first to the human beings in the audience. Then you present people your information—not information to the people. Think for a moment where your emphasis is. Is it on data and facts or is it on your audience and their needs?

CASE STUDY

A large company was holding seminars on a new software program for its IT staff. The presenter wanted the staff to grasp some basic concepts related to a change in work practices. The company had changed from a six to seven-day workweek and this affected the way information was being downloaded on the computers. There was now no day for downloading.

The title of the presenter's talk was "Triggers and Batches." I sent him to look up the word "batches" in a dictionary. He returned laughing and said that the definition was perfect for his concept. He said that they could no longer put batches of material in the computer but now had to feed it in small bits over each day—much like the Pizza Hut conveyor belt style of fulfilling specific orders for pizzas. For his introduction he created a cartoon of a baker putting in a batch of loaves and a conveyor belt full of pizzas. Even though he was talking to very knowledgeable IT staff, they immediately got the picture because of their own experiences with something as common as baking bread or making pizzas. They did not forget his message—he talked first to humans, then to the computer designers.

Some pitfalls and words to avoid in introductions:

- I would like to talk to you . . . (just do it)
- I am going to talk about . . . (again, just do it)
- I hope you will . . . (weakens)
- Jokes that have nothing to do with the topic.
- Insincere greetings. When you say, "Good morning, ladies and gentlemen," you must mean it. Look at your audience, not your notes, when you include a greeting and mentally give them time to reply. Those words need a pause afterward.
- Do not just launch into your talk without a break.

Tip: To create a pause, you can repeat your greeting once more silently to yourself.

BODY OF THE TALK

Now that you have people interested, give them specific information and detail. Return to your mind-map for the organization of appropriate concepts and headings. I had one client who organized his presentation by having a picture for each main heading. He then gave specific information by talking about the various elements in each picture.

There are a variety of ways of presenting the body of your talk: in-depth brainstorming as a group or in syndicate, questions and answers specific to the issues you want discussed, role plays, mini-dramas, or a simple, direct presentation. You must decide whether you wish to talk or facilitate. The more you are able to allow your audience to take part, the more they will own the topic. However, facilitation needs careful planning and the ability to respond quickly and think on your feet. It demands flexibility and spontaneity.

Be adaptable enough to be able to shorten, lengthen, or rearrange the order of your points. Their survival and yours are not dependent on getting every word that you have planned. Be observant of the needs of your audience and change the pace or direction when necessary.

SUMMARY OF PRESENTATION

This section can be powerful, persuasive, or gentle depending on the message you choose to deliver. It is useful to include benefits and emotional comparisons like: "people who manage this way are less frustrated and enjoy their work"; "employees who follow these guidelines will save themselves time and energy and the company will see a higher profit"; "the way to keep your customers happy is to . . ."; and so forth. You may repeat your main message. For example: "If you take only one idea away with you today, I would like for it to be . . ."

PRESENTATION TOOLS

After you have decided on the primary message and purpose of your presentation, you can make some choices about how to present the material. This is determined somewhat by the size of your audience, the kind of atmosphere you wish to create (casual, serious, etc.), the available equipment, seating and platform arrangements. Ask questions about these things ahead of time so that there are no unpleasant surprises. Do not be afraid to request the arrangements you want. Too many times the organizers of presentation events make assumptions about how they are given. For example, many seminars are set up around big tables with no space left to maneuver chairs. If you are planning group interaction, this can be disastrous.

When you know your material well, do it with few or no notes. You may want to have a very brief one page outline to keep you on track. Ideally, the introduction will be completely spontaneous. For the rest of your information you may use notes, cards, speak to your slides or pictures. Make sure you get to a presentation or seminar early to check the setup, your slides, overhead, proper pens. More important, you want to get a feel for the space and make it your home.

EFFECTIVE USE OF SLIDES

Putting important points on a slide or overhead is useful. The "visual" majority of your audience will appreciate this. Wherever possible, think in pictures. Out of this may come some clever ways to put across your ideas. Unfortunately, the common practice is to put words and complicated graphs on slides. Simplicity is the key. If the viewer cannot see at a glance the purpose of the slide, they are then too busy looking to listen to you.

Some presenters use their slides as keynotes for memory. This is acceptable as long as each word and sentence is *not* read to the audience. They can read for themselves. It is better for you to explain why those points are there and the specific information related to them. The objective is to maintain a spontaneous, flexible, and comfortable format. Trust your knowledge; you do not need to read the slides.

HANDOUTS MADE FROM SLIDES

It is the custom to reproduce slide materials and use them as handouts. Handouts of slides are more useful to the presenter than the audience. Often they are used, quite legitimately, as reminders for the speaker and to highlight main points for the audience. Sometimes they provide something to do for a bored audience. However, more often than not, people use them as an easy shortcut and the listener is left with a wad of paper that makes no sense later. It is far better to condense the material into one or two pages of reminders. This means you have to rethink your information and make it useful for the audience rather than yourself.

INTERACTIVE PRESENTATION AND FACILITATION

The skill of interactive presentation lies in making it easy for your audience to respond. The value of interaction is that it gives your audience the responsibility of doing some work and for thinking for themselves. Also they are more likely to own or share the outcome. It is a form of acknowledgment for you to allow them to have their say. Many decisions are made without consulting staff. This is a way to include them in both planning and decisions.

BRAINSTORMING

When you want to find out quickly what the group is thinking, use a one-word brainstorm. This can be done with small or large groups. There are a number of ways to do this. How you word your question(s) for the brainstorm is extremely important. The more specific your question, the more specific the answer you will receive.

The following is an example of a question that will elicit a short response without lengthy statements. What is the first word that comes to mind when I say the word "manage"? This kind of one-word response is useful when you want to get a quick picture of the thinking of your group. It takes no time and can provide a good introduction or a provocative discussion later. I have seen this used in a group of over two hundred people.

In this case, a small piece of paper was placed on the chairs of the participants before the talk began. During the opening remarks they were asked to write the word that arose when the term alliance was mentioned. The papers were then passed to the end of the rows, collated and put up for the audience to see in a later part of the presentation. The positive associations were put on one side, the negative on the other. The sense of the group reaction to the term was readily apparent.

During a brainstorming session it is important that you include every person and accept every word offered. You can also add your own. If they do not come up with one of your key words, put theirs up first and then suggest the one word they did not think of, or ask permission to add yours. You are in charge of the discussion so you can choose the words that are key to your message to move further into your presentation.

SYNDICATE OR BREAK-OUT GROUPS

Done well, syndicate groups will make your presentation for you. Sometimes it is nice to let them do all the work. Your job is to oversee, accept what they have to offer and shape the message. This takes careful and thoughtful planning. Getting the response you want will depend directly on the way you present the questions or issues and your clarity about the outcome you want.

Issues or questions that are too general will generate too many ideas and will lack focus. For example: "What are the problems in your department relating to supply management?" This question could generate many answers, a lot of negativity, and no steps to a solution. A better way of presenting the issue is: "What are the three main issues relating to 'supply management' in your department? What is working well at the moment? What problem areas need immediate focus? Come up with three ways of solving these areas."

A WORD ABOUT SCIENTIFIC OR TECHNICAL PAPERS

It is common to have ten to twenty minutes to present material at conferences. This material usually is a report of research and/or highly specific findings. It is the fashion to use the paper to be submitted for publication as the basis of the oral presentation. Unfortunately this is often boring, filled with excess information, and the real excitement and passion about the research is omitted.

Focus your attention on the one thing you would like your audience to take away from your presentation. When speakers are intent on delivering vast amounts of information, it leads to excess material being crammed into a short period of time and a speaker who talks too quickly and overrunning the time allotted. When in doubt, say less.

Data and specific lists are best shown as simple graphs and summarized during your talk. After an audience has heard six speakers pour out technological data and jargon in a period of an hour and a half, they are more than saturated. People cannot retain this detail in their heads, therefore create handouts that can be read at their leisure. Your job is to create so much interest that each person will want to go away and read them.

Your audience does not need to know everything that you have learned in order to present the paper. You are there because you have something to offer from your perspective. Others may be knowledgeable in your field. However, they will not know the information in the way that you do.

Presenters who dare to be different have presentations that are remembered. When there are "assembly-line" type talks at conferences, they all begin to sound the same. This puts an audience to sleep quickly. It is important to be different (and interesting) in this situation. It is your responsibility to keep the audience awake.

Share your information and your enthusiasm with your audience. Speak to them as if they were friends in your home. Scientific and technical presentations can be made exciting, interesting, and fun.

PRESENTATIONS AS A PART OF A JOB INTERVIEW

It is common for interviewees to have to give a short presentation. Do not forget that in the last instance, it is your choice as to whether you want that job. In your interview and presentation you will want to know if you wish to work with these people and this company. Sometime during the interview make sure that you find out where they want the company or section to go and what are the current problems. This will assist you in analyzing their needs and wishes and enable you to speak specifically to these during your presentation.

Timing Your Talk

Experienced speakers and classroom teachers know how to keep to a schedule when presenting. They have learned over time just how much time they need for the amount of information they wish to relay. Inexperienced speakers can find timing difficult. Timing your talk by speaking it or reading it aloud is an essential part of your preparation.

If you are reading your presentation, you can easily time it. A single-spaced page of text read at a reasonable pace will take approximately two and a half to three minutes. Taking less time will indicate to you that you are reading too fast.

While speaking with notes or to slides is more spontaneous, it is less easy to time. However, as a rough guideline, a twenty-minute talk should have about five to seven slides and no more than four main points. I once watched in horror as a speaker, who had been given strict instructions to give a twenty-minute talk, appeared with about forty overheads. She spoke for well over an hour, oblivious to the fact that there were other speakers.

While most audiences will love you if you finish your presentation early, the opposite may happen if you run over. When your presentation goes over your allotted time, you become extremely unpopular with your audience, the next speaker and the organizers of the seminar. Even if you think that every word you have prepared needs to be delivered, your audience does not. They have lost interest and concentration at this point. It is much better to stop short, do a quick summary of the material you are currently presenting and cut to the end of your presentation.

When you are unsure of your timing or afraid that you will go over, ask a friend or colleague in the audience or the person in charge of the event to signal to you when you have five minutes remaining. That way, you will not be surprised and be caught without enough time to close your presentation in a logical way.

GIVING YOUR PRESENTATION

Presenting yourself well and receiving feedback and acknowledgment that comes from your audience is an exhilarating experience. First-time actors and singers, and sometimes teachers, find themselves on a real high when they experience the wave of energy that comes to from the audience. Speakers who have the same experience grow to love the interaction with audiences, large or small.

To present well, you need to take some concepts and tools from earlier sections. The most important one is the concept of personal space. Make sure that you have visualized yourself doing well and feeling "at home" as you plan your presentation and immediately preceding it. Remember that you can expand your space to include any size audience or room. Welcome the audience into your home.

Think of your center as being located between your pubic bone and your navel. Breathe in and out of that area and support your voice from there. If you are using a microphone, remember that it is there purely to magnify the sound you put into it. Using a microphone is not an excuse to produce a flimsy, unsupported voice

Just before you speak make sure you sit quietly with both feet firmly on the floor, breathing deeply and observing what is happening around you. Do not memorize your opening lines. Focus on the one thing you want the audience to take away from your talk. Remember that as long as you are fully focused on your message, so is your audience. The minute your mind begins to worry, become self-conscious or lose focus the audience focuses on you, not your message.

While you are speaking, plant your feet on the floor. Grounding is important for your energy, nerves, and voice. Move only with a purpose, such as to get to the slides, flipchart, or to talk to someone specifically. Mindless pacing uses your brain power for movement rather than the message. The message is at its best and effective when you are integrated visually, vocally, and textually.

If you lose track of where you are or make a mistake, pause for a moment, take a deep breath and let your audience know what has happened. They are sympathetic and probably aware that something is causing you discomfort. Your acknowledgment of the situation will help put you and your audience at ease.

USING YOUR HANDS

We use our hands comfortably and naturally in everyday life. However when we are told to keep them still, we tend to develop extraneous twitches of hands, heads, shoulders, hips, and feet as substitutes for using them in a talk. People who live whole days, weeks, and months without thinking once about what to do with their hands, become paranoid about them when faced with a presentation. Some of this paranoia has been given to them by well-meaning consultants, who have told them to keep their hands still.

Hands are part of the visual aspects of your presentation. As long as they move in tandem with the messages and words you are using, they are fine. One purpose of the children's story exercise is to show you ways of using your hands effectively. Some people have been taught to fold their hands in front in the "fig-leaf" or "crotch" position. Keep in mind, however, that wherever you keep your hands stationary will call attention to that part of the body.

You choose what you would like to emphasize. Hands look perfectly normal hanging by your sides or using them expressively and with purpose. Frozen hand positions look far more awkward than using them to express the message. If you are worried about this, record your presentation on video so you can see for yourself.

Think of your presentation as sharing your information with your audience. You are not talking at people or trying to give them "information indigestion." No talk about any subject ever has to be indigestible or boring.

WHAT IF . . . ?

Presentations are rarely, if ever, perfect. Knowing this is the first step to remaining centered when something does go amiss. It is worth considering some of the things that might create a momentary panic and cause you to lose confidence during a talk. For example, just before you get up to speak, you discover you have on mismatched socks.

The first thing you need to know is that you will probably be the only one in the whole auditorium or room that knows it. When you are involved completely and totally in your presentation, your audience will be focused on that as well. However, when a speaker is boring, members of an audience will begin to look around for something to interest them. It could well be your socks.

CASE STUDY

A number of years ago I needed some shoes to wear with the gown I was wearing for a concert (solo) I was to give. Hastily, I ran into the shoe shop and tried on several pairs of shoes. My choice came down to two almost identical pairs. The only difference was that one pair had slightly higher heels. I chose the pair with the lower heels. They were duly boxed and handed to me. The night of the concert I dressed backstage and put my shoes on last. Surprise! The salesperson at the shoe store had put in a mixed pair of shoes—one each of the different heel heights. There was no choice except to use them, smile and walk on stage as if my legs were even. Fortunately, there was only a few millimeters difference in the size, and even more fortunately there were not two right shoes in the box, and thank God for the long dress. I sang the concert with no mishaps, physically or musically, and was relieved when the end arrived. In talking with friends and concertgoers later, I found that not a single person had noticed the difference in my shoes. Thankfully, they had all been occupied with the music instead. Moral: Always double-check all the clothing you plan to wear the day before as well as the day of your presentation.

Losing Your Place

This is more of an issue when you read a speech. Make sure you have the text in large print with adequate line spacing. If you do find yourself lost, take a deep breath, stop to find your place and continue. Remember that time is going slowly for you and fast for your audience. They are most likely to perceive your momentary stop as a pause and welcome the chance to catch up with you.

Today, the practice of using slides, overheads, or notecards tends to keep the speaker from getting lost as well as staying on track. If you are worried about straying from your subject, give yourself a time for each part of your talk and check your watch periodically to make sure you are where you planned to be. If you do lose your place or skip something you wanted to say, simply let the audience know what you have done and backtrack to that item.

Having a Slide in the Wrong Place

It does not matter whether you placed it in the wrong place, put it in upside down, or whether the technician did it. Do not bother to try to place blame but simply explain what has happened and correct it if possible within a short time. It is maddening for the audience and you if technical problems appear to take a great deal of time to correct. If the slide cannot be moved easily, you will have to flip back and forth until you have finished speaking about that part of your presentation.

Something Wrong with the Visual Aids, No Slide or Overhead Projector

When Murphy's Law is in full force, there is little you can do except improvise. However, when in doubt, err on the side of simplicity. Do not attempt to read large amounts of data to an audience. Instead describe the picture you were planning to show or tell a story around the data. If the visual information or picture was critical to your presentation, ask the members of your audience to draw or outline how they might see this picture. In other words, turn the situation around and get your audience to do the work. Your presentation may be far more spontaneous and better than you planned.

> **CASE HISTORY**
>
> I once was told at the last minute that I had no slide projector for an anatomy lecture on the larynx. Anatomy is difficult without pictures and I was not good at drawing the structures. What followed was one of the best classes I had ever given. I asked the class to get out their anatomy books and together, we all made models of the larynx out of notebook paper, tape, and staples. They never forgot the cartilages of the larynx.

No Microphone in a Large Space

In this case remember that you have included the whole audience in your personal space. It will then be easier to fill that space with your voice. You will need to support your voice with the muscles of the abdomen so you will be much more physically active. Ask people in different areas of the room or auditorium to let you know when they cannot understand or hear you. Think of yourself as an actor or actress on a large stage.

It's My First Time Speaking in Public

Giving a first performance of any kind is likely to be nerve wracking. If you are totally calm, you will probably make history as being the first ever to be so. The best way to allay fear is to practice a lot and visualize yourself being at ease on the day. Practice talking aloud to yourself in front of a mirror and talk about your subject with willing friends and colleagues.

If your mind goes blank, take a deep breath and slowly check your notes. Time will be going incredibly slowly for you so you will feel you are taking hours when it is really only seconds. No audience I know has ever left in mid-sentence.

Quiet shaking hands by placing them firmly on the podium. However do not grip so tightly that your hands turn white. The best way to alleviate nervous hands and mannerisms is to use your hands meaningfully. Reread the children's story exercise and the section above on hands.

Remember you are speaking because you are sharing your knowledge. You would not be there if the subject matter were not part of your professional expertise or within your scope of knowledge.

There Is a Question I Cannot Answer

Honesty is best. When you do not know the answer to a question, say so. Bluffing your way through invites far more embarrassment than saying you do not know. Offer to find out the answer or to send that person to someone who is knowledgeable in that area. Remember you are not God and being human is OK.

When the question is irrelevant quickly find a nice way to ask that person how it applies to the information in your talk. If they can apply it, clarify the question. If they cannot, tell them that you will be happy to discuss it with them later. Make a point to see them after the talk so they will not feel neglected.

A Person Tries to Take Over Your Talk by Making a Long Statement

There are some people who feel a need to let an audience know about their personal beliefs and knowledge—even to take the opportunity to show off. They do not have a question but begin to state a personal opinion and possibly start a debate. When the statement appears to be inappropriate or overly long, it best to find the earliest opportunity to interrupt nicely. As the speaker, you have every right to ask such a person if they are asking a question or making a statement. They will then need to define what they are doing. You can suggest to them that this time is set aside for questions. Perhaps you could meet them afterwards and discuss their points.

If their point is valid and you feel comfortable with letting them talk, then do so. However, it is your time and you must take charge of it. Once their main point has been made, summarize their point and move on.

You Have a Misguided Supporter

Occasionally a friend will try to help you out and add information that is not appropriate or is off the point. Simply thank them for their point and continue your presentation.

There Are Unwanted Interruptions or Hecklers

This is an unlikely situation in the normal presentation setting. However, interruptions and hecklers can appear in debates and in political and controversial situations. You must be careful to "fuel gauge" the situation and the people. If the interference is mostly innocent fun, you can usually stop it by inviting those people to demonstrate or share what they were discussing with the whole group. Most of the time they are embarrassed and stop immediately.

In the first instance of heckling, politely ignore it and continue your talk. However, if it becomes serious you may need to ask for help from the organizers of the event. I had a friend who often spoke on controversial subjects and knew she would be heckled or shouted down. I suggested that she put her information on slides or overheads and then it would not matter if she could not be heard. This is an extreme case and it would occur rarely.

People Get Restless

When people become restless in a talk it can be for a number of reasons. For the insecure speaker, it is easiest to think that you are being boring. That is a possibility. However, when people have been sitting for long periods of time listening to a number of speakers, it is normal. When you notice restlessness, there are a number of things you can do to change the energy: get everyone to stand up and stretch; ask them a question; get them to share information on the topic with the person sitting beside them; do a quick brainstorm; or take a five minute-break. Rather than just giving information, find a way to get your audience to give it to you.

Silence or Little Response to Questions You Ask

When you get little response to your questions first rephrase them in case they have not been understood. If there is still no response, give them a question and ask them to share answers with the people near them. Sometimes members of an audience are unwilling to answer a question in public where they might seem inadequate. This is particularly true with young people and meetings where junior staff and senior executives are both in attendance. They will happily talk with each other, but are not forthcoming in addressing the whole group.

Very rarely is the audience, or anyone in it, your enemy. However this is often the perception. When you expect an audience, or anyone else for that matter, to be an enemy you are setting up a negative situation that invites negative reaction. Make friends with your audience, respect them and their knowledge, speak positively about your subject and be a good listener when someone takes issue with what you have said. Involve your audience in the process by asking them questions and making them think. This is the best way for information to be shared and owned by everyone.

SUMMARY

In conclusion, remember that presentation is an art when you:

1. Are *yourself*—your best self—as if the audience is sitting and listening to you in your own living room.
2. Are *gracious*—be the host or hostess to your audience—as if you are offering something valuable to each person without being pretentious.
3. Speak with *enthusiasm*—show your interest and passion in the subject and allow the audience to be included in your personal relationship with the topic
4. *Create space* for the audience to absorb and understand what you are saying. They need time to see, hear, and experience the information you are giving them.
5. Keep your information *simple*—Put complicated subject matter in simple form on handouts where they will have a chance to read it over and over when they do not understand it or wish to think about it more carefully. Absorbing oral information is difficult so be considerate of your audience when planning your presentation. Remember the "fuel" gauge.
6. Allow your audience to *participate* in some way—Do not do the thinking for your audience. They need active participation if they are to get anything out of your talk. Do not let them become "couch potatoes" when you speak—this applies to both large and small group presentations.
7. *Prepare* your presentation by talking it over with a number of people first. Find out what makes sense to other people, friends, and colleagues. Talking about your material clarifies it in your own mind and allows you to know when you are too complicated. You may find what you thought was clear in your mind sounds disorganized when stated aloud.

SECTION 9: ACTION PLANNING AND SUMMARY

ACTION PLANNING

Choose one thing only to work on for a day or a week, if necessary. Remind yourself of the thing you wish to change by leaving Post-it-notes in obvious places such as your bathroom mirror, the dashboard of the car, your desk, by the telephone, the top of your lecture or presentation notes, or anyplace your eyes naturally fall during the day. These notes may contain a word, simple phrase or a symbol such as an arrow for "tall." Your concentration has to be on your work so the notes will serve as polite reminders in the off-moments.

More is not necessarily better. So engage in any of the exercises such as those on posture, voice, awareness, 180-degree vision, listening, or remaining still for three minutes. Write yourself notes to use as reminders for the rest of the day.

Create a Three-Tiered Action Plan

1. First outline, mind map, or list an overall picture of how you would like to be perceived or see yourself in five years. What personal characteristics would you like to have? Which values are dear to you? What role would you like to have in your profession? What characteristics, personal and professional, would you consider ideal for someone in that role? Which of these do you have now?

2. Next, make a list of all the things you do best. This can include anything from your professional skills to your hobbies—even DIY or reading to your children. Do not be modest. This is a list for you. If you could do anything you wanted to do professionally, what would it be? What further skills would you like to have to accomplish this? List the simplest, first steps you can take toward accomplishing your goals.

3. Create a list of priorities gathered from the answers to the questions above. Determine the easiest possible way to begin. What small things can you begin to practice, think, or do now? Mark a start-time in your diary.

SUMMARY

Personal power is taking charge of how you feel about your life and knowing that you have choices in how you lead it. All the sections in this book have been dedicated to helping you see and understand some of the choices you have. You do have the choice and the ability to change. It is not dependent on anyone else around you.

As mentioned earlier, many of our problems lie in our perceptions. Yes, they have been carefully taught in some instances. When we are taught only one way or one answer for something, it makes everything else seem wrong. After years of such thinking, it is difficult to look afresh at what we do and how we are. We become full of ironbound ideas and change with difficulty. Personal power is given away to these preconceptions and misconceptions.

Such preconceptions and lack of sensitivity are large obstacles to understanding ourselves and those around us. We begin to define who we are by what we do and create identity problems. In this instance, personal power has been given away to what we do. Emphasis on work and earning power can cause confusion as to who we are—and what our motivations for going to work are.

You cannot require another person to take on the changes you are making. They will have a different list. We only make changes when we are ready. The pieces of the puzzle fit only when other pieces are in place. The responsibility and choice are purely yours for yourself—not anyone else—not the world.

Ways of Maintaining Your Personal Power:

1. Make sure you do one thing each week that is special to you. You are worth it! Have a massage, engage in a sport or hobby, go to an art class, or sing.
2. Be aware of maintaining a dynamic rather than a static posture. Do not drag yourself down.
3. Schedule, and adhere to, short periods of quiet time. These periods can be as short as three minutes. You are in charge of your time.
4. Remember to acknowledge those around you. You are never too busy to see, smile or speak to those near you.
5. Enjoy and value your friends and colleagues. Allow them their own opinions. You can do your best when you allow others to do theirs.
6. Take a serious look at your values and the way in which they relate to your everyday life and work. It is virtually impossible to work with a personal value system which does not match the one that exists in your job. When this mismatch of values occurs, it depletes your energy.

7. Know that your self-worth and self-esteem are not attached to your wealth, position, or those with whom you associate. Self-worth comes from self-knowledge, self-respect, and self-acceptance.
8. Want to be where you are at all times.

Using These Tools Wisely

This book is full of tools for your personal development. You know what you want and need. You can choose few or many of these tools that you feel will help you. The desire to change will cause your "computer" to begin to program itself. Enjoy the process of growth.

Laugh at yourself. Share the experiences, happy, sad, or otherwise, and the doing of these exercises with your family and friends. Make presence and personal power into a community endeavor. These are not secret attainments only for the privileged. They are available to everyone. The by-products of your efforts will lead to increased trust in yourself and greater confidence.

Confidence—from *confidere*—"with full trust."

NOTES

1. Michael Argyle, Veronica Salter, Hilary Nicholson, Marilyn Williams, and Philip Burgess, *British Journal of Social and Clinical Psychology* 9 (September 1970): 222–31.

The Incredible Shrinking Singer

Rebuilding Your Confidence

An Interview with Meribeth Dayme
by Cynthia Vaughn[1]

1999

> *I have observed people physically shrink in front of my eyes when performing, speaking, or holding conversations with people or audiences they perceive to be important. These moments of shrinking are times when personal power has been given away.*
>
> Meribeth Bunch Dayme

As early as you can remember, your voice drew attention—it made you "special." Your music teachers said, "She has real talent," or "He's gonna make it!" You won the competitions, you earned the scholarships, you played the leading roles, you got a manager, you signed the contracts, and you impressed the reviewers. But with each step forward and upward, there are more people to please, and more pressure to succeed, as you unwittingly give away bits of your personal power and find yourself constantly doubting your own abilities. Perhaps you are an experienced singer going through a "slump," or seeing roles go to younger singers. You may be a singer who has had success on one level, and now face the unknown challenges of the next professional arena. You may even be returning to singing after a voluntary or forced "break," such as an illness, the birth of a child, a career change, or relocation. How do you regroup and rebuild your confidence?

    I recently spoke with *Creating Confidence* author Meribeth Bunch from her home in London. "One of the biggest problems for any singer," she told me, "is that of identifying the 'core' and the 'voice' as being the same thing. As soon as we perceive an insult to the voice, performance, or audition, we take it personally, and give away personal power to an external force. It is easy, then, to blame others."

We also blame ourselves. "The self-critic is the largest obstacle any of us face, particularly the older we become. By then we have heard 'right' and 'wrong' so much that they have become parasites. The self-critic becomes the voice inside the head that tries to speak at the same time we are singing. When we try to satisfy the self-critic, the message, presence, and performance all go out the window!"

To prove her point in lessons and workshops, Bunch tries the following experiment. "I stand behind a singer and become their self-critic. As they are performing, I whisper lots of negative observations in their ear. And they seize up completely, because they can't do both at once. Think about it—if the brain is busy talking while you are singing, it's like having a radio on. It's amazing what happens when the mind is quiet and supposedly blank. Athletes call this being 'in the zone.'"

One of the most difficult things for a performer to do is to develop an innate sense of self that is not dependent on what others think. Bunch prefers to accept exactly what singers tell her about themselves and let them change their minds later without having made a judgment. "I find out what their goals are, where they want to be, and how they want to sound ideally. We also have a discussion about the attitudes and thoughts that contribute to personal presence and space they have around them. That usually boggles them! Then I have them sing while I make a videotape. We work on the congruence of the message, and especially on staying present—which is quickly evident in the eyes. You can see the second they 'leave town'!"

Bunch tells of a soprano sent by her teacher for a consultation and video session. "She was a bit afraid at first, but later when I asked her what she was taking away from the session, her answer blew my mind. She was overjoyed because she looked like a 'normal' person. I shudder to think what she thought of herself before the session." Bunch adds, "Singers needs to hear and see for themselves how they appear and sound. As long as singers, particularly classical singers, refuse to videotape and look at themselves, they will always need to go to others for approval."

When she works with singers, Bunch trains them to be in the present. "The critically important attitude is simply this: I want to be here!" She cautions not to be stuck in the past or distracted by the future. "One of the ways we hang ourselves up is to try to recreate the great rehearsal, performance, audition we had—whenever. When we do this, we are forever disappointed that we can't get the same feeling. We must instead recreate each time we sing."

And what about the singer who is singing a small role, and desperately wants and "deserves" the lead role? "The person who is trying to be in the future is not in the present, and is probably not performing optimally. Do the small role wonderfully well! One of the sad aspects of the teaching of singing is that no attention is paid to presence from the beginning. From the first moment of making sound, the face and eyes need to be present. Even the warm-up is about the enjoyment of singing, not just a means to an end."

Bunch believes that there is a dual responsibility for the singer to maintain his or her own integrity or personal power, and for the voice teacher to find a way to "honor" the singer. "We need feedback on the voice that we can trust. However, gut feelings need to be acknowledged and honored. For example, if we are losing confidence because a teacher is subtly or otherwise trying to discourage us, we need to know when it is time to part company. We have given away our personal power to that teacher (or coach, manager, etc.), and feel we are failures because we cannot do what they are asking. We keep trying to prove ourselves to the person in front of us when we need to prove ourselves to ourselves. By constantly walking back into this situation, we crush our confidence and spirit. There is so much nurturing needed—not spoiling and false praise, but nourishment of the individual as a human being."

What is "personal power"? According to Bunch, personal power is an innate sense of yourself that is not dependent on what you believe other people think. It is the ability and confidence to find out or ask what you need to know to do your job or task well. It is the ability to listen to comments and criticism and pursue them positively until a way is found to resolve the situation with integrity and without emotional attachment to the outcome. Finally, personal power is the ability to recognize and take care of your own needs. In doing so, you are far better able to maintain your energy and sense of self-worth, and you will be free to share and to give others what they may need at the time.

NOTE

1. This article was originally published as "The Incredible Shrinking Singer" in *Classical Singer* 12, no. 4 (April 1999): 14–15. It later appeared in the NATS newsletter *Inter Nos* 53, no. 1 (Spring 2020): 13–17, and is reprinted again in this volume with permission of *Classical Singer*.

Suggestions for Further Reading

compiled by Meribeth Dayme

Bolte Taylor, Jill. *My Stroke of Insight: A Brain Scientist's Personal Journey.* New York: Viking Press, 2007.

Braden, Gregg. *The Divine Matrix: Bridging Time, Space, Miracles, and Belief.* Carlsbad, CA: Hay House, 2007.

Chia, Mantak. *Taoist Ways to Transform Stress into Vitality.* Thailand/US: Healing Tao Books, 1986.

Dayme, Meribeth. *Dynamics of the Singing Voice,* fifth ed. New York: Springer, 2009.

Dayme, Meribeth and Cynthia Vaughn. *The Singing Book,* third ed. New York: W.W. Norton & Company, 2013.

Dispenza, Joe. *You Are the Placebo: Making Your Mind Matter.* Carlsbad, CA: Hay House, 2014.

Edwards, Gill. *Conscious Medicine: Creating Health and Well-Being in a Conscious Universe.* London: Piatkus Books, 2010.

Fritz, Robert. *The Path of Least Resistance: Learning to Become the Creative Force in Your Own Life.* New York: Ballantine Books, 1989.

Green, Brian. *The Elegant Universe: Superstrings, Hidden Dimensions, and the Quest for the Ultimate Theory.* New York: W.W. Norton & Company, 2010.

Hawkins, David R. *Power versus Force: The Hidden Determinants of Human Behavior.* Carlsbad, CA: Hay House, 2012.

Hunt, Valerie V. *Infinite Mind: Science of the Human Vibrations of Consciousness,* second ed. Malibu, CA: Malibu Publishing, 1996.

Langer, Ellen J. *Counterclockwise: Mindful Health and the Power of Possibility.* New York: Ballantine Books, 2009.

Langer, Ellen J. *The Power of Mindful Learning.* Boston: Da Capo Lifelong Books, 2016.

Lipton, Bruce H. *The Biology of Belief: Unleashing the Power of Consciousness, Matter, and Miracles.* Carlsbad, CA: Hay House, 2010.

Lipton, Bruce H. *Spontaneous Evolution: Our Positive Future and a Way to Get There from Here.* Carlsbad, CA: Hay House, 2013.

Myss, Caroline. *Defy Gravity: Healing beyond the Bounds of Reason.* Carlsbad, CA: Hay House, 2011.

Norretranders, Tor. *The User Illusion: Cutting Consciousness down to Size.* London, UK: Penguin Books, 1999.

Pink, Daniel H. *A Whole New Mind: Why Right-Brainers Will Rule the Future.* New York: Riverhead Books, 2006.

Ristad, Eloise. *A Soprano on Her Head: Right-Side-Up Reflections on Life and Other Performances.* Lafayette, CA: Real People Press, 1981.

Tolle, Ekhart. *A New Earth: Awakening Your Life's Purpose.* London, UK: Penguin Life, 2005.

Zander, Benjamin, and Rosamund Stone Zander. *The Art of Possibility: Transforming Professional and Personal Life.* Boston: Harvard Business School Press, 2000

Index

Note: Page numbers in *italics* refer to photos or images.

abdominal area, 36, 214
accuracy in singing, 160–61
acknowledgment of others, 190–91
acting and miming, 170
action plans, 54–56, 260
advanced Coresinging, 60–61
affirmations, 106–7
Alexander Technique, 179
anatomy studies, 5
anxiety: bodily reactions to, 87n19; minimizing, 15, 35, 53, 105, 106, 130, 163; triggers for, 90, 130
AOL chat rooms, xv–xvi
applied kinesiology, 20–22, *21*
art exercises: children's "paint and sing," 115–16; colored marker activity, xviii–xix; "drawing the song," 106; "sing the colors," 116, 122; teen/tween "paint and sing," 121
articulation of words, 168–69, 216–18, 224–25
The Art of Possibility (Zander and Zander), 92, 93
"Ask me a question" statement, 76–77
assessments of staff, 183–84
AT (autogenic training), 97–98

athletes: energy fields and, 7; intent of, 28; Meribeth Dayme's sports experiences, 147–49; mindful preparation, 29; peak performance and health, 172; practices and, 13–14, 51; self-criticism and, 193; in the zone, 28, 64, 264
ATM (Awareness through Movement) lessons, 105
Atteshhilis, Stylianos (Daskalos), 180
attitudes, 198
audience feedback, 258. *See also* presentations
auditions, 179
autogenic training (AT), 97–98
awareness: about, 12–13, 35, 64; breath control, 36–38; exercises for, 40–41, 123–24; expanding, 15–16; external, 12–13, 40–41; five senses and, 108; internal, 13, 41–42; "Invisible Sphere" exercise, 123–24; during performances, 57; physical, 79; of teachers, 58. *See also* anxiety
Awareness through Movement (ATM) lessons, 105

back pain, 206

balance and alignment: centering, 33; in communication, 188–89; dynamic balance, 11–12, 30–31, 33, 58, 59–60; health and, 206–8; for singing, *165*, 165–66. *See also* posture
beards, 209
bioscalar energy, 40
Blades, Elizabeth, 101–11
blues scale, 138
"Body Awareness for Musicians" course, 109
"body" exercise, 118–20
body language, 175–76, 208
body of presentations, 247
Bones for Life practice, 85n1
brainstorming sessions, 249–50
The Brain That Changes Itself (Doidge), 27
break-out groups, 250
breath: about, 167; alignment linked to, 207; breath loop, 39; centering with, 30–31; chakras, 39; controlling with awareness, 36–38; energy fields and, 12; Hoberman mini sphere, 38, *38,* 42n4; matching with others, 230; during performances, 57; scalar breathing, 39–40; stretching and breathing exercises, 212; "this little light" exercise, 118, 122; voice effectiveness and, 213–14
Bunch, Meribeth. *See* Dayme, Meribeth

carotid pulse, 41–42
centering the body. *See* balance and alignment
chakras, *7,* 39, 104
Chandler, Kim, 54
chaos theory, 74, 86n8
character(s), 45, 78
charades game, 47–48
chest cavity, 36–37
chi, 26, 62n3
children's stories, 220–21, 241
Classical Singer magazine, xvi

classical singing, 162
colds, 172–73
collective consciousness, 28
communication: about, 190–91; as aim of singers, 77–78; balancing body, voice, and words, 188–89; common scenarios, 186–88; community and, 185–86; listening, 226–27; rapport, 227–33; training in, 183; user-friendly formats, 184. *See also* language; presence; presentations
community, 185–86
computer analogy, 226
confidence: characteristics of, 203; eroding with self-criticism, 131, 192–93, 198, 264; personal power, 181–84, 261–62; rebuilding, 263–65. *See also* communication; presence; presentations
Confucius, 17n7
consciousness, 27, 28. *See also* higher consciousness
consonants, 168, 169
CoreSinging: applying approach, 66–67; elements in all stages and levels, 3; feedback on, 143; history, 5–6; principles, 4–5; significance of name, 101; teachers' certification course, xvii–xix, 102–3. *See also* awareness; energy; imagination; performances; practice sessions
COVID-19, 90
Creating Confidence (Dayme), xvi, xvii. *See also* communication; confidence; presence; presentations
criticism. *See* feedback; self-criticism
cultural influences, 200

Dalcroze eurythmics, 109
dance, 53, 150
Dayme, Meribeth, *5, 148*; as artist, 151, *152*; biographical sketch, 147–53; Blades and, 102–3; college experiences, 149–50; dance lessons, 150; death of, xviii; as dog lover,

150–51, *151*; early years, 147–49, 150; legacy, xiii–xiv; personality of, 127, 143; piano lessons, 149; at summer camp, 149; unpublished poem, *155*
deadpan face, 217
Dear Evan Hansen, 92
detachment, 24–25
Deutsch, Diana, 93–94
Dispenza, Joe, 7
diversion, art of, 28
Doidge, Norman, 7
"Down by the Salley Gardens" (Yeats), 46
"drawing the song" exercise, *9, 49,* 49–50, 77, 83, 95, 106
drive to sing, 159
dualism, 90
Dyer, Wayne, 106–7
dynamic balance, 11–12, 30–31, 33, 58, 59–60
Dynamics of the Singing Voice (Dayme), ix, xi, xiii, xv, 5, 71, 102

earth energy *(jing),* 26
Eastern cultures and philosophies: in balance and breath, 11, 12; chakras, *7,* 39, 104; CoreSinging approach and, 3, 6, 90–91; energy and, 22–23, *23,* 29, 30–31, 63–64; intent as everything, 7, 14; moving meditations, 179; tai chi, 26, 179. *See also* qigong
EFT (Emotional Freedom Technique), 109, 111n15, 178
Eight-Piece Brocades, 104, 125n1, 129
Emotional Freedom Technique (EFT), 109, 111n15, 178
emotions, 67, 84–85, 161, 216. *See also* anxiety; expressiveness
energy: about, 6–7, 19, *23,* 32–33, 63–64; anatomy and, 22–24; balance and, 11–12, 30–31; clearing, 25–26; grounding exercises, 15, 30–31; intention as vital to, 7–8, 29, 97–98;

language and, 24, 30, 33, 66–67; levels of consciousness and, 27–31; muscle manipulation *versus,* 32; as negative, 98; performing and, 57–58; "room feedback" exercise, 118–20; similarity of individuals in, 228; of teachers, 58; testing, 20–22, *21*; types, 26–27; working with, 24–26, 29–30. *See also* breath; tune in/up/out guidelines
"energy drainers," 186–87
expectations: leaving behind, 30, 81–83; as negative energy, 44; rules for teens/tweens, 117; staying open without, 8. *See also* self-criticism
experimentation, 16
expressiveness, 219–20, 223–25
external awareness, 40–41
eyes, 105, 195–97

failure, 75, 80–81, 86n9. *See also* expectations
fame, 160
feedback, 234–38
Feldenkrais, Moshé, 73, 104–5
FI (Functional Integration), 105
"find your superpower" exercise, 114–15
Fitzgerald, Ella, 67
"fluffy stuff" exercise, 114, 122
free choice, 86n14
fuel gauge analogy, 241
Functional Integration (FI), 105
fun in learning, 8, 43–44, 54, 94–96. *See also* imagination; play; practice sessions
Funky 'n Fun training, 54

Gaelic language, 95–96
genetic factors in presence, 200
Godden, Rumer, 101
"Going to the Beach" meditation, 107–8
Goldman, Jonathan, 97
gratitude, 24, 32–33

grounding and balance, 30–31, 79, 253. *See also* posture

habits, 86n12, 87–88n21
hairstyles, 208–9
Hamilton, David R., 91
hammock analogy, 82–83
hand movements/placement, 253, 256
handouts, 245, 249, 251
head alignment, 207–8
head-turning exercises, 37–38
Hemsley, Thomas, 97
higher consciousness, 21–22, 25, 27–28, 29
Hill, Michael, 89–100
Hill, Susanne Bunch, 147–53
hoarseness, 161, 173
Hoberman mini sphere, 38, *38,* 42n4, 93
Hoch, Matthew, xiii–xiv, xviii, xix, 103
A House with Four Rooms (Godden), 101
"How Was That?" question, 75–76
human energy field, 22–24, *23*
Hunt, Valerie V., xiv, 6–7, 39–40, 97
hyperactivity, 175

ICVT (International Congress of Voice Teachers), 102
imagination: about, 64–65; creating characters, 45; "drawing the song" exercise, 49–50; importance of, 8, 10, 198–99; joy of learning, 43–44; learning text through, 44–45; memorizing text through, 46–48; pictures evoking, 223; tune in/up/out guidelines, 52–53. *See also* fun in learning; movement; play
improvisation, 171
intentions: mindful preparation of, 29–30; for performance, 14–15, 56; for practice sessions, 11; reminding students of, 33; setting, 92, 96, 97–98; vital to energy, 7–8, 29, 97–98
International Congress of Voice Teachers (ICVT), 102
interruptions in presentations, 257–58
introductions to presentations, 246–47
"Invisible Sphere" exercise, 123–24
"I Want to Be Here" concept, 190, 198, 227, 264

Jacobowski, Joan, 149
job interview presentations, 251
joints of the body, 206–7
journals, 60, 109, 130–31

Langer, Ellen, 11, 14
language: articulation of words, 168–69, 216–18, 224–25; building rapport with, 231; Gaelic, 95–96; as positive energy, 24, 30, 33, 66–67; taking responsibility for, 66–67; um's and er's, 242. *See also* self-criticism
laryngitis, 173
larynx, 167–68, 214–15
learning: as multifaceted, 10–11; procedural, 76; to read music, 162; taking responsibility for, 66–67
left brain, 65
life force (chi), 22–23, 26
Lipton, Bruce, 7
listening, 226–27, 232
"The Little Book About Singing" (Dayme): auditions, 179; facts about singing, 157; presence, 175–77; quiz, 158–64; singing with spirit, 180; things to include in practice, 170–71; tuning your instrument, 165–69; vocal health, 172–74; voice tool bag, 178–79
love of music, 160

The Magician's Way (Whitecloud), 75, 86n9
McTaggart, Lynne, 7–8
meditation, 107–8, 178, 179
melodies and scales, 138
mental presence, 176
mentors, 183
microphones, 163, 176–77, 252, 256

miming exercises, 170
mind energy *(shen)*, 26
mindfulness, 84–85
mindful preparation, 29–30, 67. *See also* intentions
mind-maps, 243–44, 246, 247
mixed age groups, 122–24
mock performances, 11
modal improvisation, 140
moustaches, 209
mouth chamber, 37
movement, 10, 31, 48, 120–21
MPA (music performance anxiety), 90
MTD (muscle tension dysphonia), 72
muscle manipulation, 32
muscle tension dysphonia (MTD), 72
muscle testing, 20–22, *21*
muscular movement, 42n3
music performance anxiety (MPA), 90
myofascial release, 109

nasal sounds, 168
National Association of Teachers of Singing (NATS), xv, xviii, 71, 102–3
negative thoughts, 59
neurolinguistic programming (NLP), 179
neuroplasticity, 26–27
neutrality of the environment, 84–85
Newton's third law, 73–74
NLP (neurolinguistic programming), 179
Nørretanders, Tor, xiv

ocean analogy, 82
off-pitch singing, 162
open questions, 227
O-ring energy tests, 20–22, *21*

paint and sing exercises, 115–16, 121
pantomiming exercises, 115–16
pentatonic scales, 136–37
performances: about, 65–66; acting and, 163; auditions, 179; energy of, 57–58; large audiences, 61; as part of every practice, 53, 60, 130, 171; preparing for, 14–16, 56–57; presence in, 175–77; risks in, 161; teachers and, 58. *See also* presentations
The Performer's Voice (Bunch), xvii
peripheral vision, 176, 196–97
personal power. *See* confidence
personal space, 24–25, 194, 219, 252–53. *See also* energy
Pert, Candace, 98
pharynx, 215–16
physical alignment. *See* balance and alignment; energy; posture
physical exercise, 164
pictures, 184, 246, 247
pitch pipe, 178
play: with children, 113–17; importance of, 15, 96, 117; mixed age groups, 122–24; in practice, 65; with teens and tweens, 117–22. *See also* fun in learning; imagination
posture: body language, 208; defined, 204–5; difficulty of directing changes in, 203–4; guidelines and exercises, 210–12; hairstyles, 208–9; head alignment, 207–8; health and energy linked to, 32, 206–7; importance of, 162; matching with others, 230; presence and, 195; relaxed, 205; varieties of, 79; voice and, 209–10. *See also* balance and alignment; energy
Practice Guide, 131, *132*
practice journals, 60
practice sessions: about, 65; acting and miming in, 163; creating guidelines for, 56; elements of, 13–14; importance of, 10–11, 57, 129–32; including performances in, 15, 53, 60, 130, 171; intentions for, 10–11; modeled by teachers, 58; new approach to, 51–56; planning for, 54–56, 131, *132,* 170; pleasure of, 87–88n21; visualization in, 14–15. *See also* videotapes; warm-ups

"Prescription for Practice" notepad, 55, 55–56
presence: creating, 194–97; feeling at home, 200–201; hand movements/placement, 253, 256; invisible aspects, 197–200; observations and exercises, 201–2; in performance, 175–77; personal space and, 194, 219, 252–53; physical indicators, 194–97
presentations: about, 239, 259; action planning, 260; apologies in, 242; creative approaches to, 242–45; handouts, 245, 249, 251; interactions in, 249–50; interesting/boring aspects of, 239–41; in job interviews, 251; personal power during, 261–62; personal space in, 194, 219, 252–53; sections of, 246–48; slides, 245, 248–49, 255–56, 258; timing of, 251–52; tools for, 248–49; "what-if?" scenarios, 254–58. *See also* performances
procedural learning, 76
professional-level scales, 142
proprioception, 107–8
pulse, 13, 41–42

qigong: as backstage exercise, 57; balance and, 11–12, 26; children's activities, 114; Eight-Piece Brocades, 104, 125n1, 129; flow of movement in, 31; "fluffy stuff" exercise, 114, 122; "this little light" exercise, 118, 122; tuning in with, 52
quantum physics, 74
quotations, 106–7

radial pulse, 41–42
"rapping the lyrics" exercise, 128–29
rapport, 227–33
readiness, state of, 67
Received Pronunciation (RP) voice, 94–95
Reiki, 102, 110n4

"Releasing the Eyes" lesson, 105
resonance in the voice, 168, 215–16, 224
respiratory diseases, 172–73
rhythms of the body, 13
right brain, 65
Ristad, Elousie, 65
role of the "other," 182, 183
"roller coastering" of vowels, 46–48, *47*, 95
"room feedback" exercise, 118–20
Rooney, Trish, 127–44
RP (Received Pronunciation) voice, 94–95

scaffolding analogy, 93
scalar breathing, 39–40
scales: blues, 138; Dorian, 139; interval exercises, 134; melodies and, 138; minor, 139; not beginning with, 53; pentatonic, 136–37, 139; triad patterns, 135; variations in, 10, 52, 54, 60–61, 133–34; whole-tone, 140–41
science, singing as, 6, 89–90
scientific papers, 250–51
self-criticism, 131, 192–93, 198, 264
self-energy testing, 20–22, *21*
semioccluded vocal tract (SOVT) exercises, 37, 46, 54, 135
"shrinking singers," 263–65
silliness. *See* fun in learning; play
Singing and Imagination (Hemsley), 97
The Singing Book (Bunch and Vaughn), xvii, xviii, 71, 103
singing IQ test, 158–64
"sing the colors" exercise, 116, 122
slides, 245, 248–49, 255–56, 258
"slow break" exercise, 108
smiles, 217
song texts, 10
A Soprano in Her Head (Ristad), 65
sound engineers, 163, 176–77
SOVT (semioccluded vocal tract) exercises, 37, 46, 54, 135

So You Want to Sing with Awareness (Hoch), 103
space (personal), 25–26, 194, 219, 252–53. *See also* energy
A Spectrum of Voices (Blades), 103, 104, 110
"Speech to Song Illusion," 93–94
spirit, singing with, 180
"Spring Birthday Walk" (poem), *155*
"stomping" exercise, 136, 144n8
Streisand, Barbra, 96–97
subconsciousness, 27
summary of presentations, 247
superpowers exercise, 114–15
Sussuma, Robert, 74
syndicate groups, 250

tai chi, 26, 179
tapping, 109, 111n15
teachers: certification course for CoreSinging, xvii–xix, 102–3; choosing, 162, 265; role of, 58–61, 98
technical papers, 250–51
"tell them" technique of presentations, 240
tension in the face and neck, 217, 218, 224
text: importance of, 163; learning, 44–45, 94–95; memorizing, 46–48; working with, 128–29
theme songs, 141
"this little light" exercise, 118, 122
thought patterns, 197–98
Titze, Ingo, 74
Tommasini, Anthony, 96–97
trust, 106–7
Tsao, Jesse, 31
tune in/up/out guidelines, 14, 40–41, 52–53, 104–6
twang-based exercises, 92, 99n6

"uhming and chewing," 46, 52, 53–54, 95
"Un bel dì, vedremo," 80

"unwelcome givers," 187–88

values, 232
Vaughn, Cynthia, xv–xix, xvii, 98, 102, 103, 263–65
Velarde, Rachel, 71–88
"Velcro hand" process, 76
Vennard, William, xiii–xiv, 5
videotapes, 66, 170, 178, 237, 264
visual awareness, 195–97
visualization, 14–15, 178, 199, 252
vocal folds, 214–15
vocal health, 172–74
vocalises, 54, 61
VocaList LISTSERV, xv
vocal nodules, 173–74
vocal presence, 176–77
voice: about, 213–14; articulation of words, 168–69, 216–18, 224–25; balancing, 188–89; common habits interfering with, 217–18, 222–23; exercises for, 223–25; expressiveness, 219–20, 225; hoarseness, 161, 172; importance of, 161; knowledge of, 164; matching with others, 230; pain with singing, 162; physical alignment and, 209–10; resonance, 215–16, 224; sound source, 214–15; tuning your instrument, 165–69
The Voice of Ireland (singing competition), 127
voice tool bag, 178–79
vowels, 46–48, *47*, 95, 168

warm-ups: about, 10; effective when short, 179; "Invisible Sphere" exercise, 123–24; physical and vocal, 53–54, 170, 172; scales and, 133–34; "Yes, with Guidelines" exercise, 122–23
"Waving through a Window," 92
"what-if?" scenarios, 254–58
"What Was It?" question, 75
Whitecloud, William, 75, 86n9

Why Woo-Woo Works (Hamilton), 91
wisdom, 17n7, 236
Woods, Aimee, 113–25
work behavior, 182
worksheets, 131, *132*

Yeats, William Butler, 46

"Yes, with Guidelines" exercise, 122–23
"You Are the Sunshine of My Life" exercise, 141

Zander, Benjamin, 92, 93
Zander, Rosamund S., 92, 93

About the Editors and Contributors

Cynthia Vaughn is a respected singer, voice teacher, author, and clinician. She and the late Meribeth Dayme coauthored *The Singing Book*, a leading college voice class textbook and song anthology, which was one of many products of their twenty-year collaboration and friendship. She is associate editor for "Independent Voices" articles and interviews in *Inter Nos*, the semiannual newsletter of the National Association of Teachers of Singing (NATS). A certified CoreSinging instructor, Vaughn has a decades-long association with Dayme and intimate knowledge of her methods. She holds an MA in vocal performance from San Jose State University, a BA in vocal performance from California State University, East Bay, and completed her doctoral coursework at University of Northern Colorado. After a decade on the voice faculty of Colorado State University, she founded Magnolia Music Studio in 2008.

Matthew Hoch joined the faculty of Auburn University in 2012, where he was tenured in 2015 and promoted to the rank of professor in 2020. His research program focuses on the scholarship of voice pedagogy and the practical applications of singing voice research in the applied voice studio. Hoch's published bibliography on these topics includes eight books as single author, first author, or editor and many peer-reviewed articles in over a dozen academic and professional journals. He holds the BM degree from Ithaca College, MM from the Hartt School, DMA from the New England Conservatory, and a certificate in vocology from the National Center for Voice and Speech. Hoch is the 2016 winner of the Van L. Lawrence Fellowship, awarded jointly by the Voice Foundation and NATS. He is a certified CoreSinging instructor and one of the last students of Dayme, completing his certification shortly before her passing in 2019.

* * * * *

Elizabeth Blades earned her MM and DMA degrees in vocal performance and literature at the Eastman School of Music. She is currently visiting professor of voice at Alfred University. Previous appointments include positions at Heidelberg University in Tiffin, Ohio, where she was associate professor of music, coordinator of vocal studies, and director of opera; and Nazareth College in Rochester, New York, where she was a visiting professor of music. Blades is the author of *A Spectrum of Voices: Prominent American Voice Teachers Discuss the Teaching of Singing* and *Singing with Your Whole Self: A Singer's Guide to Feldenkrais Awareness through Movement*, coauthored with Samuel H. Nelson. She regularly presents at national and international workshops to advance understanding of the impact Feldenkrais work can have for performance enhancement. She is also an active performer with experiences in many forms of voice performance, including opera, oratorio, art song, music theater, and folk/Celtic. In 2010, Blades was invited to be one of the first seven American voice teachers to receive training and certification as a CoreSinging teacher. She is the founder and director of Harmony House Online Music Studio.

Michael Hill is an experienced voice coach, singer, and freelance broadcaster, with a particular interest in how voice research, psychology, and pedagogy can be applied to help people express themselves freely and confidently. Hill's vocal coaching has embraced a wide range of different performers and styles. He has taught singing and accents to television actors, coached West End singers, helped lawyers with public speaking, and even trained international metalcore bands to grunt safely on tour. Hill has given master classes for a variety of respected institutions, including the Royal Conservatoire of Scotland, the World Voice Consortium, and Clinical Excellence Networks within the Royal College of Speech and Language Therapists. Research projects include the forthcoming book, *Great Gaelic Singers*, and a pilot study on the effectiveness of autogenic training in reducing self-perceived vocal and performance issues. Hill also continues to sing, perform, and broadcast on a variety of projects including a recent series of *Story Time* episodes for BBC Alba. He is currently senior lecturer at the Leeds Conservatoire, where he teaches students in the BA in popular music program.

Trish Rooney lectures at the Munster Technological University (MTU) Cork School of Music, where she teaches voice, popular music history, and research and is the course coordinator of the MA program in contemporary commercial music (CCM). She is a director and principal of the Academy of Popular

Music, Ireland's leading popular music secondary school and an exams officer for Vocal Health Education, UK. Rooney is a certified CoreSinging teacher and a coach for Vocology in Practice. She is on the editorial board of the *International Journal of Learning, Teaching, and Educational Research* and regularly reviews articles for other peer-reviewed journals. Rooney has worked extensively in the music industry as a performer, backing singer, and flutist and has served as vocal coach for *The Voice of Ireland*.

Rachel Velarde, mezzo-soprano, is professor of music (voice) at Grand Canyon University. Her main areas of interest are vocal performance, vocal literature, voice science, and voice pedagogy. She began teaching private voice and piano lessons in 1993 and became a member of NATS in 1996, serving three terms as president of the Valley of the Sun NATS chapter and four years as the district governor of Arizona. She also serves as the director of membership for the Pan American Vocology Association (PAVA). In 2012, Velarde received an honorable mention for the Van L. Lawrence Fellowship and completed Wicklund singing voice specialist (SVS) certification, learning how to better habilitate singers medically diagnosed with voice disorders. She completed the Summer Vocology Institute in summer 2021, earning a certificate in vocology from the National Center for Voice and Speech. A 2017 CoreSinging graduate, Velarde completed her Bones for Life teacher certification, a program of somatic awareness developed by Ruthy Alon and inspired by the Feldenkrais Method, in November 2021.

Aimee Woods is a private studio singing teacher, performer, and director based in Fort Collins, Colorado. She earned her MM degree in vocal performance from Colorado State University and her BM in vocal performance from University of Northern Colorado. In addition to teaching at Songwoods Studio, she serves as the music director for Fort Collins Children's Theatre. Woods teaches all ages and styles and is sought after as a rock/pop vocal coach, working with several local band singers and singer/songwriters. Woods is currently vice president of the Colorado/Wyoming NATS and has served on the voice faculty of Front Range Community College in Fort Collins. She has performed professional opera and musical theatre along the Colorado front range, including First Lady in *Die Zauberflöte* with Loveland Opera Theater and Kaye in *The Taffetas* at local dinner theaters. Woods holds a certificate from Internazionali di Musica at the University of Urbino, Italy, and is a certified CoreSinging teacher.

www.ingramcontent.com/pod-product-compliance
Lightning Source LLC
Chambersburg PA
CBHW032128010526
44111CB00033B/196